CONTENTS

ABBREVIATIONS

beg	beginning
ch	chain
cm	centimetre(s)
cont	continu(e)(ing)
C2[4:6]B	cable 2[4:6] back (see page 45)
C2[4:6]F	cable 2[4:6] forward (see page 45)
Cr2B	cross 2 back (see page 45)
Cr2F	cross 2 forward (see page 45)
dc	double crochet
dec	decrease(e)(ing)
foll	follow(ing)
g st	garter stitch (knit every row)
inc	increas(e)(ing)
K	knit
kw	knitwise
LH	left hand
M1	make 1: pick up strand between stitch just worked and next stitch on LH needle and knit into back of it
mm	millimetre(s)
oz	ounce(s)
P	purl

patt	pattern
psso	pass slipped stitch over
pw	purlwise
rem	remain(ing)
rep	repeat
rev st st	reverse stocking stitch (1 row P, 1 row K)
RH	right hand
skpo	slip 1, knit 1, pass slipped stitch over
sl	slip
sl st	slip stitch (crochet)
st(s)	stitches
st st	stocking stitch (1 row K, 1 row P)
tbl	through back of loop(s)
tog	together
Tw2PL	Twist 2 left purlwise (see page 44)
Tw2PR	Twist 2 right purlwise (see page 44)
Tw2L	Twist 2 left (see page 43)
Tw2R	Twist 2 right (see page 43)
wyb	with yarn at back
wyf	with yarn at front
yf	yarn forward
yon	yarn over needle
yrn	yarn round needle

INTRODUCTION

In recent years there has been a revival of interest in knitting. Top designers have demonstrated that this versatile craft is capable of producing high-fashion garments. Yarn manufacturers vie with each other in producing yarns designed for a wide spectrum of knitwear – from classic designs, traditionally knitted in high-quality wool, to practical, easy-care garments for children to glamorous, extravagant fashions for evening. In short, the creative possibilities of knitting have never been greater.

The Complete Step by Step Knitting Book will introduce you to the pleasures of knitting and help you to develop the techniques you need to tackle any knitting pattern – or even design your own. Chapter 1 provides information on yarns and the simple, inexpensive equipment required and describes the basic knitting skills: the knit stitch, the purl stitch, casting on and casting off.

Chapter 2 shows you how to follow a knitting pattern and construct a garment. Once you have grasped the simple but crucial principle of achieving the right tension and can shape a fabric and pick up stitches, you can consider yourself a capable knitter.

The following three chapters will greatly enlarge your repertoire of techniques, enabling you to produce appealing textured fabrics including cables, bobbles and smocking (chapter 3); tubular fabric and medallions (chapter 4) and the whole variety of multicoloured effects (chapter 5).

Chapter 6 demonstrates how you can use decorative techniques and trimmings to give a plain knitted garment a distinctive finishing touch. This is followed by a chapter containing a variety of sophisticated techniques – such as invisible casting on and off, grafting and working a hem – which will increase your expertise and give your work a professional finish.

Chapter 8 is a collection of patterns for all the family, specially chosen to give you an opportunity to apply the many knitting skills you have learned.

The knitter who wishes to exercise her own creativity at every stage of the knitting process will find plenty of help in the last chapter, which includes simple alterations to a pattern, such as substituting a different yarn or stitch, as well as guidance in designing a garment from scratch.

Chapters 1-7 include a collection of stitch patterns appropriate to the topics covered in them. And throughout the book you will find hints for making your knitting easier and more successful.

This beautiful stitch pattern, called Candle Flames, exemplifies the fascinating motifs and textures possible in knitting. For instructions, see page 100.

1 *The Basics*

*Y*ARNS

Much of the pleasure of knitting lies in the yarn itself. Hand knitting is a very tactile activity, and a yarn that is pleasing to touch and appropriate for the project will greatly enhance your enjoyment of the work and your pride in the finished garment.

There is a vast range of yarns available today – not only the classic smooth yarns, which never go out of fashion, but also a dazzling variety of unusual textures and fibres, from glossy silk, to velvety chenille, to chunky bouclé, in every imaginable hue. The endless creative possibilities they offer are one good reason for learning to design your own knitting; but even if you are using a published pattern, as most knitters do, you will find it worthwhile to become familiar with the different yarns available so that you can make a wise choice of yarn and pattern.

FIBRE CONTENT

Yarns are made of many different fibres and combinations of fibres, both natural and synthetic.

Natural fibres *Wool* is the traditional favourite among natural fibres. It is warm, relatively light-weight and elastic. This last quality makes it easy to knit with and means that the finished garment will – if cared for properly – hold its shape. Some wools are even machine washable.

Wool varies considerably in texture, according to the sheep from which it came and the spinning and finishing methods applied to it. The softest quality is Botany wool, which comes from merino sheep raised in Australia. Lambswool, too, is very soft, coming from the first shearing of the young animal.

Mohair is the fluffy hair of the angora goat. Despite its delicate appearance, it is strong, though not very elastic. Kid mohair is softer than ordinary mohair from the adult animal, and more expensive. Mohair is often combined with other fibres, such as wool or acrylic, for economy.

Angora is the fur of the angora rabbit. It is feather-soft and very expensive. Because it has a tendency to shed, it is not recommended for gar-ments for babies, who might choke on the fibres.

Cashmere comes from the Himalayan goat. An extremely soft and luxurious fibre, it is usually blended with other fibres.

Alpaca is the hair of the llama. It is often added to wool yarns to provide extra softness.

Silk, which is spun from the cocoon of the silkworm, is a luxurious fibre with a strength that belies its softness. Pure silk yarn normally has a glossy finish and comes in beautifully rich colours. Silk is also found combined with other fibres, such as wool and mohair.

Cotton is obtained from the seedheads of the cotton plant. Yarns made of cotton are cool and thus ideal for summer garments. Although some-what expensive, cotton is hard-wearing and good value. Cotton that has been mercerized is particu-larly strong and lustrous. Cotton's only drawbacks are its lack of elasticity, which makes it rather hard to knit with, and its density, which makes it slow to dry after laundering.

Linen is a very strong fibre, taken from the stem of the flax plant. It has a naturally slubbed texture and is often combined with cotton.

Synthetic fibres In recent years, synthetics have been much improved. They have certain practical advantages over most natural fibres, being strong, lightweight, resistant to moths and, in many cases,

This assortment of yarns gives an idea of the marvellous variety of textures available.

***Top needle** (left to right): mohair-cotton-nylon slub; kid mohair; mohair-nylon; nylon ribbon yarn; mohair-nylon; mohair-wool-nylon; space-dyed mohair-nylon; mohair-acrylic-polyester double-strand knop; nylon-mohair-wool acrylic novelty yarn; silk-rayon space-dyed slub yarn; three viscose-polyester glitter yarns.*

***Middle needle** multi-textured cotton-viscose blend; chunky cotton-linen slub; cotton-linen slub; mercerized cotton; matt cotton; mercerized cotton; cotton-viscose slub; mercerized cotton crepe; cotton-rayon; cotton-polyester chenille; mercerized cotton; acrylic-wool perlé; cotton bouclé; viscose novelty yarn; acrylic crepe baby yarn; acrylic three-ply baby yarn.*

***Bottom needle** natural wool; multicoloured wool-alpaca; angora-wool-silk multicoloured; thick-and-thin space-dyed wool; wool Aran yarn; wool-alpaca; flecked wool Aran yarn; wool-acrylic-mohair; softly spun wool; wool-silk knop; Shetland two-ply wool (two weights); wool double-knitting; shaded Shetland four-ply wool.*

machine washable. They are also relatively inexpensive. For these reasons, they are often added to natural fibres.

The main synthetic fibres are *acrylic*, *polyamide*, (including nylon), *polyester*, and *viscose* (including rayon). Of these, the commonest is acrylic, which is very soft and lightweight. A special category of synthetic is the *metallic* fibres, which are derived from aluminium.

Yarns made of 100 percent synthetic fibres are not so satisfying to use as those made of natural fibres or natural-synthetic blends. They are less pleasing to the touch, and garments made from them are apt to lose their shape.

CONSTRUCTION

The character of a yarn is determined not only by its fibre content but also by the spinning and finishing methods used in its manufacture.

Size Yarns vary enormously in size, or thickness (also called their weight). The smooth, so-called 'classic' yarns fall into seven categories: two-ply, three-ply, four-ply, double knitting, Aran-weight, chunky and extra-chunky. Within these categories there is some variation, but it is usually possible to substitute one yarn for another in the same category (see page 208).

The word 'ply' is used in two ways. Literally, it means an individual strand of fibre. A ply can be of any thickness; therefore, a yarn consisting of two plies might well be thicker than one containing four. However, in categorizing yarns we use the names 'two-ply', 'three-ply' and 'four-ply' to designate yarns that not only are so constructed but also conform to an accepted size category. Moreover, a textured yarn may also be described in relation to these categories; for example, 'knits as four-ply' means that the yarn (irrespective of its construction) will yield roughly the same number of stitches and rows over a given measurement as a standard four-ply yarn. This information is especially useful if you are substituting a yarn or designing a garment from scratch.

Finish In the spinning process, all sorts of different finishes may be applied to the fibres. The plies may be twisted loosely or firmly, to produce a wide range of textures, from soft to very firm. In general, the tighter the twist, the harder-wearing the yarn.

Slubbed yarns are irregularly spun, so that they have thick and thin stretches. They give a pleasing variation of texture to plain stitch patterns, but are less successful than the smooth yarns when worked in complex stitch patterns, as they obscure the detail somewhat; however, they can be quite effective in some larger lace and cable patterns.

Bouclé yarns have a crinkly texture produced by catching up one of the plies so that it forms a little loop around the other(s).

Knop yarns are similar in construction to bouclé yarns, but more irregular, with large loops at more widely spaced intervals. They produce a fuzzy, knobbly fabric.

Chenille yarns have a dense, velvety texture. Although very attractive, they are not easy to knit with.

Multicoloured efects can be produced by spinning together plies of different colour, or, for a subtler effect, different shades of the same colour. Flecked tweed yarns are the classic example of a multicoloured yarn. From time to time, fashion favours the technique of space-dyeing yarns, so that the colours change along the length. Such yarns can be fun to use, although you may sometimes find that you prefer the effect in the ball to that of the knitted fabric.

Novelty yarns come and go with the latest fashion trends. They may include woven ribbon and rag yarns, blends of metallic and cotton fibres, thin strands of suede – whatever.

The choice of yarns available at a given time is, of course, dictated by fashion. When the fashion is for colour-patterned knitting, as in the early 1990s, the more unusual textures, which do not lend themselves to these designs, tend to disappear.

BUYING YARN

When buying yarn, it is important to read the information on the ball band. This will include the fibre content, blocking/pressing instructions, recommendations for care of the garment, and the weight of the ball or skein. In some cases it may also give a recommended needle size and the number of stitches and rows produced in stocking stitch using those needles (see 'Tension', page 25). This last information is very useful if you wish to substitute a different yarn for the one recommended by the pattern (see page 208).

One essential piece of information on the ball band is the dye lot number. Make sure that all the yarn is from the same dye lot, for even a minor variation can be quite noticeable on the garment. Buy all the yarn required for the garment at the same time; later on, that particular dye lot may no longer be available.

If you are not fortunate enough to live near a good yarn shop, don't despair. Some shops offer a mail-order service, and there are many mail-order suppliers. Refer to the suggestions on page 222.

The seven basic weights of smooth yarn (right). From top to bottom: two-ply, three-ply, four-ply, double knitting, Aran, chunky (Icelandic type) and extra-chunky.

This yarn label (right) gives all the information a purchaser might need, including the recommended needles and suggested tension over stocking stitch.

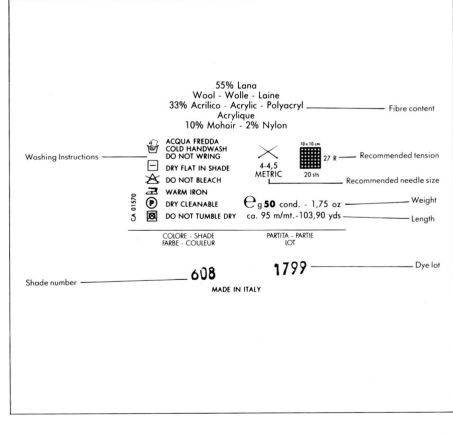

55% Lana
Wool - Wolle - Laine
33% Acrilico - Acrylic - Polyacryl —————— Fibre content
Acrylique
10% Mohair - 2% Nylon

Washing Instructions ———
ACQUA FREDDA
COLD HANDWASH
DO NOT WRING
DRY FLAT IN SHADE
DO NOT BLEACH
WARM IRON
DRY CLEANABLE
DO NOT TUMBLE DRY

CA 01570

4-4,5
METRIC

10 x 10 cm
27 R ——— Recommended tension
20 sts
——— Recommended needle size

g **50** cond. - 1,75 oz ——————— Weight
ca. 95 m/mt.-103,90 yds ——————— Length

COLORE - SHADE   PARTITA - PARTIE
FARBE - COULEUR   LOT

Shade number ———————— **608**   **1799** ——————— Dye lot

MADE IN ITALY

*E*QUIPMENT

Little in the way of special equipment is required for hand knitting. The one essential item, of course, is the needles. These come in a variety of sizes (see page 221) and types, which you can acquire gradually as the need arises. There are also various other accessories which will come in handy occasionally; their uses are described below.

Needles are made of several different materials: metal and plastic are the commonest today, but bamboo and sometimes wood can also be found. Metal needles are generally the easiest to work with, as the stitches slide easily along them; plastic tends to be rather sticky, although some people prefer it because it is warmer to the touch. You may sometimes find needles made with rigid points attached to a flexible length of plastic. These are useful for knitting heavy items, as the whole weight of the work does not need to be supported by the hands.

Other types of needle include circular and double-pointed needles, for working in the round, and cable needles, used in cable stitch patterns.

If you take good care of your needles they should last for many years. Store them in a large flat box or special needle case, so that they do not become bent. Never use a needle with a jagged point, which will split the yarn.

Equipment (opposite) needed for knitting. Some of these items are essential, some optional. Clockwise from upper left:

Bamboo needles
Plastic needles
Plastic-coated metal needles
Metal needles
Set of four double-pointed needles – used for tubular knitting and for medallions
Crochet hook – used for working crocheted edges and button loops and for darning in yarn ends

Two styles of cable needle – the bend prevents the held stitches from slipping off; a straight cable needle will do the job

Stitch holder – a double-pointed needle or a length of yarn may be used instead; ordinary safety pins are best where only a few stitches must be held

Tapestry needle – used for seaming and for working embroidery on knitting

Stitch stoppers or needle guards – used to prevent the work from slipping off the needle when it is put away; an elastic band will serve the same purpose, but stoppers will also protect the needle points

Scissors for cutting yarn – a pair of embroidery scissors is also useful, especially when undoing work knitted with fuzzy yarns

Needle gauge – useful for checking sizes of double-pointed and circular needles (marked only on the package) and when using needles sized according to a different system from the one used in the pattern

Bamboo needles with flexible plastic ends – useful when knitting large, heavy items which would add weight to ordinary straight needles

Circular needle (also called a twin pin) – used for tubular or straight knitting

Ring markers – used to mark the beginning of rounds in tubular knitting and certain key points in a pattern

Glass-headed pins – used for blocking pieces of knitting

Bobbin – used for holding small amounts of yarn when working with two or more colours across a row

Knitter's pins – used for holding two sections together when seaming and for marking divisions on edges when picking up a specified number of stitches; ordinary glass-headed pins will do

Tape measure

Other useful equipment includes a row counter, a spray bottle for wet blocking, an iron (preferably steam), a cotton pressing cloth and an ironing board with a well-padded surface or a large square or rectangular padded board. A purpose-made knitting bag is a handy, attractive way of keeping your knitting clean and tidy; some bags have wooden frames which allow them to stand on the floor when in use and then fold up for carrying or storing. A folder or notebook for storing patterns is also useful

CASTING ON

The first step in beginning a piece of knitting is to place the required number of stitches on the needle. This is called casting on. There are several different methods of casting on, producing edges suitable for different kinds of work. Although you need learn only one method to start with, it is a good idea eventually to learn several methods. Some of the most-often-used methods are shown here; two advanced ones, on pages 86–87.

The easiest method for the beginner is the double cast-on. Although it may look like a form of cat's cradle, it requires no knitting experience, whereas the cable and thumb cast-on methods require you to hold the yarn as for knitting (see page 16). The single cast-on is the simplest of all methods; however, because the loops formed are difficult to work into evenly, it is not recommended for the novice.

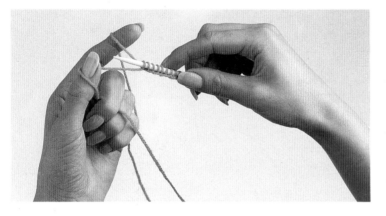

Double cast-on

Multiply the number of stitches required by 2cm/¾", and measure off this length of yarn. Wind the yarn around the fingers of your left hand as shown: up between the third and little fingers, around the little finger, over all four fingers, then clockwise around the thumb; finally take the yarn between the second and third fingers and hold

it gently but firmly. Spread the thumb and index finger apart to tension the yarn.

1 Slip the point of the needle up through the thumb loop (a).
2 Take it over and under the yarn extending to the index finger (b), thus forming a loop on the needle; as you do so, rotate your left hand towards you (you may do this instinctively, as it feels natural).
3 Bring the needle back through the thumb loop.
4 Slip the thumb out of the loop, and use it to pull down the free length of yarn (c).
This completes the first stitch. Repeat steps 1–4. The edge produced is quite flexible, yet firm, and thus a good one for ribbing.

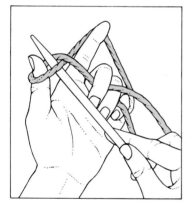

a

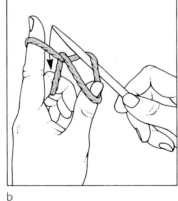

b

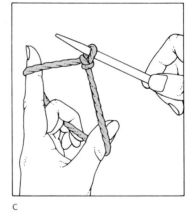

c

Slip knot

For the remaining cast-on methods, begin by making a slip knot on the needle. First make a loop in the yarn (a). Slip the point of the needle through the loop, then pull on both ends of the yarn to tighten the knot (b).

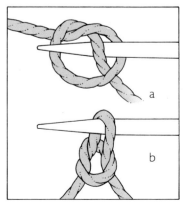

a

b

If you tend to cast on tightly, use needles a size or two larger than specified by the pattern for the casting on. Then change to the correct needles for the first row.

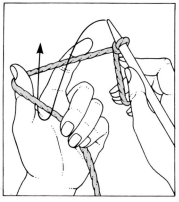

a

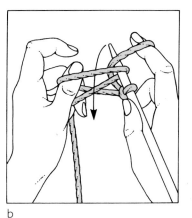

b

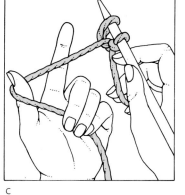

c

Thumb method

The edge produced by this method is the same as for the double cast-on. Multiply the number of stitches by 2cm/¾" and measure off this length of yarn; make a slip knot slightly beyond this point. Hold the short end of yarn in your left hand as shown. Wrap the yarn from the ball around the little finger of your right hand, as for knitting

(see page 16).
1 Take the point of the needle up under the front strand of yarn lying between the fingers and thumb of the left hand, thus forming a new loop on the needle (a).
2 Now bring the right-hand (ball) yarn under and over the point of the needle. Holding both lengths fairly taut, bring the needle down through the left-hand loop as

shown by the arrow (b).
3 Slip the thumb out of the loop, and use it to pull on the short end of yarn as shown to complete the new stitch.
Repeat steps 1–3.

Single cast-on

This method produces a soft, flexible edge. Begin by making a slip knot near the end of the yarn. Wind the yarn around the thumb, and hold it with three fingers.
1 Bring the needle up through the loop as shown by the arrow (a).
2 Slip the thumb out of the loop, and use it to pull the yarn gently downwards, forming a stitch (b).
Repeat steps 1 and 2.

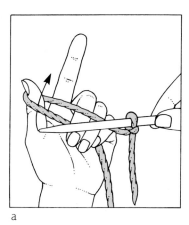

a

a

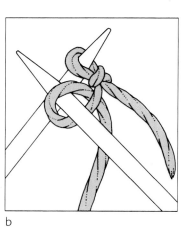

b

c

Cable method

This method produces an attractive, smooth edge, suitable for various fabrics. Begin with a slip knot, near the end of the yarn.
1 Holding the loose end firmly, insert the right-hand needle under the left, to the left of the slip knot.
2 Take the main yarn under and over the right-hand needle, from

left to right (a).
3 Draw the loop on the right-hand needle through to the front (b), and place it over the left-hand needle.
4 Insert the right-hand needle between the two stitches (c). Take the yarn under and over it, as in step 2, draw the loop through, and place it on the needle.
Repeat step 4.

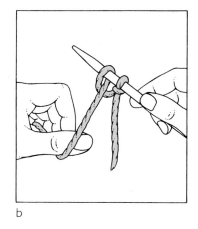

b

For an extra-flexible edge, use the double or thumb method and use two needles, held together, instead of one. When the stitches have been cast on, remove one of the needles. The large loops will be easy to work into.

HOLDING THE YARN

Once you have cast some stitches onto a needle, you are ready to begin knitting. There are several ways of holding the yarn and needles; the two basic methods are shown here.

The right-hand method of holding the yarn is used in English-speaking countries and in Western Europe generally. The left-hand method is used in Central and Eastern Europe. Each method produces exactly the same results. Try both and see which is more comfortable for you. It is a good idea to learn to use both methods, as some multi-coloured knitting requires you to work with two different colours simultaneously.

Whichever method you use, the yarn must be wound loosely around the fingers to keep it slightly tensioned, so that the stitches will be smooth and even. You may find at first that you prefer to wrap the yarn twice around the little finger.

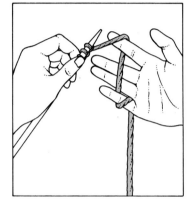

Right-hand method

Take the needle with the cast-on stitches in the left hand. Wind the yarn around the fingers of the right hand as shown.

Take the needle in the right hand so that it lies between the thumb and the rest of the hand as shown (in practice, the needle is often picked up before the yarn). Insert the needle into the first stitch on the left-hand needle, and slide the right hand forward to take the yarn around the point of the right-hand needle. In the photograph the needles are shown forming the knit stitch.

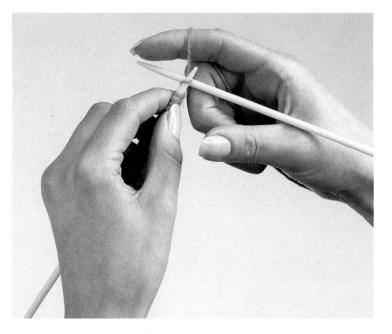

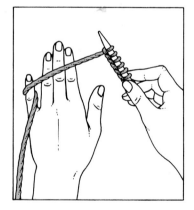

Left-hand method

Take the needle with the cast-on stitches in the right hand. Wind the yarn around the fingers of the left hand as shown.

Transfer the needle with the stitches to the left hand, and raise the index finger to tension the yarn. Take the working needle in the right hand, with the thumb in front and the fingers in back. Insert the needle into the first stitch, then rotate the left hand to bring the yarn around the point of the needle. In the photograph the needles are shown forming the knit stitch.

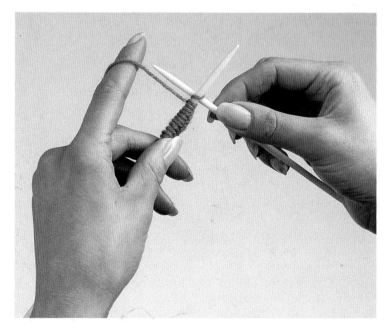

Knit & Purl

Most knitting is based on combinations of just two basic stitches: the knit stitch and the purl stitch. Once you have mastered these two stitches, you can work many different stitch patterns.

Begin by casting on about 25 or 30 stitches, using a double knitting yarn in a light colour, preferably all wool or a wool mix, for its resilience. Practise the knit stitch until you can work it fairly smoothly. Then practise the purl stitch.

Garter stitch (right).
This simple stitch pattern is produced by knitting every row. The fabric has a distinct horizontal ridge and is quite stretchy.

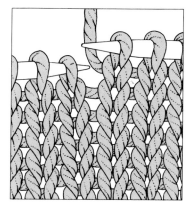

a

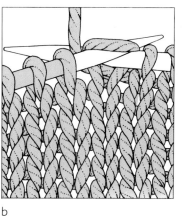

b

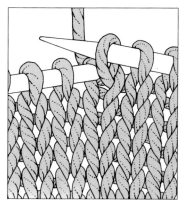

c

The knit stitch

1 Hold the needle with the stitches to be knitted in the left hand with the yarn behind (a).
2 Insert the RH needle into a stitch from front to back (b). Take the yarn over it, forming a loop.
3 Bring the needle and the new loop to the front of the work, and slide the original stitch off the LH needle (c).

The purl stitch

1 Hold the stitches to be purled in the left hand, with the yarn at the front of the work (a).
2 Insert the RH needle through the front of the stitch, from back to front (b). Take the yarn over and under, forming a loop.
3 Take the needle and the new loop through to the back; slide the stitch off the LH needle (c).

a

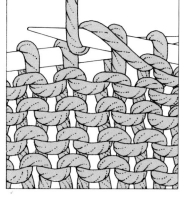

b

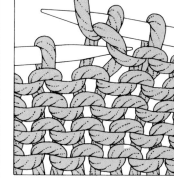

c

Stocking stitch (far left).
The most widely used of all stitch patterns, this is produced by knitting all the stitches on the right-side rows and purling on the wrong-side rows. The fabric is very smooth and slightly elastic.

Reverse stocking stitch (left). This is simply the 'wrong' side of stocking stitch. It is sometimes used in preference to stocking stitch where a slightly more textured effect is desired, and it also serves as the background fabric for cable patterns (see page 50).

17

*V*ARIATIONS

Once you have learned to knit and purl in the usual way, it is easy to learn a few variations on these basic techniques. One of these is working into the back of the stitch rather than into the front of it. This technique is sometimes required when increasing stitches (see Chapter 2) and in some stitch patterns.

It is possible to produce a variation of stocking stitch by working all the knit stitches through the back; the purl stitches are worked through the front as usual. The knitted stitches are twisted, and the fabric is unusually firm.

Another technique is simply to slip a stitch off the left-hand needle onto the right without working it. Slipped stitches are used in some methods of decreasing and in some multicolour patterns (see page 72).

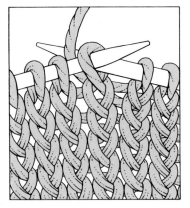

Knitting through the back of the loop
Insert the RH needle behind the LH needle and through the back of the stitch, and take the yarn under and over the needle, forming a knit stitch in the usual way. Pull the new stitch through, and slip the original stitch off the LH needle. The new stitch is slightly twisted.

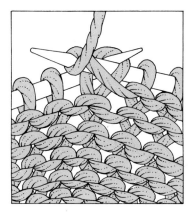

Purling through the back of the loop
This involves turning the RH needle briefly to point from left to right, then inserting it from back to front through the back of the loop as shown. Form a purl stitch in the usual way, and slip the original stitch off the LH needle. The new stitch is slightly twisted.

Slipping a stitch knitwise
Insert the needle into the front of the stitch as if to knit it, but do not form a new stitch; simply slip the original stitch onto the RH needle. The same technique is used to slip a purl stitch knitwise.
Unless the pattern instructions state otherwise, the yarn is held as for the preceding stitch: at the back if this was a knit stitch; at the front if it was a purl stitch.

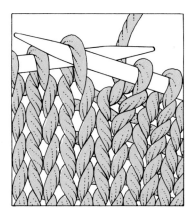

Slipping a stitch purlwise
Insert the needle into the stitch from back to front, as if you were going to purl it, then simply slip it onto the RH needle. The same technique is used to slip a P stitch purlwise.
Unless the pattern instructions state otherwise, the yarn is held as for the preceding stitch.

Single rib (left).
There are many different rib patterns; this one is the simplest. To work it, first cast on an even number of stitches. Knit the first stitch, then purl the second; repeat to the end of the row. The second row and all following rows are worked in the same way.
For double rib, knit 2
stitches, then purl 2, alternately. Some other rib patterns are shown in the Stitch Pattern pages of this book.
Note that when changing from knit to purl or vice versa one takes the yarn straight back or forward — not over the needle.

CASTING OFF

To end a piece of knitting, you 'cast off' the stitches. This technique is also used to reduce the number of stitches at the side of a piece of knitting – for example, when shaping an armhole – or in the middle, when working a horizontal buttonhole or, sometimes, when shaping a neckline. There are several methods of casting off, but the most commonly used is the one shown here. This basic method is varied slightly when casting off a ribbed fabric; this produces a softer, slightly more elastic edge than the basic method.

It is very easy to make the mistake of casting off too tightly, thus producing an edge that is shorter than the width of the fabric. To avoid this, use a needle one or two sizes larger than those used for the main fabric when casting off.

When you have learned the basic cast-off method, try the advanced methods shown on pages 88–89.

Basic cast-off

1 Knit the first two stitches.

2 Slip the LH needle into the first stitch on the RH needle, and lift it over the second stitch and off the needle. Repeat steps 1 and 2 until one stitch remains. Break the yarn and draw it firmly through the last stitch.

If casting off on the purled side of a stocking stitch fabric, you may prefer to purl the stitches instead

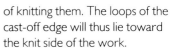

of knitting them. The loops of the cast-off edge will thus lie toward the knit side of the work.

Casting off in rib

Work all the stitches as if continuing in the pattern: thus purl stitches will be purled, rather than knitted. Lift the first stitch over the second as usual.

Achieving an even cast-off in rib is not easy, even for experienced knitters. Practise on a spare piece of ribbing, keeping a fairly loose tension and working as evenly as possible.

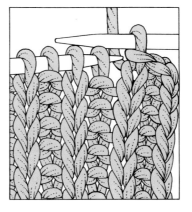

Cast-off edges (left). The sample at top has been cast off knitwise in the usual way. The one at bottom has been cast off in single rib.

LEFT-HANDED KNITTERS

If you are left-handed, you may find the 'Continental' method of holding the yarn relatively easy to learn, as the work is more evenly divided between the two hands than it is in the right-hand method.

The alternative is to use the right-hand method *reversed*, holding the needle with the stitches in the right hand, wrapping the yarn around the fingers of the left hand, and using the left hand to work the stitches. If you choose this method, you will find it helpful, when following the instructions in this book, to hold the book up to a mirror. (A mirror is not necessary if you use the left-hand method, as you can work exactly as shown.)

$\mathscr{S}$IMPLE TEXTURES

Some of the most popular stitch patterns are also among the simplest. These are combinations of knitting and purling. Cast on a number of stitches divisible by the stitch multiple, plus extra stitches as required. Work until the swatch is as deep as it is wide, and cast off.

MOSS STITCH

multiple of 2
Row 1 ✣K1, P1; rep from ✣.
Row 2 ✣P1, K1; rep from ✣.

MOSS STITCH RIB

multiple of 4
Row 1 ✣K3, P1; rep from ✣.
Row 2 ✣K2, P1; rep from ✣.

IRISH MOSS STITCH

multiple of 2
Rows 1 and 2 ✣K1, P1; rep from ✣.
Rows 3 and 4 ✣P1; K1, rep from ✣.

DIAMOND SEED

multiple of 8
Row 1 ✣P1, K7; rep from ✣.
Rows 2 and 8 ✣K1, P5, K1, P1; rep from ✣.
Rows 3 and 7 ✣K2, P1, K3, P1, K1; rep from ✣.
Rows 4 and 6 ✣P2, K1, P1, K1, P3; rep from ✣.
Row 5 ✣K4, P1, K3; rep from ✣.

ROMAN STITCH

multiple of 2
Rows 1 and 3 Knit.
Rows 2 and 4 Purl.
Row 5 ✫K1, P1; rep from ✫.
Row 6 ✫P1, K1; rep from ✫.

SIMPLE SEED

multiple of 4
Row 1 ✫K3, P1; rep from ✫.
Rows 2 and 4 Purl.
Row 3 Knit.
Row 5 ✫K1, P1, K3; rep from ✫ to last 3 sts, P1, K2.
Rows 6 and 8 Purl.
Row 7 Knit.

CHEVRON SEED

multiple of 8
Row 1 ✫P1, K3; rep from ✫.
Row 2 ✫K1, P5, K1, P1; rep from ✫.
Row 3 ✫K2, P1, K3, P1, K1; rep from ✫.
Row 4 ✫P2, K1, P1, K1, P3; rep from ✫.

EVEN BASKETWEAVE

multiple of 8, plus 4 extra
Row 1 (RS) K4, ✫P4, K4; rep from ✫.
Row 2 P4, ✫K4, P4; rep from ✫.
Rows 3 and 4 as Rows 1 and 2.
Row 5 and 7 as Row 2.
Row 6 and 8 as Row 1.

21

MORE SIMPLE TEXTURES

Here are some more useful stitch patterns to learn. They include two attractive rib patterns which can easily be substituted for original rib in many cases. The twisted rib is a slightly firmer version of the basic knit 1, purl 1, and uses the technique of knitting into the back of the stitch. Farrow rib is a decorative alternative to plain rib.

Two of the patterns – woven stitch and honey-comb slip stitch – use the technique of slipping stitches described on page 18. Either could be substituted for stocking stitch or reverse stocking stitch in most patterns, provided you can obtain the required tension (see page 25).

The remaining three stitches are relatively large-scale patterns combining pleasing texture with interesting linear effects.

1 × 1 TWISTED RIB

multiple of 2
Row 1 ✶K1 tbl, P1; rep from ✶.
Row 2 as Row 1.

FARROW RIB

multiple of 3
Row 1 and every row ✶K2, P1; rep from ✶.

EMBOSSED CHEVRON

multiple of 12
Row 1 ✶K3, P5, K3, P1; rep from ✶.
Row 2 and every alternate row K the K sts and P the P sts.
Row 3 P1, ✶K3, P3; rep from ✶ to last 5 sts, K3, P2.
Row 5 P2, ✶K3, P1, K3, P5; rep from ✶ to last 10 sts, K3, P1, K3, P3.
Row 7 ✶P3, K5, P3, K1; rep from ✶.
Row 9 K1, ✶P3, K3; rep from ✶ to last 5 sts, P3, K2.
Row 11 K2, ✶P3, K1, P3, K5; rep from ✶ to last 3 sts, K3.

EMBOSSED LEAF STITCH

multiple of 10
Row 1 Purl.
Row 2 Knit.
Rows 3 and 4 Purl.
Row 5 ✿P5, K5; rep from ✿.
Row 6 ✿K1, P5, K4; rep from ✿.
Row 7 ✿P3, K5, P2; rep from ✿.
Row 8 ✿K3, P5, K2; rep from ✿.
Row 9 ✿P1, K5, K4; rep from ✿.
Row 10 Knit.
Row 11 ✿K1, P5, K4; rep from ✿.
Row 12 ✿P3, K5, P2; rep from ✿.
Row 13 as Row 8.
Row 14 as Row 9.
Row 15 ✿K5, P5; rep from ✿.
Row 16 Purl.

STEPPED PATTERN

multiple of 18
Row 1 ✿K15, P3; rep from ✿.
Row 2 and every alternate row K the K sts and P the P sts.
Row 3 ✿K15, P3; rep from ✿.
Rows 5 and 7 ✿K3, P15; rep from ✿.
Rows 9 and 11 ✿K3, P3, K12; rep from ✿.
Rows 13 and 15 ✿P6, K3, P9; rep from ✿.
Rows 17 and 19 ✿K9, P3, K6; rep from ✿.
Rows 21 and 23 ✿P12, K3, P3; rep from ✿.

WOVEN STITCH

multiple of 2
Rows 1 and 3 (WS) Purl.
Row 2 K1, ✿sl 1 wyf, K1; rep from ✿ to last st, K1.
Row 4 K1, ✿K1, sl 1 wyf; rep from ✿ to last st, K1.

HONEYCOMB SLIP STITCH

multiple of 2 plus 1 extra
Row 1 P1, ✿sl 1 pw, P1; rep from ✿.
Rows 2 and 4 Purl.
Row 3 P2, ✿sl 1 pw, P1; rep from ✿ to last st, P1.

You will sometimes hear people say, 'I can knit and purl, but I can't follow a knitting pattern.' It is true that patterns often look very complex, and to the uninitiated they may even appear to be written in a foreign language. However, it is relatively easy to learn this language, as you will discover.

SELECTING A PATTERN

First of all, it is important to select a pattern that is appropriate for your level of ability, so that it will be successful and encourage you to develop your knitting skills. If you are choosing your first pattern, try to select something that is not absolutely dependent on perfect sizing and shaping. Also, do not choose a very complicated stitch pattern.

SIZE

Check that the sizes given include one that is suitable for your measurements. It will allow some room for movement when wearing the garment.

Progressing from the first row of ribbing to the finished garment is not difficult – once you understand the basic principles and language of printed patterns.

(This is known as 'ease' or 'tolerance'.) If several sets of figures are given, the smallest one is always indicated first, with larger ones in brackets. It is a good idea to circle each figure that refers to your size.

MATERIALS AND EQUIPMENT

A printed pattern will specify all the materials and equipment necessary to complete the garment. It will state the amount and type of yarn, needle sizes, the correct tension (see page 21), and any haberdashery required, such as buttons or zips.

When you are still learning to knit, it is wise to choose the exact yarn specified in the pattern. Later, when you are more experienced, you can often substitute a different yarn for the one specified. For guidance in buying yarn, see pages 10 and 208.

SEQUENCE OF WORKING

The pattern will indicate the order in which the pieces are to be worked. It is advisable to stick to this order. Often some instructions in one piece will relate to previously completed pieces. It is also advisable to join the pieces together in the order suggested, for this may relate to some further work such as a neckband or collar.

Make it a habit to check your work as you go along, especially if it has a complicated stitch pattern. Lay it out flat in good light and look at it carefully. A check of the number of stitches on the needle will also indicate whether all is going according to plan.

KNITTING LANGUAGE

All knitting patterns use abbreviations and symbols of various kinds in order to save space. These are fairly standard, although you will find some differences in patterns produced in different English-speaking countries and in different spinners' patterns and knitting books. A full list of the abbreviations used in this book is given on page 221. Special abbreviations are explained at the beginning of a pattern.

In addition to abbreviations, patterns use symbols such as ( ), [ ] and * *. These may contain variations for different sizes, and they may also enclose a set of instructions that are to be repeated. For example, '* K1, P1, rep from * to end.' Sections of a pattern that are to be repeated may use two or more asterisks, to indicate repeats within repeats.

You will find, as you gain experience, that such symbols are easy to understand.

ENSION

A most important part of any knitting pattern is the part that states the required tension. This is the number of stitches and rows, over a given measurement, obtained by the designer of that pattern. It will be given in a form such as the following: '21 sts and 30 rows to 10cm/4″, worked over st st on 4mm needles'. Sometimes the tension will be given 'over patt' – that is, over the stitch pattern used for the main part of the garment.

No matter how experienced a knitter you are, it is essential to check your tension in order for the garment to be the correct size. To check the tension, you must knit a sample before beginning the garment itself.

It is also a good idea to re-check your tension occasionally during the course of knitting a garment to make sure it has not altered. You can do this on a completed section of the garment.

Knitting a tension swatch

1 Cast on a few more stitches than stated by the pattern for the tension. For example, if 21 stitches are required, you should cast on about 28 or 30. Work in the pattern, using the specified needles, until the work measures a little more than 10cm/4″, then cast off.

2 Pin the swatch to a flat, padded surface as shown. In some cases, such as a highly textured or lacy pattern, it may be necessary to block the work (see page 34) in order to make it as smooth as the finished garment will be.

3 Insert a pin, as shown, a few stitches in from one edge. Count off the number of stitches required for the tension and insert another pin. Measure the distance between the pins. It should be 10cm/4″ (or the measurement given). If the measurement is greater, your tension is too loose, and you should change to smaller needles. If it is shorter, your tension is too tight, and you should change to larger needles.

The row tension is measured in the same way, although if it is given over stocking stitch, you will find it easier to count it on the ridged, purl side of the work. The row tension is usually less important than the stitch tension, for shaping instructions (for armholes, neck opening, etc.) are

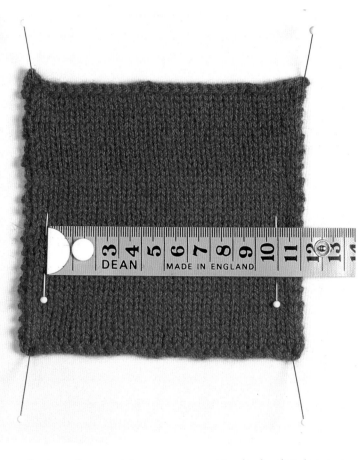

normally given after a certain measurement has been achieved, rather than after a given number of rows. However, some patterns will require a given number of pattern repeats to be completed at certain shaping points, and in such cases if the row tension varies from that required, the proportions of the garment will be incorrect.

Do not try to achieve the

correct tension by changing your way of knitting; the tension with which you knit is natural to you. Change the needle size instead.

Your tension may vary, however, if you are especially tired, or tense, or if you have not done any knitting for a while. It is a good idea, in such cases, to begin by knitting a few rows with some spare yarn and needles until you resume your natural rhythm.

Complex stitch patterns

It is often perplexing to a beginner to be given the tension over the garment's stitch pattern if the pattern is a complex one. How do you go about making a swatch without casting on all the stitches required for a section?

The procedure is to look at the first pattern row that contains a repeated group of stitches and calculate how many stitches are in the repeat. For example, take these instructions: '* (K1, P1, K1) into first st, P3 tog, rep from * to end.' When you have followed the first instruction, in brackets, you will have 3 stitches on the needle; when you follow the second, 'purl 3 together', you will have 1 stitch. Add the 1 to the 3 to get the number of stitches in one repeat: 4.

The number of stitches to cast on must be divisible by 4 and include a few stitches more than those specified for the tension. Add any edge stitches given in the pattern; these will be found outside the asterisks. Cast on this number and work as instructed until the swatch measures slightly more than 10cm/4″.

If the stitches are difficult to count in that particular stitch pattern, tie loops of yarn at the beginning and end of the specified number of stitches and rows. Then measure the tension between these markers.

CORRECTING MISTAKES

Every knitter occasionally makes a mistake, so it is a good idea to learn how to deal effectively with these when they occur.

First of all, keep a crochet hook within easy reach while you are knitting. This is used to pick up dropped stitches. A cable needle is also sometimes useful for holding a loose stitch while you sort out a problem. After correcting a mistake, count the stitches to make sure you have the right number.

As a general rule, the amount of yarn needed to knit one row is four times the width of the knitting. More may be required for highly textured patterns.

Picking up a ladder
If the work is in stocking stitch, insert the crochet hook from front to back through the lowest stitch, pick up the strand as shown, and pull it through to make a new stitch; repeat to the top of the ladder, and place the last stitch on the LH needle, making sure it is turned the correct way for knitting.

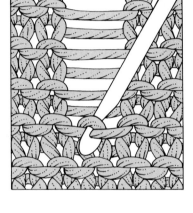

In some patterns you will need to pick up purl stitches when retrieving a ladder. The technique is basically the same as for a knit stitch, but the hook is inserted from back to front as shown.

Unpicking stitches
If you find a mistake a few rows down, it is feasible to unpick the work stitch by stitch until you reach the mistake, then correct it and proceed as usual.
To unpick a knit stitch, put the LH needle through the lower stitch. Pull the RH needle out of the stitch above it, and pull the yarn out of the loop.

To unpick a purl stitch, the process is essentially the same as for a knit stitch, but the yarn is held in front of the work.

When picking up stitches after unravelling, use a needle two or three sizes smaller than those used for the knitting. This makes the task easier and avoids pulling the stitches out of shape.

For unravelling hairy yarns, keep some sharp-pointed embroidery scissors handy to snip any caught-up fibres. Be extra careful, however, not to cut the main strand of yarn. A magnifying glass may prove useful in such cases.

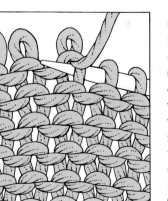

Unravelling
If the mistake is more than a few rows down, it will be quicker to unravel the work. Unravel it to one or two rows below that in which the mistake occurs, ending with the yarn at the RH edge. In some patterns it is easier to work from the right side of the fabric; in others, including stocking stitch, it is easier to work on the wrong (usually purl) side, as shown here.

Insert the needle into the stitch below the RH loop from back to front, and pull out the loop. Continue in this way to the end of the row.

Left-handed knitters may prefer to unravel the work so that the yarn is at the LH edge and then work from left to right.

SELVEDGES

A selvedge is a specially worked edge on a piece of knitting. It may be added to give a smooth, firm edge on a fabric, such as stocking stitch, that would otherwise have a rather loose one, and thus make the edges easier to handle when seaming. Or it may give a decorative finish to a piece of knitting that will not be seamed – a scarf, for example – and prevent the edges from curling, as some stitch patterns are apt to do.

Patterns rarely include selvedges in the instructions. In the case of a one-stitch selvedge, to be joined in a seam, it is not usually necessary to add extra stitches. However, if the fabric stitch pattern is a complex one, or if there is a detailed colour pattern, such as a traditional Fair Isle motif, you may wish to add a selvedge stitch to each edge, so that the pattern can run smoothly across the seam.

Single chain edge

This selvedge gives a smooth edge which is especially appropriate for pieces that will be joined edge to edge (see page 35) or where stitches will be picked up (see page 32).

Right side: slip the first stitch knitwise; knit the last stitch.
Wrong side: slip the first stitch purlwise; purl the last stitch.

Single garter edge

This method produces a firm edge on fabrics that tend to be loose, and is especially well suited to seaming with backstitch (see page 35).

Right and wrong sides: knit the first and the last stitch.

Double garter edge

This is a decorative edge which lies flat. Allow 2 extra stitches for each edge.

Right and wrong sides: slip the first stitch knitwise and knit the second stitch. At the end of the row, knit the last 2 stitches.

You will never need to join yarn in the middle of a row (except in tubular knitting – see page 62) if you always rewind a new ball before using it. Your fingers will detect any irregularities or knots in the yarn, and you can then break the yarn at such points and start a new ball.

If you clearly have enough yarn left for one row and think you may have enough for two, fasten a paper clip to the halfway point. If, after the next row, you still have about 25cm/10" to go before reaching the clip, you can complete another row.

INCREASES & DECREASES

There are many different methods of increasing and decreasing, and they are used for many different purposes. A series of increases or decreases may be used at the edge of a piece of knitting or across a row to shape it. Increases and decreases are also used decoratively to produce many interesting stitch patterns. When used for stitch patterns, increases and decreases are normally paired, so that the number of stitches on the needle remains the same. In some lace patterns there will be a temporary increase in the number of stitches, but this will be reduced to the normal number a row or two later.

A 'decorative increase' makes a hole in the fabric and is used mainly in lace patterns. It is produced by taking the yarn over or around the needle. The method varies slightly, depending on the starting position of the yarn, but the effect is the same.

a

Bar increase – knitwise

A bar increase – usually indicated in patterns as 'inc 1' – involves working twice into the same stitch. Whether worked on a knit row or a purl row, this produces a tiny horizontal strand on the knit side of the work. If worked a few stitches in from the edge, it can have a decorative effect.
1 Knit into the front of the stitch as usual, but do not slip the stitch

b

off the needle (a).
2 Now knit again into the same stitch through the back of the loop.
3 Slip the stitch off the LH needle (b). Two stitches have been made from one.

This method of increasing is often used to create fullness above the ribbing – known as a 'mass increase'.

a

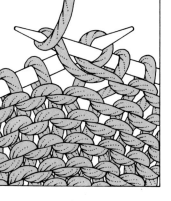

b

Bar increase – purlwise

1 Purl the stitch in the usual way, but do not slip the stitch off the needle (a).
2 Now purl again into the same stitch through the back of the loop. This entails twisting the stitch as shown (b).
3 Slip the stitch off the LH needle. In either a knit or purl bar increase the little bar produced on the knit side will appear to the

right of the first of the two stitches. Therefore, if you 'inc 1' into the 4th stitch from the RH edge, you should work across the row until there are 5 stitches remaining, and work the inc 1 into the first of these 5 stitches. On the newly worked row the bar will appear 5 stitches in from each edge.

Making one knit stitch

This kind of increase is usually written 'M1'.
1 Insert the LH needle from the front to back under the strand lying between the two adjacent stitches on the LH and RH needles (a).
2 Knit into the back of the new loop just formed on the LH needle (b).
3 Slip the loop off the needle (c).

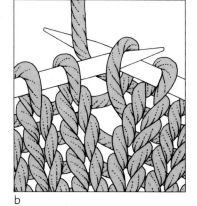

a

b

c

Making one purl stitch

This also is abbreviated as 'MI'.

I Insert the LH needle from front to back under the strand lying between the two adjacent stitches on the LH and RH needles (a).

2 Purl into the back of the new loop just formed, twisting it as shown to make this possible (b).

3 Slip the loop off the LH needle (c).

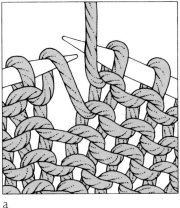

a

b

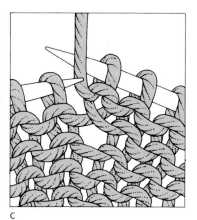

c

a

b

Lifted increase – knitwise

Like the 'MI' increase, this type of increase is inconspicuous.

I With the RH needle, pull up the stitch lying directly below the next stitch on the LH needle, from front to back, and knit into it (a).

2 Now knit into the next stitch on the LH needle (b).

To become familiar with the different effects produced with increases and decreases, cast on about 20 stitches and work in stocking stitch using a smooth yarn, practising the techniques shown here. On each increase/decrease row, attach a little tag identifying the method used. Keep the sample for future reference.

a

b

Lifted increase – purlwise

I With the RH needle, pull up the stitch lying directly below the next stitch on the LH needle, from back to front, and purl into it (a).

2 Now purl into the next stitch on the LH needle (b).

Yarn forward

This is worked between two knit stitches.

I Bring the yarn to the front of the work, then back over the needle.

2 Knit the stitch in the usual way (a). An extra loop has been formed on the needle (b).

3 On the next row, purl into this loop (c) as if it were a stitch (or work as given in the pattern).

a

b

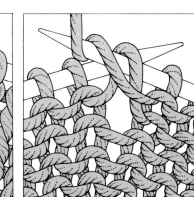

c

Yarn round needle

This is worked between two purl stitches, or between a knit and a purl stitch. Begin with the yarn at the front of the work.

1 Take the yarn over the needle and to the front, thus taking it completely around the needle (a).
2 Purl the stitch as usual. An extra loop has been formed (b).
3 On the next row work into this loop as if it were a stitch (c).

a

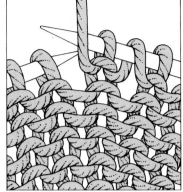

b

c

Yarn over needle

This is worked between a purl stitch and a knit stitch. The yarn will thus be at the front of the work.

1 Take the yarn back over the needle.
2 Knit the next stitch in the usual way.
3 On the next row, work into the new loop as instructed by the pattern.

DECREASING

There are fewer methods of decreasing than of increasing. Like increases, however, they produce different effects on the fabric and can be employed either inconspicuously or decoratively.

On raglan armholes a decorative type of decreasing – called 'fully fashioned' shaping – is often used. The decreases are worked two stitches in from the edge. At the right-hand edge a slipstitch decrease is worked on the third and fourth stitches from the edge; at the left-hand edge the third and fourth stitches are knitted together.

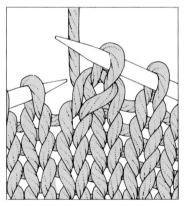

a

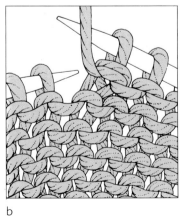

b

Knitting two stitches together

The instructions for this technique are 'K2tog'.
1 Insert the RH needle knitwise into the second stitch on the LH needle and then into the first stitch (a).
2 Knit the 2 stitches together, and slip the original stitch off the LH needle (b).

a

b

Purling two stitches together

The instructions for this technique are 'P2tog'.
1 Insert the RH needle purlwise into the first stitch on the LH needle and then into the second stitch (a).
2 Purl the 2 stitches together, and slip the original stitch off the LH needle (b).

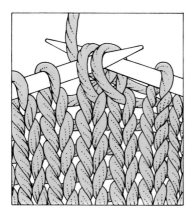

Knitting together 'tbl'

When stitches are knitted together normally, they will slant slightly to the right. In some cases a slant to the left will be required. In this case the stitches are knitted through the backs of the loops; the instructions are 'K2tog tbl'.

1 Insert the RH needle through the backs of the first and second stitches on the LH needle.
2 Knit the stitches together.

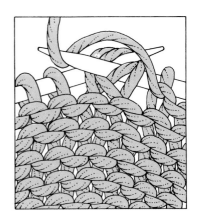

Purling together 'tbl'

When stitches are purled together normally, they will slant to the right on the knit side of the work. To achieve a slant to the left, they are purled through the backs of the loops, and the instructions are 'P2tog tbl'.

1 Insert the RH needle from back to front through the second stitch and then the first stitch.
2 Purl the two stitches together.

Slipstitch decrease, knitwise

Like knitting two together tbl, this produces a distinct slant to the left. Instructions are: 'slip one, knit one, pass slipped stitch over', or 'sl 1, K1, psso' (sometimes 'skpo').

1 Slip the first stitch on the LH needle knitwise (a).
2 Knit the next stitch (b).
3 Insert the LH needle into the slipped stitch, and lift it over the knitted stitch (c).

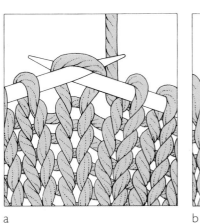

a

b

c

Slipstitch decrease, purlwise

The instructions are: 'slip one, purl one, pass slipped stitch over', or 'sl 1, P1, psso'.

1 With the yarn at the front, slip the first stitch purlwise (a).
2 Purl the next stitch in the usual way (b).
3 Insert the LH needle into the slipped stitch and lift it over the purled stitch (c).

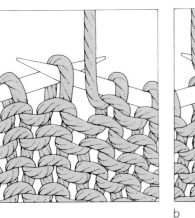

a

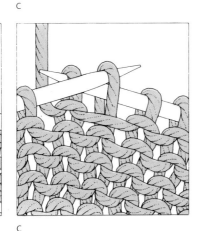

b

c

a

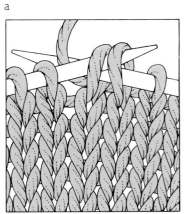

b

Slip, slip, knit decrease

This is similar to an ordinary knitwise slipstitch decrease but produces a smoother effect, which may be preferred in some lace patterns, for example. It is abbreviated 'ssk'.

1 Slip the first stitch knitwise, then slip the second knitwise (a).
2 Insert the LH needle into the front of the two slipped stitches, without removing them from the

RH needle; then knit them together through the backs of the loops with the RH needle (b).

Picking Up Stitches

Stitches are often held without being cast off, on a spare needle or stitch holder, and then worked into later after another part of the garment has been completed. For example, the stitches of a pocket lining will not be cast off but held on a spare needle until the pocket is the correct depth and then incorporated into the main section (see page 95).

A double-pointed needle is often the most convenient tool for this purpose, as the stitches can then be worked into from either end. If only a few stitches are to be held, a safety pin or a length of yarn will do. Whether the stitches to be held are knit or purl stitches, always slip them purlwise (see page 18), so that they will be facing the correct way for being worked into.

In some cases, new stitches will need to be picked up from a cast-off edge or side edge; this is called 'K up' or 'pick up and K'. It involves attaching the yarn to the edge and drawing it through the knitting at short intervals. Picking up can be done with either a knitting needle or a crochet hook.

The pattern will specify how many stitches are to be picked up. It is important to space them evenly, which can be tricky on a curved edge. Using large pins, mark the halfway point of the edge, then divide each of these two sections in half. Further subdivisions may sometimes be necessary. Divide the number of stitches to be picked up by the number of sections, and space these groups of stitches accordingly. Count the stitches in each section and then count the total, to make sure you have the required number.

Pins inserted along the curved section of a neckline to facilitate even spacing when picking up stitches.

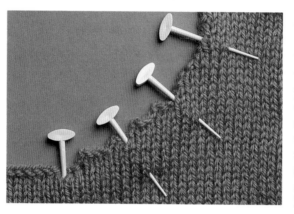

Picking up stitches on a cast-off edge

1 Fasten the yarn inconspicuously just under the edge.
2 Insert the needle from front to back through the first edge stitch.
3 Take the yarn under and over the needle to form a loop, and draw the loop through to the front. Repeat to the end.

The first row will be worked on the wrong side.

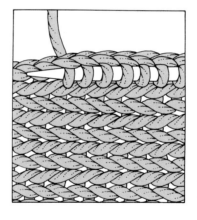

Picking up stitches on a side edge

The method is essentially the same as when picking up cast-off stitches. In this case, however, you will probably need to plan the spacing of the stitches, as for a curved edge, since working into every stitch or every other stitch may yield too many or too few. Work one stitch in from the edge, taking care not to encroach on the next line of stitches.

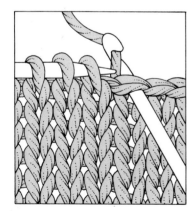

a

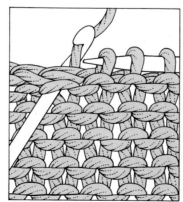

b

Picking up stitches with a crochet hook

1 Fasten the yarn just under the LH edge. Using a crochet hook, pull a loop through to the front of the work (a).
2 Insert the needle into this loop, and pull the yarn slightly to make it snug. Repeat all along the edge.

Left-handed knitters may prefer to work this method from the wrong side of the work, moving from right to left (b).

BUTTONHOLES

Many garments are fastened with buttons, and therefore making buttonholes is an important skill to learn. Buttonholes are not difficult. The easiest is the eyelet buttonhole; this is used on baby clothes, but is also suitable for some adults' garments. If the knitting is in a medium-weight yarn the hole produced will accommodate a flat button with a diameter of up to 1.5cm/⅝in.

Horizontal buttonholes are often worked in a ribbed band, worked on stitches picked up along the centre front edge of a cardigan or jacket, so that the ribs are at a right angle to the jacket and the buttonholes run vertically. A true vertical buttonhole is best used only for purely decorative fastenings, as it is the weakest of the three kinds of buttonhole.

Buttonholes can be strengthened and neatened using the techniques shown on page 97.

a

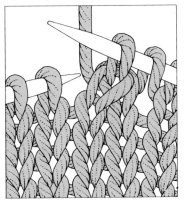

b

Eyelet buttonhole
Work to the position of the buttonhole.
1 Bring the yarn forward (see page 29) to make a new stitch. Insert the needle knitwise into the next 2 stitches (a).
2 Knit the stitches together to decrease one stitch (b).
On the following row, work into the new loop.

Horizontal buttonhole
On the right side, work to the position for the buttonhole.
1 Cast off the specified number of stitches (a). Work to the end.
2 On the wrong side, cast on the same number of stitches as were cast off (b), using the single cast-on (see page 15).
3 On the next row, work into the back of the cast-on stitches for a neat finished effect (c).

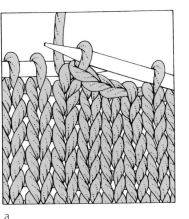

a

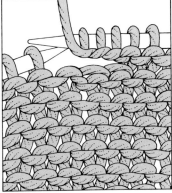

b

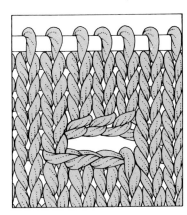

c

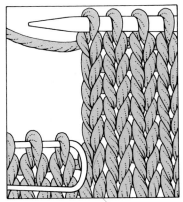

a

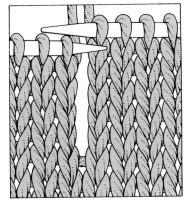

b

Vertical buttonhole
On the right side, work up to the position of the buttonhole.
1 Slip the remaining stitches onto a stitch holder.
2 Turn the work and continue on these stitches for the specified number of rows, ending with a right-side row (a). Do not break off the yarn.
3 Join a new length of yarn to the buttonhole edge of the held stitches. Using the needle already in the RH stitches, work to the end, then turn and continue on these stitches until there is one row less than on the RH side (b).
4 Fasten off the second length of yarn, and continue working to the end of the row. A smoother edge will result if the first stitch on every other row, at the buttonhole edge, is slipped, rather than worked into.

BLOCKING & PRESSING

This detail of a sleeve shows the proper way to insert pins – at intervals of about 2cm/ ¾". Note that the ribbing is not pinned. (The motif is the half diamond cable with bobbles – see page 52.)

After spending hours knitting a garment, it is important not to skimp on the making-up process. A little care and attention at this stage will ensure that your knitting skills will show to best advantage.

Before joining the pieces of knitting, you will probably need to block them to shape, and possibly press them. The treatment you choose depends on the fibre content of the yarn and also on the stitch pattern. The garment pattern instructions will usually specify how the work is to be treated; fibre content – and sometimes information on pressing – will also be given on the ball band. Some yarns, such as pure acrylic, should be neither blocked nor pressed.

If the stitch pattern is a textured one, the fabric should not be pressed, whatever the fibre content of the yarn.

For blocking or pressing you will need a firm, flat surface – which can be a board, a table top, or even the floor – well padded with an old blanket and a sheet or towel; an ironing board can be used for small pieces. You will also need some rustproof pins; for pressing, pins with ordinary heads are required.

WET BLOCKING

Pin the piece right side up to the flat surface, following the measurements given (sometimes in diagram form) in the pattern. Make sure that the knitting runs straight and that the shape is not distorted. Insert the pins at intervals of about 2cm/¾". Do not pin the ribbing.

Dampen the work thoroughly with cool water, using a spray bottle (the kind used to spray plants is ideal). Or dab it gently all over with a wet sponge. Leave the knitting to dry completely.

STEAM BLOCKING

This treatment is suitable for natural fibres, which will tolerate heat. First pin the pieces to the work surface as for ordinary blocking.

To apply steam, use either a steam iron and a dry pressing cloth or a dry iron and a damp cloth. Place the cloth over the work and hold the iron just above it, allowing the steam to penetrate the knitting. Allow the work to dry before removing the pins.

PRESSING

Pin the pieces to the flat surface as for blocking, but place them wrong side up. Do not pin the ribbing. Place the pins close together and insert them diagonally all the way into the padded surface.

Use a steam iron and a dry cloth or a dry iron and a damp cloth. For natural-synthetic blends use a dry, cool iron over a dry cloth.

Do *not* slide the iron over the surface; instead, place it lightly on one area for a second or two, lift it off, and place it on another area. Allow the work to cool before removing it from the board.

SEAMS

There are several different ways of joining pieces of knitting, suitable for different parts of a garment. An edge-to-edge seam, for example, is ideal for joining a button or buttonhole band to a front edge, and is especially appropriate for baby clothes, as there is no extra bulk on the wrong side to irritate delicate skin. A flat seam is sometimes used for ribbing, although it is not quite so strong as the edge-to-edge seam. Backstitch is the preferred method where strength is required – as in a side seam.

Some edges may be grafted, rather than sewn together; for this advanced technique see page 90.

The yarn used for knitting the garment can normally be used for the sewing. However, if this yarn is a chunky weight, or has a slubbed texture, you should work the stitching with a lighter-weight yarn in the same colour. Always fasten the yarn with a couple of backstitches.

Yarns used for the stitching should be darned into the edges of the work with the tapestry needle for a short distance. Ends left from the knitting are treated the same way.

a

b

Edge-to-edge seam

Place both pieces right side up on a flat surface.

1 Fasten the yarn to the wrong side, on the RH edge, and bring it to the right side (a).

2 Take it across and through the stitch directly opposite on the LH edge; pull the yarn to draw the edges together, then work into the next stitch on the RH edge. Continue in this way to the top of the seam, pulling the yarn as you go to bring the edges smoothly together (b).

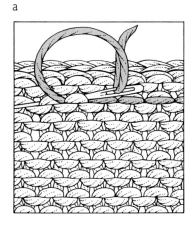

Backstitch seam

Pin the two pieces together with right sides facing.

1 Fasten the yarn at the RH corner.

2 Work from right to left, taking the yarn across two stitches on the under side, then back over one stitch on top, so that the stitches meet end to end as shown. On the other side, the stitches overlap.

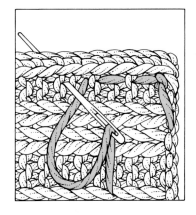

Flat seam

This seam consists of running stitches, worked close together, and may be used on ribbing that will not be subjected to strain.

1 Place the two pieces together with right sides facing. Fasten the thread at the end.

2 Work from right to left, one stitch in from the edge, taking the yarn straight up and down over one stitch at a time.

Setting in a sleeve

A sleeve with a curved sleeve head is set into the armhole after joining the adjacent seams.

1 Turn the main part of the garment wrong side out. Insert a pin into the front and back edges halfway between the two seams.

2 Turn the sleeve right side out, and insert pins at the centre point and halfway down.

3 Position the sleeve inside the

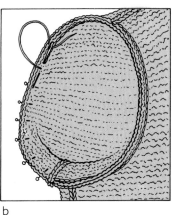

armhole, and pin the edges together, matching the pins and seams. Add more pins around the edge, placing them about 2 or 3cm/¾ – 1″ apart and easing the sleeve to fit the armhole, if necessary. You may wish to tack the edges together.

4 Work around the armhole, about 5mm/¼″ from the edge, using backstitch and working from the sleeve side.

a

b

MORE COMPLEX TEXTURES

These patterns suggest the infinite possibilities available through the techniques of increasing and decreasing. Daisy stitch and coral knit stitch illustrate the 'crunchy' textures that can be achieved by alternately increasing and then decreasing the stitches that make up the fabric. Nut pattern employs basically the same principle to form little clusters over the fabric. It resembles the bobble patterns shown on pages 52–53.

Leaf and chevron patterns are examples of linear effects formed through increases and decreases. In chevron the downward points are formed by decreasing, the upward ones by increasing. The pointed/scalloped edge of these patterns is less apparent when worked above ribbing.

In fisherman's rib the stitches are not actually increased, but a technique similar to a lifted increase is used to create a softly elastic texture.

NUT PATTERN

multiple of 4
Row 1 ✢P3, (K1, yf, K1) into next st; rep from ✢.
Rows 2 and 3 ✢P3, K3; rep from ✢.
Row 4 ✢P3 tog, K3; rep from ✢.
Row 5 Purl.
Row 6 Knit.
Row 7 ✢P1, (K1, yf, K1) into next st, P2; rep from ✢.
Row 8 K2, ✢P3, K3; rep from ✢ to last 4 sts, P3, K1.
Row 9 P1, ✢K3, P3; rep from ✢ to last 5 sts, K3, P2.
Row 10 K2, ✢P3 tog, K3; rep from ✢ to last 4 sts, P3 tog, K1.
Row 11 Purl.
Row 12 Knit.

CORAL KNOT STITCH

multiple of 2 plus 2 extra
Row 1 K1, ✢K2 tog; rep from ✢ to last st, K1.
Row 2 K1, ✢K1, pick up strand between this and next st and K it; rep from ✢ to last st, K1.
Row 3 Knit.
Row 4 Purl.

FISHERMAN'S RIB

multiple of 2
Row 1 Purl.
Row 2 ✢P1, K next st in the row below; rep from ✢ to last 2 sts, P2.
Repeat Row 2 throughout.

LEAF PATTERN

multiple of 24 plus 1 extra

Note 'K up 1': Pick up a stitch (see page 32).

Row 1 K1, *K up 1, sl 1., K1, psso, K4, K2 tog, K3, K up 1, K1, K up 1, K3, sl 1, K1, psso, K4, K2 tog, K up 1, K1; rep from *.

Row 2 and every alternate row Purl.

Row 3 K1, * K up 1, K1, sl 1, K1, psso, K2, K2 tog, K4, K up 1, K1, K up 1, K4, sl 1, K1, psso, K2, K2 tog, K1, K up 1, K1; rep from *.

Row 5 K1, *K up 1, K2, sl 1, K1, psso, K2 tog, K5, K up 1, K1, K up 1, K5, sl 1, K1, psso, K2 tog, K2, K up 1, K1; rep from *.

Row 7 K1, *K up 1, K3, sl 1, K1, psso, K4, K2 tog, K up 1, K1, K up 1, sl 1, K1, psso, K4, K2 tog, K3, K up 1, K1; rep from *.

Row 9 K1, *K up 1, K4, sl 1, K1, psso, K2, K2 tog, K1, K up 1, K1, K up 1, K1, sl 1, K1, psso, K2, K2 tog, K4, K up 1, K1; rep from *.

Row 11 K1, *K up 1, K5, sl 1, K1, psso, K2 tog, K2, K up 1, K1, K up 1, K2, sl 1, K1, psso, K2 tog, K5, K up 1, K1; rep from *.

Row 12 as Row 2.

DAISY STITCH

multiple of 4, plus 1 extra

Rows 1 and 3 (RS) Knit.

Row 2 K1, *P3 tog, yon ,P same 3 sts tog again, K1; rep from *.

Row 4 K1, P1, K1, *P3 tog, yon, P same 3 sts tog again, K1; rep from * to last 2 sts, P1, K1.

CHEVRON

multiple of 13 plus 2 extra

Row 1 *K2, M1, K4, sl 1, K2 tog, psso, K4, M1; rep from *.

Row 2 Purl.

LACE PATTERNS

For many people lace patterns are the most tempting of all types of knitting. The complementary relationship of the knitted fabric itself and the pattern of holes is especially pleasing.

The character of a lace pattern can change quite dramatically, depending on the yarn it is worked in. Try some of these patterns in several different yarns: fine baby yarns, soft mohair blends, crisp cotton yarns, glitter yarns. As a general rule, however, the yarn should not be too thick. The samples on this page are worked in soft silk and wool-silk yarns; those on the next two pages in a four-ply wool.

If you are beginning a lace pattern at the edge, without any ribbing, it is best to use the single cast-on (see page 15), which produces a soft edge.

SNOWDROP LACE

multiple of 8 plus 5 extra
Rows 1 and 3 K1, ✳yf, sl 1 pw, K2 tog, psso, yf, K5; rep from ✳ to last 4 sts, yf, sl 1, K2 tog, psso, yf, K1.
Row 2 and every alternate row Purl.
Row 5 K1, ✳K3, yf, sl 1, K1, psso, K1, K2 tog, yf; rep from ✳ to last 4 sts, K4.
Row 7 K1, ✳ yf, sl 1, K2 tog, psso, yf, K1; rep from ✳ to last 4 sts, yf, sl 1, K2 tog, psso, yf, K1.

VINE LACE

multiple of 9 plus 4 extra
Row 1 and every alternate row (WS) Purl.
Row 2 K3, ✳yf, K2, sl 1, K1, psso, K2 tog, K2, yf, K1; rep from ✳ to last st, K1.
Row 4 K2, ✳yf, K2, sl 1, K1, psso, K2 tog, K2, yf, K1; rep from ✳ to last 2 sts, K2.

QUATREFOIL EYELET

multiple of 8
Row 1 and every alternate row (WS) Purl.
Row 2 Knit.
Row 4 K3, ✳yf, sl 1, K1, psso, K6; rep from ✳ ending last rep K3 instead of K6.
Row 6 K1, ✳K2 tog, yf, K1, yf, sl 1, K1, psso, K3; rep from ✳ ending last rep K2 instead of K3.
Row 8 as Row 4.
Row 10 Knit.
Row 12 K7, ✳yf, sl 1, K1, psso, K6; rep from ✳ to last st, K1.
Row 14 K5, ✳K2 tog, yf, K1, yf, sl 1, K1, psso, K3; rep from ✳ to last 3 sts, K3.
Row 16 as Row 12.

CHEVRON LACE

multiple of 8 plus 1 extra (multiple is increased 1 st in Row 9, reduced in Row 10)

Row 1 *K5 , yf, K2 tog, K1; rep from * to last st, K1.
Row 2 and every alternate row Purl.
Row 3 *K3, K2 tog tbl, yf, K1, yf, K2 tog; rep from * to last st, K1.
Row 5 K1, *K1, K2 tog tbl, yf, K3, yf, K2 tog; rep from *.
Row 7 *yf, K2 tog tbl, return st to left needle, pass next st over it and put st back on right needle, yf, K5; rep from * to last st K1.
Row 9 *K1, K into front and back of next st, K6; rep from * to last st, K1.
Row 11 *K2 tog, K4, yf, K2 tog, K1; rep from * to last st, K1.
Row 12 Purl.
Rep rows 3–12.

VANDYKE STITCH

multiple of 10

Row 1 *yf, sl 1, K 1, psso, K8; rep from *.
Row 2 and every alternate row Purl.
Row 3 *K1, yf, sl 1, K1, psso, K5, K2 tog, yf; rep from * ending last rep K2.
Row 5 *K2, yf, sl 1, K1, psso, K3, K2 tog , yf, K1; rep from *.
Row 7 *K5, yf, sl 1, K1, psso, K3; rep from *.
Row 9 *K3, K2 tog, yf, K1, yf, sl 1, K1, psso, K2; rep from *.
Row 11 *K2, K2 tog, yf, K3, yf, sl 1, K1, psso, K1; rep from *.

OPENWORK DIAMOND PATTERN

multiple of 10 plus 2 extra

Row 1 K1, *K1, yf, sl 1, K1, psso, K5, K2 tog, yf, rep from * to last st, K1.
Row 2 and every alternate row Purl.
Row 3 K1, *K2, yf, sl 1, K1, psso, K3, K2 tog, yf, K1; rep from * to last st, K1.
Row 5 K1, *K1, yf, sl 1, K1, psso, yf, sl 1, K1, psso, K1, K2 tog, yf, K2 tog, yf; rep from * to last st, K1.
Row 7 K1, *K2, yf, sl 1, K1, psso, yf, sl 1, K2 tog, psso, yf, K2 tog, yf, K1; rep from * to last st, K1.
Row 9 K1, *K3, K2 tog, yf, K1, yf, sl 1, K1, psso, K2; rep from * to last st, K1.
Row 11 K1, *K2, K2 tog, yf, K3, yf, sl 1, K1, psso, K1; rep from * to last st, K1.
Row 13 K1, *K1, K2 tog, yf, K2 tog, yf, K1, yf, sl 1, K1, psso, yf, sl 1, K1, psso; rep from * to last st, K1.
Row 15 K2 tog, *yf, K2 tog, yf, K3, yf,sl 1, K1, psso, yf, sl 1, K1, psso, K1, yf, sl 1, K2 tog, psso; rep from * to last 2 sts, K2.

FERN LACE

multiple of 10 plus 1 extra
Row 1 and every alternate row (WS) Purl.
Row 2 K3, ✿K2 tog, yf, K1, yf, ssk, K5; rep from ✿, ending last rep K3.
Row 4 K2, ✿K2 tog, (K1, yf) twice, K1, ssk, K3; rep from ✿, ending last rep K2.
Row 6 K1, ✿K2 tog, K2, yf, K1, yf, K2, ssk, K1; rep from ✿.
Row 8 K2 tog, ✿K3, yf, K1, yf, K3, sl 1, K2 tog, psso; rep from ✿ to last 9 sts, K3, yf, K1, yf, K3, ssk.
Row 10 K1, ✿yf, ssk, K5, K2 tog, yf, K1; rep from ✿.
Row 12 K1, ✿yf, K1, ssk, K3, K2 tog, K1, yf, K1; rep from ✿.
Row 14 K1, ✿yf, K2, ssk, K1, K2 tog, K2, yf, K1; rep from ✿.
Row 16 K1, ✿yf, K3, sl 1, K2 tog, psso, K3, yf, K1; rep from ✿.

CURVING LATTICE LACE

multiple of 13 plus 2 extra
Row 1 K1, ✿K2, sl 1, K1, psso, K4, K2 tog, K2, yf, K1, yf; rep from ✿ to last st, K1.
Row 2 and every alternate row Purl.
Row 3 K1, ✿yf, K2, sl 1, K1, psso, K2, K2 tog, K2, yf, K3; rep from ✿ to last st, K1.
Row 5 K1, ✿K1, yf, K2, sl 1, K1, psso, K2 tog, K2, yf, K4; rep from ✿ to last st, K1.
Row 7 K1, ✿yf, K1, yf, K2, sl 1, K1, psso, K4, K2 tog, K2; rep from ✿ to last st, K1.
Row 9 K1, ✿K3, yf, K2, sl 1, K1, psso, K2, K2 tog, K2, yf; rep from ✿ to last st, K1.
Row 11 K1, ✿K4, yf, K2, sl 1, K1, psso, K2 tog, K2, yf, K1; rep from ✿ to last st, K1.
Row 12 Purl.

OPEN CHEVRON LACE

multiple of 12 plus 1 extra
Row 1 and every alternate row (WS) Purl.
Row 2 K4, ✿K2 tog, yf, K1, yf, sl 1, K1, psso, K7; rep from ✿ ending last rep K4.
Row 4 K3, ✿K2 tog, yf, K3, yf, sl 1, K1, psso, K5; rep from ✿ ending last rep K3.
Row 6 K2, ✿(K2 tog, yf) twice, K1, (yf, sl 1, K1, psso) twice, K3; rep from ✿ ending last rep K2.
Row 8 K1, ✿(K2 tog, yf) twice, K3, (yf, sl 1, K1, psso) twice, K1; rep from ✿.
Row 10 K2 tog, ✿yf, K2 tog, yf, K5, yf, sl 1, K1, psso, yf, sl 1, K2 tog, psso; rep from ✿ ending last rep sl 1, K1, psso.
Row 12 K1, ✿K2 tog, yf, K1, yf, sl 1, K1, psso, K1; rep from ✿.
Row 14 K2 tog, ✿yf, K3, yf, sl 1, K2 tog, psso; rep from ✿ ending last rep sl 1, K1, psso.

ENGLISH MESH LACE

multiple of 6 plus 1 extra
Row 1 and every alternate row (WS) Purl.
Row 2 K1, ✿yf, ssk, K1, K2 tog, yf, K1; rep from ✿.
Row 4 K1 ✿yf, K1, sl 1, K2 tog, psso, K1, yf, K1; rep from ✿.
Row 6 K1, ✿K2 tog, yf, K1, yf, ssk, K1; rep from ✿.
Row 8 K2 tog, ✿(K1, yf) twice, K1, sl 1, K2 tog, psso; rep from ✿ to last 5 sts, (K1, yf) twice, K1, ssk.

FALLING LEAF PATTERN

multiple of 10 plus 1 extra
Row 1 K1, ✿yf, K3, sl 1, K2 tog, psso, K3, yf, K1; rep from ✿.
Row 2 and every alternate row Purl.
Row 3 K1, ✿K1, yf, K2, sl 1, K2 tog, psso, K2, yf, K2; rep from ✿.
Row 5 K1, ✿K2, yf, K1, sl 1, K2 tog, psso, K1, yf, K3; rep from ✿.
Row 7 K1, ✿K3, yf, sl 1, K2 tog, psso, yf, K4; rep from ✿.
Row 9 K2 tog, ✿K3, yf, K1, yf, K3, sl 1, K2 tog, psso; rep from ✿ to last 9 sts, K3, yf, K1, yf, K3, sl 1, K1, psso.
Row 11 K2 tog, ✿K2, yf, K3, yf, K2, sl 1, K2 tog, psso; rep from ✿ to last 9 sts, K2, yf, K3, yf, K2, sl 1, K1, psso.
Row 13 K2 tog, ✿K1, yf, K5, yf, K1, sl 1, K2 tog, psso; rep from ✿ to last 9 sts, K1, yf, K5, yf, K1, sl 1, K1, psso.
Row 15 K2 tog, ✿yf, K7, yf, sl 1, K2 tog, psso; rep from ✿ to last 9 sts, yf, K7, yf, sl 1, K1, psso.
Row 16 as Row 2.

FISHTAIL LACE

multiple of 10 plus 1 extra
Row 1 (RS) K1, ✿yf, K3, sl 1, K2 tog, psso, K3, yf, K1; rep from ✿.
Row 2 and every alternate row Purl.
Row 3 K1, ✿K1, yf, K2, sl 1, K2 tog, psso, K2, yf, K2; rep from ✿.
Row 5 K1, ✿K2, yf, K1, sl 1, K2 tog, psso, K1, yf, K3; rep from ✿.
Row 7 K1, ✿K3, yf, sl 1, K2 tog, psso, yf, K4; rep from ✿.
Row 8 as Row 2.

3 Special Textures

Once you have mastered the basic knitting skills and can follow a pattern, why not try some more adventurous stitch patterns? The techniques described in this chapter require some facility in handling yarn and needles, but the fascinating results are well worth the effort. With only a little practice you can produce gracefully coiling cables, large and small bobbles, knitted smocking and shaggy looped pile fabrics. The versatility of knitting is amply demonstrated in these pages.

It is well worthwhile experimenting with different yarns to see how many varied effects are possible using these stitches. For example, cables are often worked in Aran yarn, as part of a traditional Aran-style sweater; but they can look especially beautiful in a glossy cotton or silk yarn, and they also lend themselves well to mohair and angora yarns. Bobbles are normally worked in smooth yarns, such as wool double-knitting; in cotton they have a crisper texture.

Twisted stitches and a cable (above) are shown in this sample. At left, two stitches have been twisted right on every fourth row. At right, a 'cable 6 forward' has been worked on every sixth row.

Working a cable (left).
In this photograph interlaced cable (see page 51) is being worked. Two stitches are held at the front, while the next is about to be purled.

Twisted Stitches & Cables

Some of the most beautiful of all stitch patterns involve crossing stitches over each other – that is, changing the sequence in which they are worked. Among the most familiar of these are found in Aran knitting, with its rich variety of rope-like cables, plaits, zigzags and honeycomb effects.

Stitches can be crossed in many different ways. Some crossing techniques are worked entirely on the main pair of needles; these are often referred to as 'twisting' the stitches. Up to four stitches can be twisted on the two needles, to produce mock cables which are virtually indistinguishable from those produced with a cable needle.

It is important, when twisting stitches, to keep a loose tension on the twist row and on those preceding and following it. This makes the work easier and reduces strain on the yarn. When cabling, always use a cable needle no larger – and preferably smaller – than the main needles, in order to avoid distorting the stitches.

Cables may coil either to the right – called 'cable back' – or to the left – called 'cable forward'. The basic cable can be worked over 4, 6 or 8 stitches.

Different effects are achieved by varying the number of rows between cable rows. Working the cable every sixth row produces a graceful coil; on every fourth row, a thick, rope-like effect; on every tenth or twelfth row, a flat effect like a twisted ribbon. A novel effect can be produced by using a contrasting colour for half of the cable stitches. The cable shown opposite is worked over 6 stitches, but the same technique is used whatever the number.

VARIATIONS ON CABLING

The basic cable technique can be used to move a single stitch or a group of stitches across the fabric, forming more complex cable and lattice patterns. The illustrations on page 45 show how to move a single knit stitch to the right or the left on a background of reverse stocking stitch. The same basic method can be used to move different numbers of stitches at a time. To become familiar with cabling techniques, make a sample, using Aran or double knitting yarn.

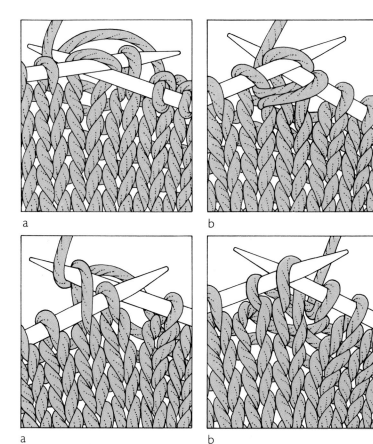

a   b

a   b

Twist 2 right (abbreviated Tw2R)
1 Take the RH needle in front of the first stitch on the LH needle and knit into the second stitch (a). Do not let the first stitch slip off the needle.
2 Knit into the first stitch (b) and slip both stitches off the LH needle.
On the next row, purl into the twisted stitches as usual.
The stitches twist to the right.

Twist 2 left (abbreviated Tw2L)
1 Take the RH needle behind the first stitch on the LH needle, and knit into the second stitch through the back of the loop (a).
2 Knit into the first stitch, also through the back of the loop (b).
On the next row, purl into the twisted stitches as usual.
The stitches now twist to the left.

a

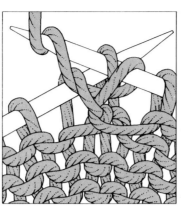

b

Twist 2 right purlwise
(abbreviated Tw2PR)

1 Take the RH needle in front of the first stitch on the LH needle and purl into the second stitch (a).
2 Purl into the first stitch (b). Slip both stitches off the LH needle. On the next row, knit into the twisted stitches as usual.
The stitches twist to the right on the knit side of the work.

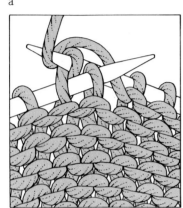

a

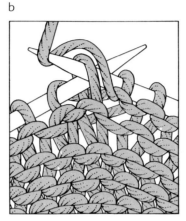

b

Twist 2 left purlwise
(abbreviated Tw2PL)

1 Take the RH needle and yarn behind the first stitch on the LH needle, and purl into the back of the second stitch, twisting it as shown (a). Take care not to let the first stitch slip off the needle.
2 Purl into the front of the first stitch (b), and let both stitches slip off the needle.
On the next row, knit into the twisted stitches as usual.
The stitches twist to the left on the knit side of the work.

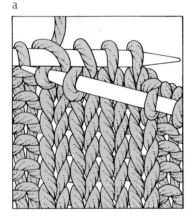

a

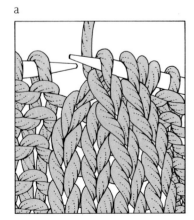

b

Mock cable back
This mock cable contains 4 stitches.

1 Take the RH needle in front of the first 2 stitches and knit the third stitch.
2 Knit the fourth stitch (a). Leave all 4 stitches on the LH needle.
3 Knit the second stitch on the LH needle (a).
4 Knit the first stitch. Slip all 4 stitches off the needle (b).

On the following row, purl these stitches, remembering to keep the tension fairly loose.
The resulting cable twists to the right.

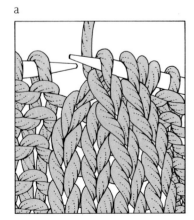

Mock cable forward
For this mock cable, knit the third and fourth stitches through the back of the loops. Then knit the first stitch through the front in the usual way, slip it off the needle, knit the second stitch through the front and slip all stitches off the needle.
The resulting cable twists to the left.

Cable 6 back (C6B)
1 Work to the position of the cable, then slip the next 3 stitches onto the cable needle and hold them at the back of the work.
2 Knit the next 3 stitches (a).
3 Knit the 3 stitches from the cable needle (b).
On the next row, purl these stitches as usual.
The cable coils to the right.

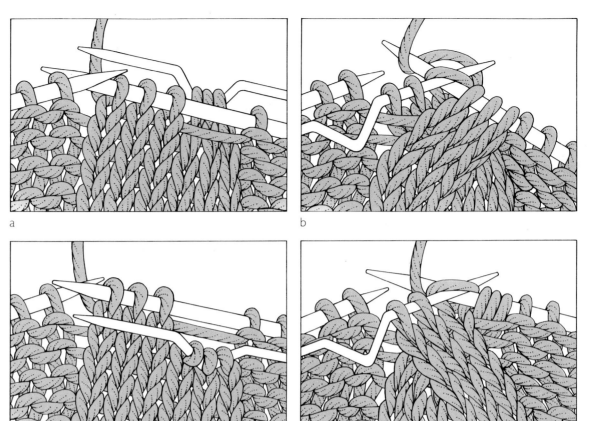

a

b

Cable 6 forward (C6F)
1 Work to the position of the cable, then slip the next 3 stitches onto the cable needle and hold them at the front of the work.
2 Knit the next 3 stitches (a).
3 Knit the 3 stitches from the cable needle (b).
On the next row, purl these stitches as usual.
The cable coils to the left.

a

b

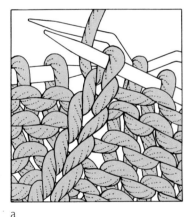

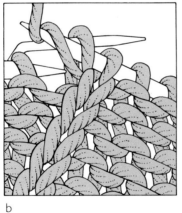

a

b

Cross 2 back (abbreviated Cr2B)
1 Slip the purl stitch immediately before the knit stitch onto a cable needle and hold it at the back of the work.
2 Knit the knit stitch (a).
3 Purl the stitch from the cable needle (b).

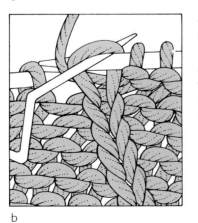

a

b

Cross 2 forward (abbreviated Cr2F)
1 Slip the knit stitch onto the cable needle and hold it at the front of the work.
2 Purl the next, purl, stitch (a).
3 Knit the stitch from the cable needle (b).

OBBLES & NOTS

Many different sizes and shapes of bobble can be produced, but they are all based on the same principle: making several stitches out of one stitch and then decreasing back to a single stitch, usually after working one or more rows on the increased stitches. The extra rows are usually worked on the bobble alone; this produces a bobble that stands out firmly from the background fabric, being attached to it only at the top and the bottom. A softer bobble is produced by working the increased stitches along with the background fabric. Small bobbles – often called knots – are made by immediately decreasing the increased stitches.

The initial increasing for a bobble can be worked in a variety of ways: by alternately knitting and purling into the stitch, by knitting into the front and back of the stitch alternately, or by taking the yarn over the needle between knit stitches.

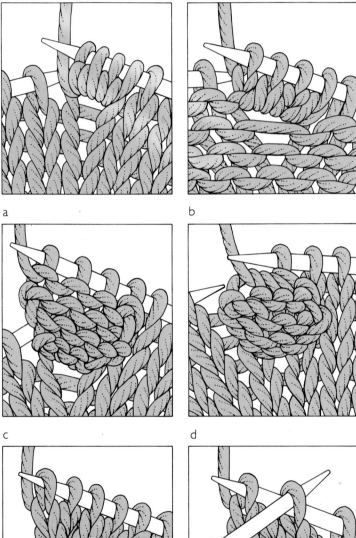

a

b

c

d

Bobble – Method 1

This bobble is worked in reverse stocking stitch and is shown on a stocking stitch fabric. For a stocking stitch bobble, reverse the 'knit' and 'purl' instructions in steps 2–4.

1 Knit, purl, knit and purl into the same stitch, thus making 4 stitches out of one (a). Turn the work.

2 Knit these 4 stitches (b). Turn.

3 Purl the stitches. Turn.

4 Repeat steps 2 and 3 once. The right (purl) side of the bobble is facing (c).

5 With the LH needle, lift the second, third and fourth stitches over the first, thus decreasing back to one stitch and completing the bobble (d).

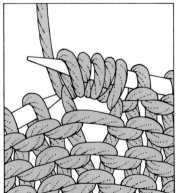

a

b

c

Bobble – Method 2

This bobble is slightly flatter than that shown in Method 1.

1 Knit 1, yarn forward, knit 1, yarn forward, knit 1 (a); Turn.

2 Purl the stitches. Turn.

3 Knit the stitches (b). Turn.

4 Purl 2 together, purl 1, purl 2 together: 3 stitches. Turn.

5 Slip 1, knit 2 together, pass the slipped stitch over (c).

a

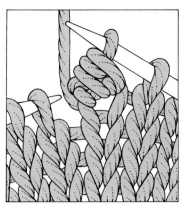

b

Knot – Method 1

This small bobble, or knot, is produced in essentially the same way as the Method 1 bobble opposite, but the increased stitches are immediately decreased.

1 Knit, purl, knit, purl and knit into the stitch, thus making 5 stitches out of one (a).

2 With the LH needle, lift the second, third, fourth and fifth stitches over the first one, thus decreasing back to one stitch and completing the knot (b).

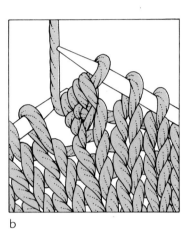

a

Knot – Method 2

This method produces a slightly flatter and smoother knot than Method 1, above.

1 Knit into the front, back, front and back of the stitch, thus making 4 stitches out of one.

2 With the LH needle, lift the second (a), third and fourth stitches over the first one, completing the knot (b).

b

CONTRASTING BOBBLES

To work a bobble or knot in a contrasting colour, simply tie the new colour to the first colour at the position for the bobble on the wrong side of the work, drop the first colour and work the bobble in the new colour. When the bobble is completed, break off the yarn and tie the ends together securely. When the knitting is completed, darn the ends into the wrong side. If a series of bobbles is to be worked across a row at short intervals, it may be preferable to weave in the contrasting yarn as shown on page 70.

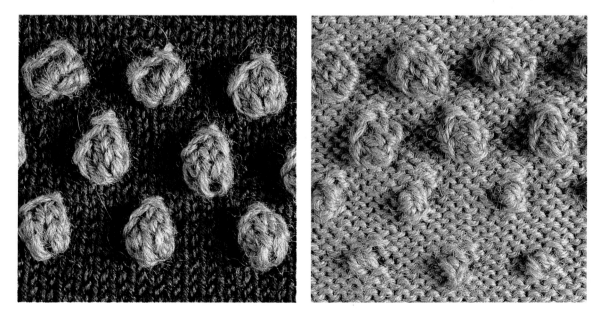

In the sample (far left), bobbles have been worked in every sixth stitch and on every sixth row and staggered evenly. The yarn has been woven in on the wrong side. The bobble shown is the one described in Method 2. The pattern requires a multiple of 6 stitches plus 5 extra.

The sample (left) shows, from top to bottom: bobbles, Method 1; bobbles, Method 2; knots, Method 1; knots, Method 2.

ELONGATED STITCHES

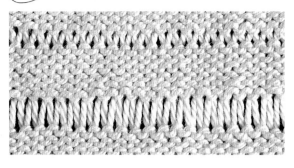

Elongated stitches (right) are shown here against reverse stocking stitch. In the top row the yarn has been taken once around the needle; in the bottom row, twice.

A variety of openwork effects can be achieved by winding the yarn two or more times around the needle, then, on the following row, working into only the first of each pair or group of loops, allowing the extra loops to unwind. The patterns using this technique – called 'dropped-stitch patterns' – range from simple bands of openwork, formed by elongating the stitches all the way across the fabric – to quite complex patterns.

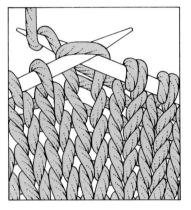 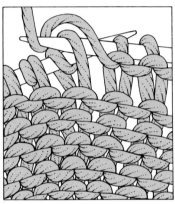

Basic elongated stitch

1 Insert the RH needle knitwise into the stitch, take the yarn twice around the needle, and draw the 2 loops through the stitch, allowing it to slip off the needle. Repeat to the end of the row,

2 On the following row, purl into the first of each pair of loops and allow the extra loop to drop off the needle.

Either the knit side or the purl side can be used as the right side of the work.

Longer stitches can be produced by winding the yarn 3 or more times around the needle.

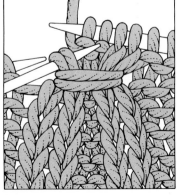

SMOCKING

A smocked fabric can be produced either by sewing a knitted fabric in a pattern (see page 83) or by knitting in the smocking as you go. The latter method, which is shown here, is based on a rib pattern, which can be varied by adjusting the thickness and/or spacing of the ribs. A cable needle is used to group stitches together so that they can be wrapped with the yarn. The grouped stitches can be wrapped before they are worked, as shown here, or worked first and then wrapped.

Smocking (right) has been knitted in, as described below.

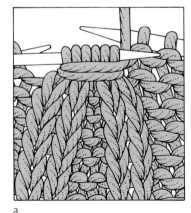

Basic ribbed smocking

Cast on a multiple of 8 stitches plus 10. Work in K2, P2 rib for 5 rows. On the 6th (right side) row, work the smocking, as follows:

1 Purl the first 2 (purl) stitches.

2 Slip the next 6 stitches onto the cable needle; hold them at front.

3 Wind the yarn twice around these stitches from left to right, pulling it firmly (a); knit 2, purl 2 (b), knit 2 from the cable needle.

4 Repeat steps 1–3 to the end.

5 Work in rib for 5 rows.

6 On the 12th row purl the first 2 stitches.

7 Slip 2 knit stitches onto the cable needle. Wind the yarn around these stitches twice, knit them, then slip them off the cable needle.

8 Purl 2 stitches, repeat steps 2 and 3 to the last 2 stitches; knit 2. These 12 rows form the pattern.

a

b

$\mathcal{L}$OOP STITCH

It is possible to produce looped pile or shaggy fabrics in knitting by winding the yarn around the thumb at regular close intervals. The loops produced in this way can be left as they are, or they can be cut for a shaggy effect.

Loop stitch is easier to work if the yarn is held in the right hand, as shown on page 16. (Left-handed knitters should reverse the movements shown here.)

Loop stitch (left) has been worked on this fabric in a staggered pattern.

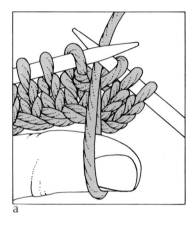

a

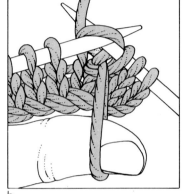

b

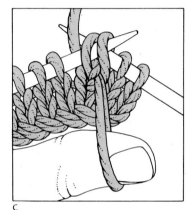

c

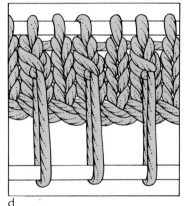

d

Working loop stitch
Begin by working 2 rows of stocking stitch, then knit one or two stitches for the selvedge.
1 Knit the next stitch, but do not let the original stitch slip off the needle. Bring the yarn forward between the needles and take it under the left thumb from back to front, making a loop of the desired length (a).
2 Knit again into the same stitch (b), and slip the original stitch off the LH needle, still keeping the thumb in the loop.
3 With the thumb still in the loop, insert the LH needle through the front of the 2 stitches just made, and knit both stitches together through the back (c). Slip the thumb out of the loop.
Work to the position of the next loop, then repeat steps 1–3. In the drawing the loops are shown separated by a single knit stitch. They may be more widely spaced

if desired.
Purl the next row. Slip the free needle through the loops, and pull them gently downwards (d).

Forming a loop (right). The length of the loop can be increased by holding the thumb lower.

CABLE PATTERNS

This selection of cable patterns suggests the rich variety of effects possible when crossing stitches with a cable needle. These samples have been worked in Aran-weight yarn, reflecting their connection with this traditional form of knitting, in which cables symbolize ropes used by fishermen. However, cables have a wonderfully versatile quality, and lend themselves equally well to fine silky yarns, crisp cottons and soft mohair yarns.

RIBBED CABLE

worked over 11 sts
Rows 1, 3 and 5 (RS) P2, K1 tbl, (P1 tbl, K1 tbl) 3 times, P2.
Row 2 and every alternate row K2, P1 tbl, (K1 tbl, P1 tbl) 3 times, K2.
Row 7 P2, sl next 4 sts onto cable needle and hold at front of work, K1 tbl, P1, K1 tbl, sl 4th st from cable needle back onto LH needle and P1, then (K1 tbl, P1, K1 tbl) from cable needle, P2.
Rows 9, 11, 13 and 15 as Row 1.
Row 16 as Row 2.

LINK CABLE

worked over 24 sts
Rows 1, 3 and 5 (RS) P6, K12, P6.
Rows 2, 4 and 6 K6, P12, K6.
Row 7 P6, C6B, C6F, P6.
Row 8 as Row 2.

DEER CABLE

worked over 20 sts
Row 1 and every alternate row (WS) K2, P16, K2.
Row 2 P2, K4, C4B, C4F, K4, P2.
Row 4 P2, K2, C4B, K4, C4F, K2, P2.
Row 6 P2, C4B, K8, C4F.

GULL STITCH

worked over 11 sts
Row 1 P2, ✲K7, P2; rep from ✲.
Row 2 K2, ✲P7, K2; rep from ✲.
Row 3 P2, ✲sl 2 sts onto cable needle and hold at back of work, K1 from LH needle, then K2 from cable needle, K1, sl 1 st onto cable needle and hold at front of work, K2 sts from LH needle, then K1 from cable needle, P2; rep from ✲.
Row 4 P2, ✲P7, K2; rep from ✲.

INTERLACED CABLE

worked over 17 sts
Note 'Cr3F': sl next 2 sts onto cable needle and hold at front of work, P1, then K2 from cable needle.
'Cr3B': sl next st onto cable needle and hold at back of work, K2, then P1 from cable needle.

Row 1 (WS) (K2, P2) twice, K1, (P2, K2) twice.
Row 2 P2, K2, P2, sl next 3 sts onto cable needle and hold at back of work, K2, sl P st from cable needle back onto LH needle and P it, K2 from cable needle, P2, K2, P2.
Row 3 as Row 1.
Row 4 P2, Cr3F, Cr3B, P1, Cr3F, Cr3B, P2.
Row 5 (K3, P4) twice, K3.
Row 6 P3, C4B, P3, C4F, P3.
Row 7 as Row 5.
Row 8 P2, Cr3B, Cr3F, P1, Cr3B, Cr3F, P2.
Row 9 as Row 1.
Row 10 P2, K2, P2, sl next 3 sts onto cable needle and hold at front of work, K2, sl P st from cable needle back onto LH needle and P it, K2 from cable needle, P2, K2, P2.
Rows 11–16 as Rows 3–8.

TRELLIS STITCH

multiple of 6 plus 2 extra
Note 'C3B': sl next 2 sts onto cable needle and hold at back of work, K1, P2 from cable needle.
'C3F': sl next st onto cable needle and leave at front of work, P2, K1 from cable needle.

Rows 1 and 3 P3, ✲K2, P4; rep from ✲ to last 5 sts, K2, P3.
Rows 2, 4 and 12 K3, ✲P2, K4; rep from ✲ to last 5 sts, P2, K3.
Row 5 P1, ✲C3B, C3F; rep from ✲ to last st, P1.
Rows 6, 8 and 10 K1, P1, ✲K4, P2; rep from ✲ to last 6 sts, K4, P1, K1.
Rows 7 and 9 P1, K1, ✲P4, K2; rep from ✲ to last 6 sts, P4, K1, P1.
Row 11 P1, ✲C3F, C3B; rep from ✲ to last st, P1.

BOBBLE PATTERNS

Bobbles are most attractive when they are combined with other elements, such as cables, eyelets and ribs. The half diamond cable with bobbles makes a striking vertical motif on a plain background (see page 34) – as does the nosegay pattern.

EYELET AND BOBBLE PATTERN

multiple of 9 plus 4 extra

Row 1 K1, *yf, sl 1, K1, psso, yf, sl 1, K1, psso, K5; rep from * to last 3 sts, K3.

Row 2 and every alternate row Purl.

Row 3 K2, *yf, sl 1, K1, psso, yf, sl 1, K1, psso, K5; rep from * to last 2 sts, K2.

Row 5 K3, *yf, sl 1, K1, psso, yf, sl 1, K1, psso, K5; rep from * to last st, K1.

Row 7 K4, *yf, sl 1, K1, psso, yf, sl 1, K1, psso, K2, **K into front and back of st twice, turn, P4, turn, K4, pass 2nd, 3rd and 4th sts over first st **, K2; rep from *.

Row 9 K3, *K2 tog, yf, K2 tog, yf, K5; rep from * to last st, K1.

Row 11 K2, *K2 tog, yf, K2 tog, yf, K5; rep from * to last 2 sts, K2.

Row 13 K1, *K2 tog, yf, K2 tog, yf, K5; rep from * to last 3 sts, K3.

Row 15 *K2 tog, yf, K2 tog, yf, K2, work from ** to **, K2; rep from * to last 4 sts, K4.

Row 16 as Row 2.

HALF DIAMOND CABLE WITH BOBBLES

worked over 19 sts

Note 'C5B': sl 3 sts onto cable needle and hold at back of work, K2, put P st onto LH needle and P it, K2 from cable needle.

'Cr3B': see p. 51.

'Cr3F': see p. 51.

Rows 1 and 3 K7, P2, K1,P2, K7.

Row 2 P7, C5B, P7.

Row 4 P6, Cr3B, P1, Cr3F, P6.

Row 5 and every alternate row K all the K sts and P all the P sts.

Row 6 P5, Cr3B, P1, *(K1, P1, K1, P1, K1, P1, K1) into next st, lift 2nd st on RH needle over first then separately over the 3rd, 4th, 5th, 6th and 7th sts*, P1, Cr3F, P5.

Row 8 P4, Cr3B, (P1, work from * to * of Row 6) twice, P1, Cr3F, P5.

Row 10 P3, Cr3B, (P1, work from * to * of Row 6) three times, P1, Cr3F, P3.

Row 12 P2, Cr3B, P2, K2, P1, K2, P2, Cr3F, P2.

Row 14 P1, Cr3B, P3, K2, P1, K2, P3, Cr3F, P1.

SIMPLE BOBBLE STITCH

multiple of 6 plus 1 extra

Row 1 ✿K3, ✿✿K into front, back and front of next st, turn and K the 3 sts, turn and P the 3 sts, turn and K the 3 sts, turn and pass the 2nd st over the first st, pass the 3rd st over the first st ✿✿, K2, rep from ✿ to last st, K1.

Row 2, 4 and 6 Purl.

Row 3 and 5 Knit.

Row 7 ✿Work from ✿✿ to ✿✿ of Row 1, K5; rep from ✿ to last st, work from ✿✿ to ✿✿.

Rows 8, 10 and 12 Purl.

Rows 9 and 11 Knit.

STEMMED BERRY PATTERN

multiple of 6 plus 5 extra

Row 1 ✿P2, (K1 into front and back) twice into next st, P2, sl 1 pw wyb; rep from ✿ to last 2 sts, P2.

Rows 2 and 4 K2, (K1, yf) four times, K2, P1; rep from ✿ to last 2 sts, K2.

Rows 3 and 5 ✿P2, K4 dropping extra loops, P2, sl 1 pw wyb; rep from ✿ to last 2 sts, P2.

Row 6 ✿K2, P4 tog, K2, P1; rep from ✿ to last 2 sts, K2.

Row 7 ✿P2, sl 1 pw wyb, P2, (K1 into front and back) twice into next st; rep from ✿ to last 2 sts, P2.

Rows 8 and 10 ✿K2, P1, K2, (K1, yf) four times; rep from ✿ to last 2 sts, K2.

Rows 9 and 11 ✿P2, sl 1 pw wyb, P2, K4 dropping extra loops; rep from ✿ to last 2 sts, P2.

Row 12 ✿K2, P1, K2, P4 tog; rep from ✿ to last 2 sts, K2.

NOSEGAY PATTERN

worked over 16 sts

Row 1 (WS) K7, P2, K7.

Row 2 P6, C2B, C2F, P6.

Row 3 K5, Cr2F, P2, Cr2B, K5.

Row 4 P4, Cr2B, C2B, C2F, Cr2F, P4.

Row 5 K3, Cr2F, K1, P4, K1, Cr2B, K3.

Row 6 P2, Cr2B, P1, Cr2B, K2, Cr2F, P1, Cr2F, P2.

Row 7 (K2, P1) twice, K1, P2, K1, (P1, K2) twice.

Row 8 P2, make bobble, P1, Cr2B, P1, K2, P1, Cr2F, P1, make bobble, P2.

Row 9 K4, P1, K2, P2, K2, P1, K4.

Row 10 P4, make bobble, P2, K2, P2, make bobble, P4.

Note 'Cr2B': sl next st onto cable needle and hold at back of work, K1, then P1 from cable needle. 'Cr2F': sl next st onto cable needle and hold at front of work, P1, then K1 from cable needle. 'Make bobble': (K1, yf, K1, yf, K1) into next st, turn, P5, turn, K5, turn, P2 tog, P1, P2 tog, turn, sl 1, K2 tog, psso.

53

PATTERN POTPOURRI

This collection of patterns includes the techniques of twisting and elongating stitches and grouping them together to create smocked effects. When practising these stitches, use a fairly stretchy yarn – a pure wool double knitting or four-ply is ideal. When you can work them smoothly, try them in some different yarns to discover their possibilities. Try smocked rib pattern, for example, in a glossy mercerized cotton, or elongated cross stitch in a glitter yarn.

ALTERNATING 2 × 2 RIB

multiple of 4 plus 2 extra
Note 'Tw2L': K 2nd st tbl, K first st tbl, sl both sts off needle.

Rows 1 and 3 ✷K2, P2; rep from ✷ to last 2 sts, K2.
Rows 2 and 4 ✷P2, K2; rep from ✷ to last 2 sts, P2.
Row 5 ✷Tw2L, P2; rep from ✷ to last 2 sts, Tw2L.
Rows 6 and 8 ✷K2, P2; rep from ✷ to last 2 sts, K2.
Rows 7 and 9 ✷P2, K2; rep from ✷ to last 2 sts, P2.
Row 10 ✷K2, P2; rep from ✷ to last 2 sts, K2.
Row 11 ✷P2, Tw2L; rep from ✷ to last 2 sts, P2.
Row 12 ✷P2, K2; rep from ✷ to last 2 sts, P2.

LINKED CHECK PATTERN

multiple of 10
Note 'Tw2R': K into front of 2nd st, then into front of first st, sl both sts off needle.
'Tw2PL': P into 2nd st, sl this st over first st and off needle, P first st tbl. (This technique varies somewhat from the Tw2PL shown on page 44.)

Row 1 ✷K4, P2, Tw2R, P2; rep from ✷.
Row 2 ✷K2, Tw2PL, K2, P4; rep from ✷.
Rows 3 and 5 as Row 1.
Rows 4 and 6 as Row 2.
Row 7 ✷P1, Tw2R, P2, K4, P1; rep from ✷.
Row 8 ✷K1, P4, K2, Tw2PL, K1; rep from ✷.
Rows 9 and 11 as Row 7.
Rows 10 and 12 as Row 8.

CROSSED-STITCH RIB

multiple of 3 plus 1 extra
Note 'Tw2R': K into front of 2nd st, K into front of first st, sl both sts off needle.

Row 1 P1, ✷Tw2R, P1; rep from ✷.
Row 2 K1, ✷P2, K1; rep from ✷.

TASSEL STITCH

multiple of 6 plus 1 extra
Row 1 ✷K4, P2; rep from ✷ to last st, K1.
Row 2 P1, ✷K2, P4; rep from ✷.
Row 3 as Row 1.
Row 4 as Row 2.
Row 5 ✷Put RH needle between 4th and 5th sts and draw through a loop, K1, P2, K3; rep from ✷ to last st, K1.
Row 6 P1, ✷P3, K2, P2 tog; rep from ✷.
Row 7 K1, ✷P2, K4; rep from ✷.
Row 8 ✷P4, K2; rep from ✷ to last st, P1.
Row 9 as Row 7.
Row 10 as Row 8.
Row 11 K3, ✷put RH needle between 4th and 5th sts and draw through a loop, K1, P2, K3; rep from ✷ to last 4 sts, K1, P2, K1.
Row 12 P1, K2, P2 tog, ✷P3, K2, P2 tog; rep from ✷ to last 3 sts, P3.

SMOCKED RIB PATTERN

multiple of 16 plus 12 extra
Row 1 K3, P6, ✷K2, P2, K2, P2, K2, P6; rep from ✷ to last 3 sts, K3.
Row 2 and every alternate row K the K sts and P the P sts.
Rows 3, 5 and 7 as Row 1.
Row 9 K3, P2, K2, P2, ✷ ✷✷sl next 10 sts onto a cable needle, wind yarn around needle 3 times back to front, and on these 10 sts work K2, P6, K2✷✷, P2, K2, P2; rep from ✷ to last 3 sts, K3.
Row 11, 13, 15 and 17 K3, P2, K2, ✷P2, K2, P6, K2, P2, K2; rep from ✷ to last 5 sts, P2, K3.
Row 19 K1, ✷rep from ✷✷ to ✷✷, P2, K2, P2; rep from ✷ to last 11 sts, ✷✷ to ✷✷, K1.

ELONGATED CROSS STITCH

worked over any number of stitches
Work in st st, g st or rev st st to position for cross st.
Next row (RS) ✷Insert needle kw into next st, take yarn under and over RH needle, under and over LH needle, and again under RH needle. Draw loop through and sl st off LH needle; rep from ✷.
Next row K or P into each st according to patt.

4

Working in Rounds

Up to this point we have concentrated on knitting back and forth in rows to produce flat pieces of fabric, which are then usually joined to make a garment. In this chapter we shall look at the technique of knitting in rounds to produce a seamless fabric – either tubular or flat. Tubular fabrics are used in many ways: for polo necks; for socks, gloves and hats; and sometimes for the main body of a sweater. Flat medallion shapes can be sewn together to make a bedspread, for example; a large medallion can make a cushion cover or a shawl.

Knitting in rounds has several advantages over knitting in rows. For one thing, the right side of the work is always facing you, which means that certain stitch patterns are easier to form; for example, stocking stitch is produced by knitting every row. Also, the fabric produced is seamless, which reduces the work involved in making up and results in a more comfortable garment. Stitch patterns can be worked using only the repeat, without any edge stitches.

Two different kinds of needles are used for knitting in rounds: sets of double-pointed needles and circular needles. In some cases they are interchangeable; in others they are not. Whichever type you are using, there are several points to remember. First of all, it is important to keep track of the beginning of each round. To do this, place a ring marker or a loop of contrasting yarn at the beginning of the round, and slip it onto the right-hand needle as you begin each new round. It may also be necessary to mark certain shaping points or pattern repeats; use markers of a different colour for this purpose.

It is also important to work the first stitch of the round – and the first stitch on a new double-pointed needle – very firmly, in order to avoid producing a ladder effect at this point in the work.

When stitches are to be picked up for working in the round – at a neckline, for example – the pattern will specify the correct number for the stitch pattern repeat. However, if you are altering a pattern in which this section is knitted flat, you may need to adjust the number of stitches to make sure you have an exact multiple of the repeat. For example, if you are working a K2, P2 rib, the total number of stitches must be divisible by 4; otherwise, the stitch pattern will not join up correctly.

USING A CIRCULAR NEEDLE

Of the two kinds of needle used for knitting in the round, the circular needle is the easier to use. Only two needle points are involved in the work, and the bulk of the knitting slides easily between them as the work progresses. Also, there is only one join – as opposed to three or more if you are using double-pointed needles – so that it is easier to produce a smooth fabric. However, the circular needle cannot be used for small items, for the knitting must be able to reach from one point to the other without stretching. To determine whether the work can be done on a circular needle, refer to the chart on page 221.

Before beginning to work with a new circular needle or one that has been coiled up in the package for some time, straighten it by soaking it in warm water for about 15 minutes then pulling it gently through your fingers.

Working quatrefoil eyelet (see page 38) in the round on a circular needle. Like most lace patterns, it is easily converted to this method simply by knitting all the purl rows of the flat knitting pattern.

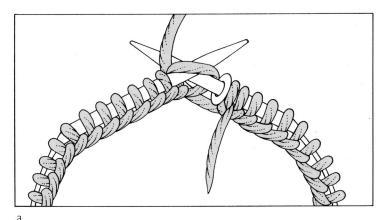

a

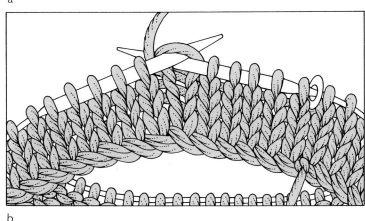

b

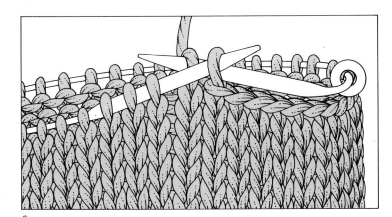

c

Tubular knitting on a circular needle

1 Cast on the required number of stitches. If you are using a single-needle method of casting on, wind an elastic band around one end to prevent the stitches from slipping off. Before beginning to knit, make sure that the stitches reach comfortably from one point to the other.

2 Hold the needle so that the end holding the last cast-on stitch is in your right hand and the one with the first cast-on stitch is in your left. Make sure that the stitches are not twisted on the needle; their lower edges should lie towards the centre of the ring.

4 Place a ring marker or a loop of contrasting yarn over the RH point. Insert the point into the first stitch on the LH needle (a), and work the first stitch, drawing the yarn firmly to prevent a gap at the join.

5 Work the first (right-side) round of the specified pattern around to the marker. Check the work to make sure there are no twists in it; if there are, you must unravel the work and start again. Slip the marker and continue with the second round of the pattern.

6 Continue working in the chosen pattern (see page 63) as set (b).

7 Cast off in the usual way (c). After drawing the thread through the last stitch, take it through the first stitch of the round.

Working in rows with a circular needle

A circular needle is also useful for working in rows. Because the weight of the work is distributed equally along the needle, this method is recommended for large, heavy pieces of knitting, which would be tiring to work on a pair of needles. Substituting a circular needle is also a good idea when knitting on a train journey, for example, when ordinary needles may be awkward.

To use a circular needle in this way, simply cast on in the chosen method. Work the first row beginning with the *last* cast-on stitch, rather than the first one, as in tubular knitting. At the end of the row, turn the needle so that the point with the last-worked stitch is in your left hand, and work the next row.

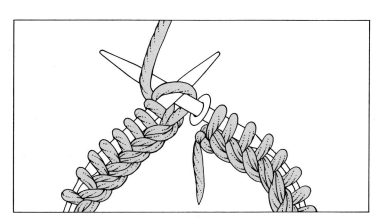

DOUBLE-POINTED NEEDLES

Double-pointed needles are usually sold in sets of four. The knitting is divided onto three needles, and the fourth is used to work the stitches. You may prefer to work with five needles. Sets of five are available in some places; or buy two sets of four.

Double-pointed needles are often used to pick up stitches around a neckline, in which case the technique is basically the same as shown on page 32. The total number of stitches may be divided evenly among the three or four needles; or the division may be based on the shape of the work: a V neck, for example, might be divided into right front, left front and back, with a needle for each.

For small items, such as socks and gloves, double-pointed needles are used from the outset of the work. In traditional Guernsey and Fair Isle knitting, sets of extra-long double-pointed needles are used to knit virtually the entire garment.

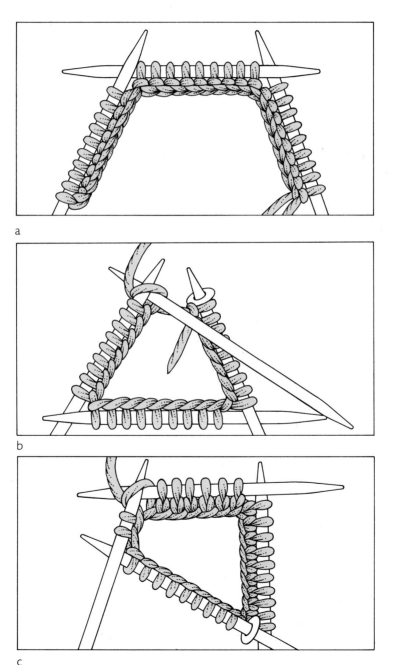

a

b

c

When resuming work on a piece of knitting worked on double-pointed needles, undo two or three stitches and work them again. They will have stretched slightly, and the interruption might (depending on the stitch pattern) be quite noticeable. The same applies to knitting worked in rows on ordinary needles, if you have had to stop in the middle of a row.

Tubular fabric on double-pointed needles

1 Begin by casting the required number of stitches onto a single-pointed needle of the same size as the double-pointed needles (or a larger size, if a loose edge is desired). The illustrations show the stitches as cast on by the thumb method, but any method could be used.

2 Slip the stitches onto the double-pointed needles, leaving one needle free for working the stitches. Here, three needles out of a set of four are used (a).

3 Arrange the needles so that their points cross as shown. Check to make sure that the stitches are not twisted. Place a ring marker over the point holding the last cast-on stitch. With the remaining needle, knit the first cast-on stitch (b); draw the yarn firmly to close the gap.

4 Continue working into all the stitches on the first needle. When this needle is free, use it to work into the stitches on the second needle (c). Continue in this way, taking care to pull the yarn firmly when working the first stitch on the new needle and slipping the marker at the beginning of each new round.

When the work is the required depth, cast off as usual. Draw the yarn through the first stitch of the round to make a neat join.

MEDALLIONS

By working in rounds and increasing in a regular sequence it is possible to make a variety of medallion shapes. Medallions have a number of different uses. A single medallion can be used as the back of a baby's bonnet or the top of a beret. If extended, it can become a shawl. Individual medallions can be sewn or crocheted together to make a tablecloth or bedspread.

Medallions are normally worked from the centre outwards, although it is also possible to work them from the outer edge inwards, by means of decreasing rather than increasing.

If the increases are worked at the same point on every round, they will form a pattern of straight lines radiating outwards from the centre. If they are moved, a swirl pattern is produced.

The type of increase worked will also affect the appearance of the medallions. Bar increases (page 28) will produce an embossed effect, raised increases a more subtle pattern. For a more decorative effect, an openwork increase is used.

Medallions must be worked on double-pointed needles (although a circular needle can be substituted on the outer rounds of a shawl). The number of needles used varies with the shape and with personal preference. A square medallion is best worked on four, knitting with a fifth; a pentagon, on five; a hexagon, on three (two sections per needle).

It must be admitted that medallion knitting is not easy. However, once you are past the first few rounds it becomes much pleasanter. For your initial practice, use a moderately stretchy, smooth yarn in a light to medium colour.

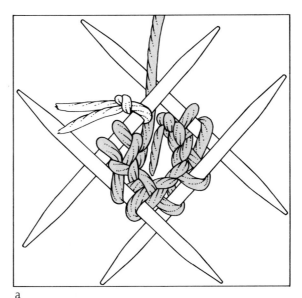

a

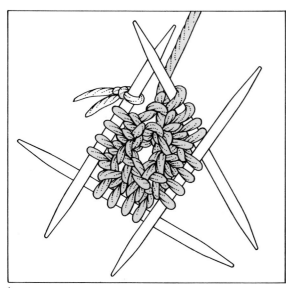

b

c

Crocheted foundation

You may find this method of beginning a medallion easier than the cast-on method, especially where there are only 8 stitches in the first round.

1 Crochet a chain (page 81) consisting of 8 stitches, including the slip loop. Join the first and last chain with a slip stitch.

2 Using 4 double-pointed needles, pick up 1 stitch for each chain. Insert the needle through the top of the chain as shown.

Working a square medallion

1 Cast 8 stitches onto a double-pointed needle using the cable method (page 15). Or you may prefer to use the French two-needle cast-on. This is like the cable method, but the needle is inserted into the stitches themselves, rather than between them.

2 Arrange the stitches on 4 needles, as shown, and tie a thread marker at the beginning of the round – just before the last cast-on stitch (a).

3 (round 1) Using the fifth needle, knit into the back of every stitch.

4 (round 2) Knit into the front and back of very stitch: 16 stitches on the needles (b).

5 (round 3) Knit every stitch in the normal way.

6 (round 4) Knit into the front and back of the first stitch, knit 1, knit into the front and back of the third stitch, knit 1. Placing the bar 1 stitch in from the corner makes the line of increasing symmetrical. Repeat on the remaining 3 sets of 4 stitches: 24 stitches. Repeat rounds 3 and 4 until the medallion is the desired size. Cast off (c).

SHAPING A GUSSET

A traditional Guernsey sweater is knitted mainly in the round. Even the sleeves are worked in this way, on stitches picked up from the yoke. The shaping incorporates an underarm gusset, which helps to make the garment comfortable. This feature is well worth including on any pullover in which ease of movement is a primary consideration.

Although a gusset can be worked separately and sewn in, it is not difficult to knit one in as shown here, while working in the round.

The garment is worked in the round up to the armpit. To indicate the side 'seams', purl a single stitch at these points on each round. At the widest part of the gusset the tubular knitting is interrupted and the front and back completed separately, working in rows. Then stitches are picked up for the sleeves and the tubular knitting recommenced. The gusset stitches are decreased down to a single purled stitch for the sleeve 'seam'.

1 To begin shaping the gusset, increase 1 stitch on either side of the 'seam' by working a 'make 1' increase (page 28) just before the purled stitch, knitting the stitch, then increasing again just after it (a).
2 On the next round, purl across all stitches.
3 On the next round, work up to the 3 gusset stitches, make 1, work across gusset, make 1.
4 Continue in this way, adding 2 stitches to the gusset on alternate rounds, until it is the desired width. Work one round straight; slip the gusset stitches onto a stitch holder (b).
5 Complete the front and back sections separately. Join the shoulder seams.
6 Using a set of double-pointed needles, knit across the gusset stitches, then pick up and knit the stitches for the sleeve from the front and back of the garment (c).
7 Work the sleeve downwards, decreasing on either side of the gusset. On the first round: Sl 1, K1, psso, K to last 2 gusset sts, K2 tog.
8 Work the next round without decreasing.
9 Continue to decrease 2 stitches on alternate rounds until 1 stitch remains in the gusset. This marks the sleeve 'seam'; purl it on every round (d).

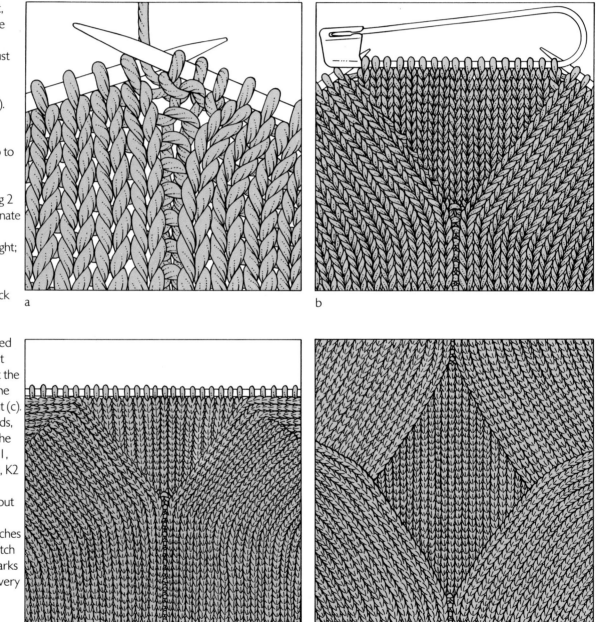

a

b

c

d

Turning a Heel

Socks are nearly always worked in the round, on double-pointed needles, in order to avoid the discomfort of a seam. The only complicated shaping involved is turning the heel, but even this is less difficult than it appears at first glance.

There are several basic methods of turning a heel, One of them, shown in these illustrations, is called a Dutch heel. The shaping involves a technique known as short-row shaping, in which some stitches are merely held on the needle while others are worked. In turning a heel the held stitches are gradually decreased and incorporated into the centre section of the heel, then the heel is rejoined to the instep stitches.

The main part of a sock is normally worked in stocking stitch, because it is smooth and comfortable. Single ribbing is the usual choice for the upper edge of the sock because it grips the ankle neatly. Take care to cast on loosely so that the edge will not be uncomfortably tight.

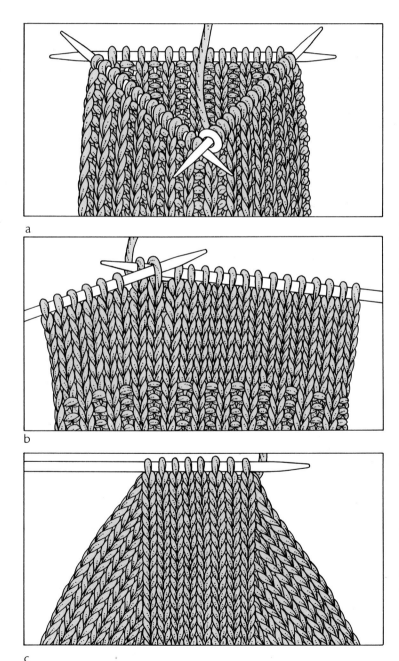

a

b

c

1 Using a set of 4 double-pointed needles, cast on the specified number of stitches for the sock. The number should be divisible by 3 and also – if you are working in K1, P1 rib – by 2. Here the number is 42.

2 Work in single rib (or other rib pattern) for the required length down to the top of the heel (a). Fasten off.

3 Now divide the heel stitches from those that will be used for the instep. The respective numbers will vary according to the pattern and the size; here, 22 stitches are used for the heel. Slip the first 11 stitches of the round and the last 11 onto one double-pointed needle. (If you prefer, you can use single-pointed needles for working the heel.) Slip the remaining instep stitches onto a spare needle; a short circular needle is convenient for this, as it holds the stitches in a curve, out of the way.

4 Rejoin the yarn to the RH edge of the heel stitches. Work in rows, in stocking stitch, until the heel is the required depth from ankle to bottom of heel, ending with a purl row.

5 On the next row, work across the first 14 stitches (the number will vary with the pattern, but should be approximately two thirds of the total), then decrease 1 stitch as follows: sl 1, K1 (b),

psso. Turn, leaving the remaining stitches unworked. There are 15 stitches on the needle.

6 Purl across the first 7 stitches, then decrease 1 stitch: P2 tog. Turn, leaving the remaining stitches unworked.

7 Continue working on the centre stitches; at the end of every row work in 1 of the held stitches, at the same time decreasing 1 stitch. On knit rows decrease as in step 5; on purl rows, as in step 6. Continue in this way until there are 8 stitches on the needle (that is, when all the held stitches have been decreased), ending with a wrong-side row (c).

8 Resume working in rounds on the 3 double-pointed needles. Work across the heel stitches, then pick up and knit the specified number along the left side of the

(continued on next page)

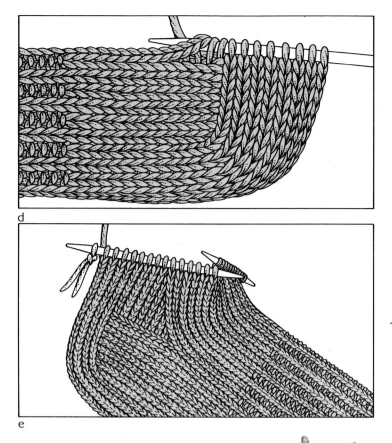

d

f

e

heel (d); here it is 10 stitches. Using a second needle, work across the instep stitches. Using a third needle, pick up 10 stitches (or the specified number) along the right side of the heel ; then knit across half of the heel stitches. Place a marker at this point to indicate the beginning of the round. At this point there are 48 stitches on the needles.

9 Work one round straight.

10 Begin to decrease the stitches to either side of the instep: work to the last 3 stitches on the first needle, K2 tog, work across the instep stitches, work the first stitch on third needle, then sl 1, K1, psso (e), work to the end.

11 Repeat this decrease round until the specified number of stitches remain on the needles (f). The sock is then worked straight until the toe shaping.

Joining in new yarn

It should not be necessary to join yarn in mid-row when working in rows, if you re-wind the yarn (see page 27); however, this cannot be avoided in circular knitting. If the fabric is smooth, it is obviously important to place the join at an inconspicuous place on the garment; on a textured fabric it may be possible to join yarn almost anywhere within the round. Either of the following two method can be used, depending on the yarn and the stitch pattern.

Threading-in method

This method of joining yarn is preferred when working stocking stitch in a smooth yarn.

1 Thread the end of the new yarn into a tapestry needle. Take it through the old yarn for about 4cm/1½″. Continue knitting, working in the joined yarn. Trim the loose ends later.

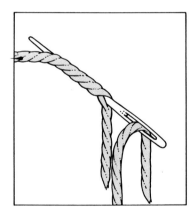

Double strand method

This method can be used if the yarn is fuzzy and the stitch pattern a textured one. The first stitch in the new yarn should be a knit stitch.

1 Having worked the last stitch in the old yarn, let this yarn drop down on the wrong side of the work.

2 Turn back the end of the new yarn for about 10cm/4″. Insert the

a

needle into the next stitch and draw through the loop of the new yarn, thus forming the first stitch in the new yarn (a).

3 Work the next two or three stitches in the double strand, then let the short end drop (b).

4 On the following round, treat these double strands as one. Trim the short end of new yarn close to the work. Darn the old yarn into the wrong side.

b

STITCH PATTERNS IN ROUNDS

Instructions for stitch patterns are normally given for working in rows. Very rarely you will find them represented by symbols on a chart; however, there is no universally agreed system of symbols for the different stitches. The knitter wishing to work in the round may therefore be put off the idea, thinking that she will be able to use only the basic stitches.

Happily, there are a great many stitch patterns that can easily be converted for working in the round. As already noted (page 56), stocking stitch is produced by knitting every round. Conversely, reverse stocking stitch results if every round is purled. For garter stitch, you knit and purl alternate rounds. For most rib patterns, you simply knit and purl the same stitches on every round. The principle, therefore, is that any stitch normally purled on a wrong-side row will be knitted when worked on the right side, and vice versa.

Any stitch pattern in which every wrong-side row is simply purled can easily be worked in the round by knitting all these rows.

If you wish to use a more complex stitch pattern, you may need first to work a sample in rows, until you become thoroughly familiar with its construction. Then write your own revised instructions and work sample in the round. Remember, when working in the round, to omit the edge stitches.

On the sample at right are some of the stitch patterns given elsewhere in the book, with instructions converted for working in the round.

SIMPLE SEED (page 21) *multiple of 8*

Row 1 ✳P1, K7; rep from ✳.
Rows 2, 3, 4 Knit.
Row 5 ✳K4, P1, K3; rep from ✳.
Rows 6 and 7 Knit.

DIAMOND SEED (Page 20) *multiple of 8*

Row 1 ✳P1, K7; rep from ✳.
Rows 2 and 8 ✳K1, P1, K5, P1; rep from ✳.
Rows 3 and 7 ✳K2, P1, K3, P1, K1; rep from ✳.
Rows 4 and 6 ✳K3, P1, K1, P1, K2; rep from ✳.
Row 5 ✳K4, P1, K3; rep from ✳.

NUT PATTERN (page 36) *multiple of 4*

Row 1 ✳P3, (K1, yon, K1) into next st; rep from ✳.
Rows 2 and 3 ✳P3, K3, rep from ✳.
Row 4 ✳P3, K3tog; rep from ✳.
Rows 5 and 6 Purl.
Row 7 ✳P1, (K1, yon, K1) into next st; rep from ✳.

Rows 8 and 9 ✳P1, K3, P2; rep from ✳.
Row 10 ✳P1, K3tog, P2, rep from ✳.
Rows 11 and 12 Purl.

IRISH MOSS (page 20) *multiple of 2*

Rows 1 and 2 ✳K1, P1; rep from ✳.
Rows 3 and 4 ✳P1, K1; rep from ✳.

EMBOSSED CHEVRON (page 22)
multiple of 12

Rows 1 and 2 ✳K3, P5, K3, P1; rep from ✳.
Rows 3 and 4 ✳P1, K3, P2; rep from ✳.
Rows 5 and 6 ✳P2, K3, P1, K3, P3; rep from ✳.
Rows 7 and 8 ✳P3, K5, P3, K1; rep from ✳.
Rows 9 and 10 ✳K1, P3, K3, P3, K2; rep from ✳.
Rows 11 and 12 ✳K2, P3, K1, P3, K3; rep from ✳.

EDALLIONS

These four medallions include the basic shapes and the different methods of placing and working increases. They have been worked here in a crisp double-knitting-weight mercerized cotton, which shows off their method of construction.

Once you have become adept at the method of working medallions you will find that they offer an enormous variety of creative possibilities. You can introduce stripes and other colour patterns. Or you can work the medallion in a stitch pattern – although it is best to work this out on paper first, at least for the first few rows to be worked in the pattern. Once the pattern is established, you should be able to bring the increased stitches into the pattern with no more difficulty than in shaping a piece of row-by-row flat knitting.

For the basic technique of working a medallion, see page 59.

MALTESE CROSS MEDALLION

Cast on 8 stitches. (In this example, a crocheted chain [see page 59] has been used as the foundation.) Arrange the stitches evenly on 4 needles, and use a fifth for the knitting.

Round 1 K every st tbl.

Round 2 *K1, yf; rep from *: 16 sts.

Round 3 and every alternate round Knit.

Round 4 K1, *yf, K2; rep from * to last st, yf, K1: 24 sts.

Round 6 K2, *yf, K2, yf, K4; rep from * ending last rep K2 instead of K4: 32 sts.

Continue in this way, increasing to either side of the 2 centre stitches on each needle, until the medallion is the required size. Cast off loosely.

For a solid medallion work as above, but work a bar increase or a 'Make 1' increase to either side of the centre 2 stitches.

SWIRL HEXAGON

Cast on 12 stitches. (A knitted foundation has been used for this example.) Divide the stitches evenly onto 3 needles, and knit with a fourth.

Round 1 K every st tbl.

Round 2 *Yf, K2; rep from *: 18 sts.

Round 3 and every alternate round Knit.

Round 4 *Yf, K3; rep from *: 24 sts.

Round 6 *Yf, K4; rep from *: 30 sts.

Continue in this way until hexagon is the required size. Cast off loosely.

CIRCULAR TARGET MEDALLION

Cast on 8 stitches. (In this example, a crocheted chain [see page 59] has been used as the foundation.) Arrange the stitches evenly on 4 needles, and use a fifth for the knitting.

Round 1 K every st tbl.
Round 2 ✬Yf, K1; rep from ✬: 16 sts.
Rounds 3, 4 and 5 Knit.
Round 6 ✬Yf, K1; rep from ✬: 16 sts.
Rounds 7–11 Knit.
Round 12 ✬Yf, K1; rep from ✬: 64 sts.
Rounds 13–19 Knit.
The example shown has been worked up to Round 14, then cast off and finished with a crocheted edging. To make the medallion larger, continue as follows:
Round 20 ✬Yf, K2; rep from ✬: 96 sts.
Rounds 21–25 Knit.
Round 26 ✬Yf, K3; rep from ✬: 128 sts.
Rounds 25–31 Knit.
Round 32 ✬Yf, K4; rep from ✬: 160 sts.
Continue in this way, working 5 plain rounds between every increase round and increasing 32 stitches on every subsequent increase round, spacing them evenly (so that, for example, round 38 will have 5 K stitches between the increases).

PENTAGON

Cast on 10 stitches. (In this example, a knitted foundation has been used.) Divide the stitches onto 3 needles as follows: needle 1, 2 sts; needle 2, 4 sts; needle 3, 4 sts. Begin by working on these 3 needles, knitting with a fourth; when the work becomes large enough to accommodate more needles, divide the stitches evenly onto 5 needles and knit with a sixth.

Round 1 K every st tbl.
Round 2 ✬K1, M1; rep from ✬: 20 sts.
Round 3 Knit.
Round 4 ✬K1, M1, K3, M1; rep from ✬: 30 sts.
Round 5 Knit.
Round 6 Knit.
Round 7 ✬K1, M1, K5, M1; rep from ✬: 40 sts.
Round 8 Knit.
Round 9 ✬K1, M1, K7, M1; rep from ✬: 50 sts.
Continue to work in this way, increasing to either side of the stitch at the beginning of each section and working 2 plain rounds and 1 plain round alternately between the increase rounds. Cast off loosely when the medallion is the required size.
For an openwork effect work a 'yarn forward' increase instead of a 'make 1' increase.

5

Colourwork

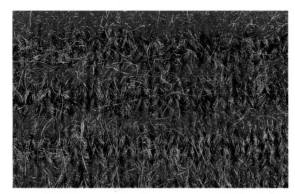

Horizontal stripes can be simply worked by changing colour at the side edge. Here the colours have been changed on every second row.

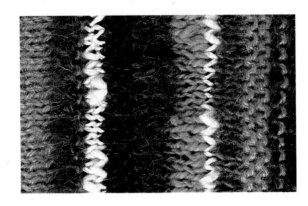

These vertical stripes are actually worked horizontally. Variety has been introduced by changing the colours at irregular intervals and by working an occasional purled row to form a ridge. This kind of striped fabric is a good way of using up oddments of yarn.

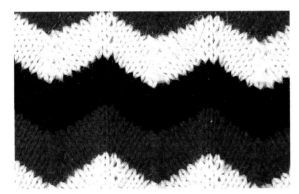

Chevron stripes have been created here by working the chevron stitch pattern given on page 37 and changing colour as for ordinary horizontal stripes.

There are many ways of combining two or more colours in a piece of knitting – some complex, some extremely simple, all capable of producing rich and exciting effects. They include simple horizontal stripes, fascinating slipstitch patterns – some with interesting textures as well – jacquard motifs and traditional Fair Isle designs.

Many commercially produced patterns include colourwork; but it is also possible to add a colour pattern to a one-colour design, thereby giving it a stamp of individuality.

HORIZONTAL STRIPES

An infinite number of effects can be created simply by working rows in different colours to produce horizontal stripes. The simplest version is a two-colour stripe, with the colours changed after a regular number of rows. Worked in stocking stitch, this has a neat, crisp appearance. More subtle effects can be achieved by using several shades of the same colour; by varying the number of rows worked, in a regular or random pattern; by using the purled side of the work, so that the colour changes have a broken appearance; or by introducing the occasional purled row on the right side of a stocking stitch fabric for textural interest.

Horizontal stripes need not run horizontally. If you work the garment from one side edge to the other – a method often used for batwing pullovers and cardigans – the stripes will run vertically. (True vertical stripes are produced by using one of the methods shown on pages 68–70.) Zigzag stripes will result if you work horizontal stripes in a chevron stitch pattern.

Discover the fun of creating your own stripe patterns by working samples in leftover yarns. Keep the samples for reference when designing.

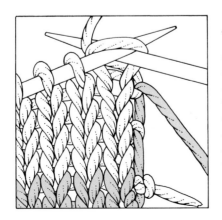

Joining new colours

1 Tie the new colour to the old one at the RH edge of the work, using a double knot. Do not cut off the old yarn.

2 Continue knitting with the new yarn. On every second row twist the two yarns around each other to help keep the edge neat. When changing back to the first colour, bring it in front of the second colour. Avoid pulling it tightly when beginning to knit with the new yarn.

If the yarn is fine, up to three colours can be carried up the side in this way. Where more colours are used, or where one colour is not used for many rows, they should be cut off and rejoined as required. This is also necessary, of course, where new colours are introduced on wrong-side rows and thus joined at the LH edge.

SLIPSTITCH COLOUR PATTERNS

Also called mosaic patterns, slipstitch patterns have the charming characteristic of looking extremely complicated but actually being quite simple to work. Only one colour is used in a row; the intermingled colour effects are achieved by slipping some stitches instead of working them, so that the colour from the previous row encroaches upon that of the row being worked. The working yarn is carried loosely behind the slipped stitches.

The fabric produced by most slipstitch patterns is a relatively dense one, because the slipped stitches tend to pull the other ones downward slightly. In some patterns the stitches also draw in slightly, so that more stitches are required for a given width than for, say, a stocking stitch fabric using the same yarn and needles. Thus it is most important, if you are planning to substitute a slipstitch pattern for another stitch, to make a good-sized tension swatch.

The stitches slipped in these patterns are always slipped purlwise, as shown in the example below. Note also that the instructions 'with yarn to front' and 'with yarn back' refer to the back and front in relation to the knitter; they do not mean the right and wrong sides of the work. The yarn is taken directly to the front or back and not taken over the needle. After slipping the stitch(es) as instructed, you must then, of course, have the yarn at the back if the next stitch is a knit stitch or at the front if it is a purl stitch.

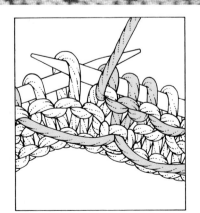

The right and wrong sides of Tricolour Wave Stripe illustrate the construction of a typical slipstitch colour pattern.

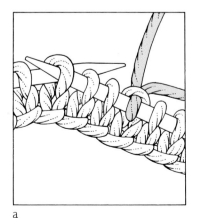

Basic slipstitch technique
The simple pattern shown here – called Tricolour Wave Stripe – will introduce you to the principles of working slipstitch colour patterns. First cast on a multiple of 4 stitches plus 1, using colour A. Purl one row.
Row 1 (right side): With B, K1, ✶ with yarn back sl 3 purlwise (a), K1, rep from ✶ to end.

Row 2: With B, P2, ✶ with yarn to front sl 1 (b), P3, rep from ✶ to last 3sts, sl 1, P2.
Row 3: With B, K to end.
Row 4: With B, P to end.
Rows 5–8: With C, rep rows 1–4.
Rows 9–12: With A, rep rows 1–4.

VERTICAL COLOUR CHANGES

Colour patterns with more than one colour in a row are worked by one of several methods: carrying, or 'stranding', the unused colour loosely along the back of the work until it is needed again; 'weaving' the unused yarn into the work at intervals, or with every alternate stitch, until it is needed; and working with several different balls of yarn, positioned across the work and picked up as required – a method sometimes called 'intarsia'.

The choice of method is dictated mainly by the type of design, but also by the weight and colour of the yarn. A repeating-motif pattern, such as a traditional Fair Isle design, that uses only two colours in any one row is normally knitted using the stranding method, with weaving incorporated where the unused yarn must span long distances. A design that includes more than two colours in a row will usually be knitted by the intarsia method, because carrying more than two colours across every row would make the work too bulky. However, a two-colour vertical stripe pattern with, say, 10 stitches in each stripe would also be knitted using the intarsia method because the stranding

method would leave long strands of yarn – likely to be snagged – on the wrong side, and weaving in the yarn might leave noticeable marks on the right side: weaving is better suited to 'busy' patterns. Care must also be taken, especially with fine yarns, that dark colours do not show through light ones on the right side. It is best to make a sample first to determine whether this is likely to be a problem.

INTARSIA METHOD

Designs requiring the intarsia method include wide vertical or diagonal stripes, large repeating motifs, individual motifs and pictorial knitting.

The first step is to prepare the yarn by winding it onto bobbins. These do not unroll as balls of yarn do, and thus are less likely to become tangled. It is possible to buy plastic bobbins at some yarn shops; however, if the yarn you are using is thick, you may prefer to make your own bobbins of the desired size from pieces of cardboard.

Motifs designed to be worked using the intarsia method can sometimes be more easily worked in Swiss darning (see page 82).

In these illustrations the fabric being worked is stocking stitch; in the case of reverse stocking stitch the yarns are held on the knit side of the work; however, the process of twisting the yarns is essentially the same: the old yarn is taken over the new yarn, which is then brought up in the correct position for working.

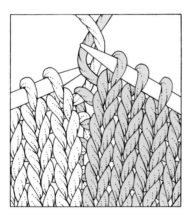

Changing colour on a knit row
Work in the first colour to the point for the colour change. If the second colour is being introduced for the first time, tie it to the first colour. On subsequent rows the procedure is as follows:
Drop the first colour *over* the second, pick up the second and continue knitting with it. In this way, the yarns are twisted around each other. If this were not done,

the two areas of colour would be separate, leaving a split in the fabric.

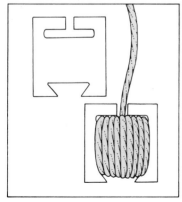

Making a bobbin
Cut a cardboard rectangle of the desired size. For thick yarns, about 5 by 8cm/2 by 3½″ will do. In each short end, cut notches as shown. Wind the yarn through the notches.

Changing colour on a purl row
Work in the first colour to the point for the colour change. Drop the first colour over the second, pick up the second and continue purling with it.
On both knit and purl rows, work the stitches before and after the change fairly tightly to avoid leaving a gap.

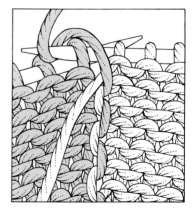

STRANDING YARNS

Stranding is the basic technique used when knitting a repeating motif using two colours that are alternated at short intervals. As a general rule yarns should not be stranded across more than five stitches; otherwise the elasticity of the work is likely to be impaired. Longer strands are also more likely to be snagged. Where yarn must be carried for more than five stitches, it should be woven into the work, using the techniques shown on page 70.

Both stranding and weaving are easier to do on knit rows than on purl rows, and this is one reason why Shetland knitters have traditionally knitted their intricately patterned sweaters in the round (see 'Working in Rounds', page 56). Whether you work in rounds or in rows, however, it is most important to hold the unused yarn loosely in order to avoid puckering the fabric. For a smooth tension it is best to hold one yarn in each hand, thus combining the right-hand and the left-hand methods (see page 16). You will find the new method awkward at first, but it is worthwhile persevering with it if you plan to do much of this kind of colour-patterned knitting.

Stranding yarn on a knit row

On the row in which the second colour is introduced, join it at the RH edge. Begin knitting in the colour specified by the pattern, carrying the other colour loosely across the back of the work.
To knit with the RH yarn, hold the LH yarn slightly under the needles (a).
To knit with the LH yarn, hold the RH yarn out of the way (b).

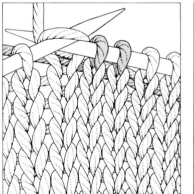

a

b

The best way of working a Fair Isle pattern is to hold one colour in each hand, as shown, knitting with them alternately and stranding or weaving the unused colour into the back of the work.

Stranding on a purl row

Here the process is the same as for a knit row, except that the stranded yarn is held at the front of the work.
To purl with the RH yarn, hold the left under the needles (a).
To purl with the LH yarn, hold the right out of the way (b).

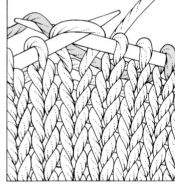

a

b

To prevent a ball of yarn from rolling around while you are knitting, simply place it in a bowl or a jar on the floor. This is especially helpful when working with two yarns simultaneously – a bowl placed on either side of you will keep the yarns from becoming tangled.

WEAVING YARNS

Before learning the weaving technique, it is advisable to master the stranding technique – if possible, holding the yarn in both hands. You will see that in stranding the unused yarn is always kept out of the way of the yarn being worked. In weaving, the unused yarn is occasionally incorporated into a stitch. This can be done on every alternate stitch, as described below; this produces a dense fabric with no loose strands on the wrong side. Or it can be done every few stitches. Avoid working the yarn into stitches directly above each other, as this may cause a visible indentation in the fabric.

For your first attempts at weaving, work in the round, as described on page 57. Alternatively, cast 50 or more stitches onto a pair of needles and work in rows, breaking off one yarn at the end of each knit row, then purling back to the right-hand edge and rejoining the contrasting colour for the next row of weaving. When you can weave on a knit row, try weaving the yarns while purling.

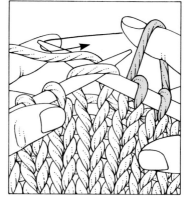

Knitting – weaving LH yarn
When knitting with the RH yarn, take the LH yarn alternately below and above the stitches.
To weave the LH yarn below, simply hold it under the work as if for stranding (see page 69).
To weave the LH yarn above, bring it over the RH needle as shown, left. Then bring the RH yarn around the needle to knit as usual; draw this loop through the stitch.

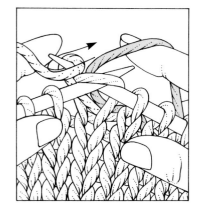

Purling – weaving in LH yarn
When purling with the RH yarn, take the LH yarn alternately below and above the stitches.
To weave the LH yarn below, simply hold it away from the work as if for stranding (see page 69).
To weave the LH yarn above, take it over the RH needle (but not all the way around it), and purl (left) with the RH yarn.

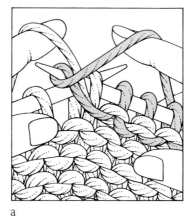

a

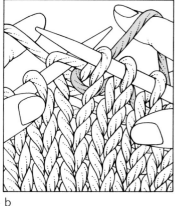

b

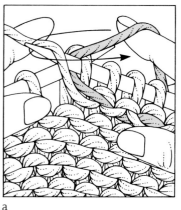

a

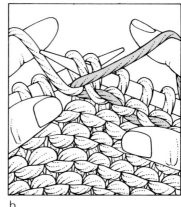

b

Knitting – weaving in RH yarn
To weave the RH yarn above, simply hold it away from the work as if for stranding (see page 69) and knit with the LH yarn.
To take the RH yarn below:
1 Bring the RH yarn around the needle as if to knit.
2 Bring the LH yarn around the needle as if to knit.

3 Reverse the RH yarn (a), taking it to the left and under the needle point – and thus off the needle.
4 Complete the stitch in the LH yarn (b).

Purling – weaving in RH yarn
To weave the RH yarn above, simply hold it away from the work as if for stranding (see page 69), and purl with the LH yarn.
To weave the RH yarn below:
1 Loop the RH yarn around the needle as shown.
2 Bring the LH yarn over the needle as if to purl.

3 Reverse the RH yarn (a), taking it to the left and under the needle point – and thus off the needle.
4 Complete the stitch in the LH yarn (b).

FOLLOWING A CHART

Individual and repeating motifs for colour patterns are often given in the form of a chart, which is easier to follow than written row-by-row instructions. The colours themselves may be shown on the chart, or they may be represented by symbols, identified in an accompanying key. Each square on the chart represents a single stitch.

The chart is worked from bottom to top. Right-side rows are normally given odd numbers; they are worked from right to left. The even-numbered, wrong-side rows are worked from left to right. This rule, however, does not apply to working in rounds (see page 56) in which all the rows are knitted from right to left.

Charts for repeating motifs normally include only the one repeat, along with any edge stitches required. The repeat itself is marked off with a heavy line; where several sizes are given there may be additional edge stitches given for the larger sizes.

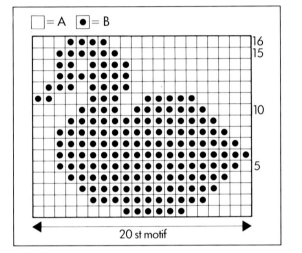

When following a chart, it is important to keep careful track of your progress. A good way of doing this is to have the chart photocopied (several times, if it is to be repeated vertically) and draw a line through each row when it is completed. If the chart is small, having it enlarged by the photocopier will make it easier to follow.

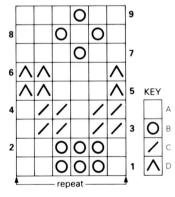

Two simple charts: one for an individual motif and one for a repeat pattern (taken from the Fair Isle accessories pattern on page 176). In the duck motif only one contrasting colour is used, represented by a dot. For this simple motif only every fifth row is marked, plus the final 16th row. The slightly more complicated Fair Isle motif uses three contrasting colours, with every row marked.

SLIPSTITCH COLOURWORK

Like most other forms of colourwork, slipstitch patterns have a marvellously versatile character. They can change beyond recognition if you play around with the choice of colours. Try substituting dark for light shades in some of these patterns.

The fabric produced by slipstitch patterns is quite dense, which makes them ideal for a jacket.

Remember that the stitches are slipped purlwise, unless otherwise stated.

THREE-COLOUR TWEED

multiple of 3 plus 1 extra
Note Colour A = dark pink, Colour B = pale pink, Colour C = green.

Row 1 (WS) With A, Knit.
Row 2 With B, K3, ✩sl 1 wyb, K2; rep from ✩ to last st, K1.
Row 3 With B, K3, ✩sl 1 wyf, K2; rep from ✩ to last st, K1.
Row 4 With C, ✩K2, sl 1 wyb; rep from ✩ to last st, K1.
Row 5 With C, K1, ✩sl 1 wyf, K2; rep from ✩.
Row 6 With A, K1, ✩sl 1 wyb, K2; rep from ✩.
Row 7 With A, ✩K2, sl 1 wyf; rep from ✩ to last st, K1.

LINKED STRIPE PATTERN

multiple of 4
Note Colour A = turquoise, Colour B = green.

Rows 1 (RS), **2, 5 and 6** With A, knit.
Row 3 and 7 With B, K1, ✩sl 2 wyb, K2; rep from ✩ ending sl 2, K1.
Rows 4 and 8 With B, P1, ✩sl 2 wyf, P2; rep from ✩ ending sl 2, P1.
Rows 9, 10, 13 and 14 With B, knit.
Rows 11 and 15 With A, K1, ✩sl 2 wyb, K2; rep from ✩ ending sl 2, K1.
Rows 12 and 16 With A, P1, ✩sl 2 wyf, P2; rep from ✩ ending sl 2, P1.

CORN ON THE COB STITCH

multiple of 2
Note Colour A = pink, Colour B = mauve.

Cast on with A and knit one row.
Row 1 (RS) With B, K1, ✳K1, sl 1 wyb; rep from ✳ ending K1.
Row 2 With B, K1, ✳ sl 1 wyf, K1 tbl; rep from ✳ ending K1.
Row 3 With A, K1, ✳sl 1 wyb, K1 tbl; rep from ✳ ending K1.
Row 4 With A, K1, ✳K1, sl 1 wyf; rep from ✳ ending K1.

SHADOW BOX PATTERN *(below)*

multiple of 4 plus 3 extra
Note Colour A = pale blue, Colour B = dark blue, Colour C = turquoise.

Row 1 (RS) With A, knit.
Row 2 With A, K1, ✳K1 wrapping yarn twice around needle, K3; rep from ✳ ending last rep K1.
Row 3 With B, K1, ✳sl 1 wyb dropping extra loop, K3; rep from ✳ ending last rep K1.
Row 4 With B, K1, ✳sl 1 wyf, K3; rep from ✳ ending sl 1, K1.
Row 5 With C, K1, ✳sl 2 wyb, K2; rep from ✳ ending sl 1, K1.
Row 6 With C, K1, sl 1 wyf, ✳P2, sl 2 wyf; rep from ✳ ending K1.

LADDERS *(left)*

multiple of 6 plus 5 extra
Note Colour A = green, Colour B = blue

Row 1 With A, K2, ✳sl 1 pw, K5; rep from ✳ to last 3 sts, sl 1 pw, K2.
Row 2 With A, P2, sl 1 pw, ✳P5, sl 1 pw; rep from ✳ to last 2 sts, P2.
Row 3 With B, ✳K5, sl 1 pw; rep from ✳ to last 5 sts, K5.
Row 4 With B, ✳K5, sl 1 pw wyf; rep from ✳ to last 5 sts, K5.

MULTICOLOURED STRIPES

multiple of 4 plus 3 extra
Note Colour A = mauve, Colour B = pale pink, Colour C = red, Colour D = dark pink.

Row 1 (WS) With A, Purl.
Row 2 With B, K2, ✳sl 1 wyb, K1; rep from ✳ to last st, K1.
Row 3 With B, P2, ✳sl 1 wyf, P1; rep from ✳ to last st, P1.
Row 4 With C, K1, ✳sl 1 wyb, K1; rep from ✳.
Row 5 With C, Purl.
Row 6 With D, K1, ✳sl 1 wyb, K3; rep from ✳ to last 2 sts, sl 1 wyb, K1.
Row 7 With D, P1, ✳sl 1 wyf, P3; rep from ✳ to last 2 sts, sl 1 wyf, P1.
Row 8 With B, K2, ✳sl 3 wyb, K1; rep from ✳ to last st, K1.
Row 9 With B, ✳P3, sl 1 wyf; rep from ✳ to last 3 sts, P3.
Row 10 With A, K1, ✳sl 1 wyb, K3; rep from ✳ to last 2 sts, sl 1 wyf, K1.

JACQUARD PATTERNS

The term 'jacquard' is commonly applied to repeating colourwork motifs. (The word is derived from a loom producing figured fabrics invented in the 18th century by Joseph Jacquard.) Depending on the scale and complexity of the motifs and whether there are only two colours in a row or more than two, they may be worked by either the intarsia or the stranding/weaving method. For the patterns shown here, the latter method is generally preferable. Note, however, that where a colour must be woven across a long distance – as in parts of the Greek key pattern – it is most important to keep the tension very smooth. Also, avoid working the yarn in at the same point on two successive rows, as this will make a visible indentation on the right side.

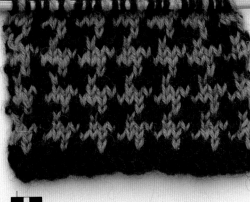

4 rows
repeat 4 sts

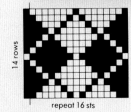

14 rows
repeat 16 sts

NOTE: In the sample two contrasting colours have been used. Light and dark can be reversed if desired.

6 rows
repeat 8 sts

NOTE: the basic repeat is only 4 stitches; a larger section is shown for clarity. In the sample, the pattern is moved 1 stitch to the right with each change of background colour.

12 rows

repeat 8 sts

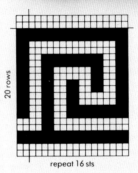

20 rows

repeat 16 sts

4 rows

repeat 4 sts

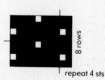

8 rows

repeat 4 sts

75

FAIR ISLE PATTERNS

Many beautiful multicoloured patterns have been created on some islands off the north coast of Scotland – the Shetlands and the nearby tiny Fair Isle. The motifs are combined and repeated in various ways to make stunning garments.

A sensitive choice of colour is the key to success in working Fair Isle patterns. Ideally, you should use special Shetland wool, which is dyed in traditional shades that blend and contrast well.

When choosing your own colour scheme, it is a good idea to photocopy the illustration in order to get a black and white representation of the colours. You can then substitute your own colours using a similar balance of lights and darks.

Although the patterns look extremely complex, they actually use only two colours in a row, and are worked using the stranding/weaving technique (see pages 69–70).

repeat 20 sts

4 rows

repeat 4 sts

4 rows

repeat 12 sts

7 rows

repeat 8 sts

9 rows

7 rows

repeat 12 sts

13 rows

33 rows

repeat 12 sts

25 rows

repeat 24 sts

13 rows

repeat 18 sts

4 rows

repeat 6 sts

77

6 Embellishments

Knitting is often embellished in some way. A twisted cord may be required around a waistline or at a neck; a crocheted edging may be used down the front opening of a cardigan; beads, sequins, or embroidery stitches may be worked into the knitting; a deep fringe may be added to a shawl to help it hang gracefully.

Conversely, knitting itself – in the form of a lacy knitted edging – can be used as the embellishment.

In the following few pages you will find instructions for all of these techniques.

DECORATIVE CORDS
Several kinds of decorative cord can be used for drawstrings or decorative ties at a neckline, for example. Experiment with these different kinds of cord, using different types of yarn, to discover their possibilities.

Knitted cord
For this cord you will need two double-pointed needles. Only one strand of yarn is used; work with the yarn still attached to the ball.
1 Cast on 2 stitches and knit them in the usual way (a).
2 Without turning the work, move the stitches towards the point of the needle, bring the yarn firmly from left to right, behind

a

the work, and knit the two stitches.
3 Continue in this way (b) until the cord is the required length. Knit the two stitches together and fasten off. The loose yarn ends can be sewn into the cord; or they can be used to attach a pompom, tassel or bead to each end.

b

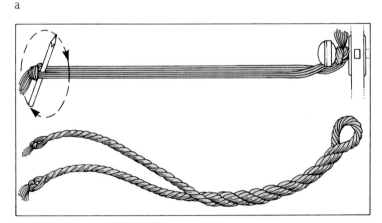

Twisted cord
The important thing to remember when making this cord is to twist the strands very tightly indeed; otherwise the finished cord will be flimsy. To estimate how many strands you will need, cut several short strands, twist them together, and then double this twisted length; add or subtract as appropriate. Cut the strands for the cord three times the finished length.
1 Knot the strands together at one end, and anchor this end to a fixed object, such as a doorknob; or ask someone to help you turn from that end.
2 Tie the strands together at the other end, and slip a pencil through the knot.
3 Holding the strands taut, turn the pencil clockwise, continuing to turn until the strands will kink up in several places if the tension is relaxed.

4 Bring the two knotted ends together, and give the cord a firm shake; it will twist around itself. Smooth out the coils, and tie a knot a short distance from the folded end. Also knot the two free ends together. Trim both ends and fluff out the strands.

Plaited cord
Cut the strands slightly longer than the required finished length of the cord, making sure that the number of strands is divisible by 3. Knot the strands together at one end, and pin the knot to a fixed object, such as the upholstered arm of a chair. Plait the strands. Knot the other end, and trim the ends if necessary.

TRIMMINGS

Many kinds of knitted garment can be decorated with fringes, tassels or pompoms. A simple fringe is the perfect finishing touch for a scarf; a more elaborate knotted one makes an elegant edging on a shawl. Pompoms make perky trimmings for hats and are favourites on children's garments. A tassel can be sewn to the ends of knitted cords or attached to the four corners of a knitted (or woven fabric) cushion cover.

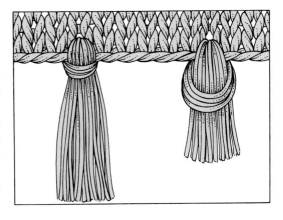

Simple fringe

This fringe is essentially a series of tassels. The strands should be about two and a half times the finished length.

1 Fold the group of strands in half. With the help of a crochet hook, draw the folded end through the edge from front to back.

2 Bring the strands through the loop, and pull downwards gently, bringing the loop up to the edge.

a

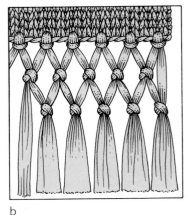

b

Knotted fringe

Elegant lattice-like effects can be created with this technique. The fringe should be at least 12cm/4½" deep; it uses fewer strands than a simple fringe.

1 Knot the strands into the edge of the fabric as for a simple fringe, placing them slightly farther apart.

2 When all the strands have been attached, take half the strands from the first group at one edge and half from the next group, and tie them together as shown. Join the remaining strands from the second group to half the strands from the third group. Continue to the end (a).

3 On the second row tie the separated strands together (b). More rows of knotting can be added if desired. An attractive variation is to join some strands with beads.

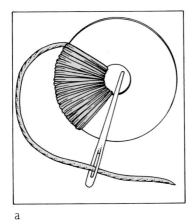

a

Pompoms

To make a pompom, first cut two identical circles from thin cardboard, the diameter of the finished pompom. In the centre of the circles draw another circle, one quarter the diameter of the outer circle. Mark the circle on one piece of cardboard, using any convenient round shape, then mark the smaller circle.

1 Cut a long length of yarn,

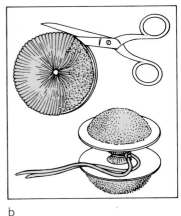

b

thread it into a tapestry needle, and wrap the yarn around the two circles (a). Add more yarn until the hole is tightly filled.

2 With sharp scissors cut around the edge of the circles (b, top).

3 Pull the cardboard circles apart slightly and tie a length of yarn firmly around the strands in the middle (b, bottom). Cut away the cardboard circles. Trim any uneven strands.

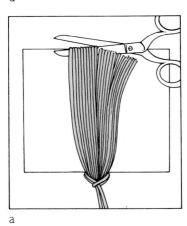

a

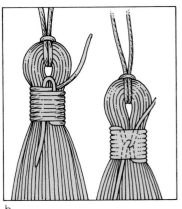

b

Tassels

From stiff cardboard cut a rectangle the length of the finished tassel.

1 Wind the yarn around the cardboard until the tassel is the desired thickness.

2 Loop a piece of yarn under the strands at one end. Cut through the other end (a).

3 Make a loop at one end of a length of yarn; holding the loop alongside the strands, wind the other end around several times. Slip the free end through the loop (b, left). Pull on the two ends to fasten them (b, right); trim the ends and push them inside.

BEADS & SEQUINS

A few beads or sequins can be sewn onto a finished piece of knitting, but if many are required and if they are to be placed evenly over part or all of the garment, they should be knitted in, using one of the methods shown below. When choosing beads or sequins for this purpose, make sure to select ones that have a hole large enough for the yarn to slip through easily; otherwise, the yarn is likely to become frayed or even break.

The simpler of the two methods for knitting with beads or sequins is the slip stitch method. The yarn-around-needle method must be used where beads are to be worked into consecutive stitches. Keeping the beads on the right side of the work requires a little more skill than in the slip stitch method. The beads or sequins can be worked into the knit side or purl side of the work. On the wrong side, work fairly tightly to hold the beads in place.

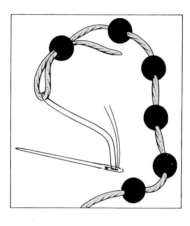

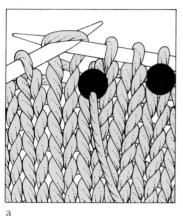

a

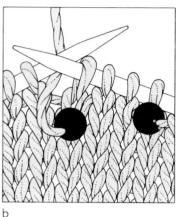

b

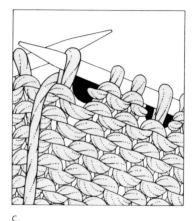

c

Threading beads onto yarn
First thread a sewing needle with a double strand of strong thread as shown. Slip the end of the yarn through the loop of thread, and turn back the end. Thread the beads or sequins onto the yarn, always keeping one bead on the loop to hold it in place.

Slip stitch method
This method can be used wherever the beads or sequins are separated by at least one stitch. It is normally worked on right-side rows, but can also be worked from the wrong side. At least two rows of knitting should be completed before beads are worked in.
I Knit up to the position for the bead. Bring the yarn forward and slip the next stitch knitwise (a).

2 Push the bead up close to the work (b) and knit the next stitch in the normal way.
If working a wrong-side row, take the yarn back to the right side of the work, slip the next stitch purlwise, push the bead up so that it lies close to the right side (c), and purl the next stitch.

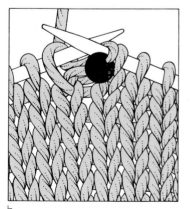

a

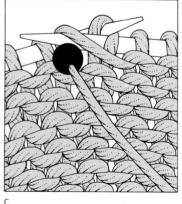

b

c

Yarn-around-needle method
I On a right-side (knit) row, insert the needle through the back of the next stitch and push a bead up close to the work (a).
2 Take the yarn around the needle, and push the bead through the stitch to the front. Complete the stitch (b).
On a wrong-side (purl) row, insert the needle purlwise through the back of the loop (c). Push the bead through the loop.

CROCHET

A knowledge of elementary crochet techniques is extremely useful for the knitter. Crochet can be used to make simple button loops – often required on baby garments – and to finish edges. It is also sometimes used to join seams.

Crochet is not difficult to learn. Only one implement is required, and mistakes are easily corrected; you simply unravel the work back to the mistake, slip the hook into the loop, and continue.

How to hold the hook and yarn is shown here. The yarn goes around the left little finger, under the third finger, then over the second and first fingers. A picot edging is being worked; the first row is double crochet and the second is 3 slip stitches, followed by 3 chain, all worked into the same double crochet.

a

b

Working a chain
The chain (abbreviated ch) is the basic stitch of crochet. A given number of chain stitches are used to begin work and are the equivalent of casting on in knitting.
1 Begin with a slip knot. Leave the hook in the loop, and grasp the base of the knot with the left thumb and forefinger.

2 Slide the hook forward under the tensioned yarn and turn it anti-clockwise, thus catching up the yarn as shown (a).
3 Still keeping the yarn tensioned, pull the hook back through the loop. A new loop has been formed.
Repeat steps 2 and 3 to make the required number of chains (b).

Slip stitch
This stitch (abbreviated sl st) is the shallowest crochet stitch. It is used to join chain to make a ring and also to join two pieces that have already been edged with double crochet. (Slip stitch is also sometimes called single crochet.) Insert the hook into the top of the stitch (or into a chain stitch). Draw a loop through the stitch and through the loop on the hook in one movement.

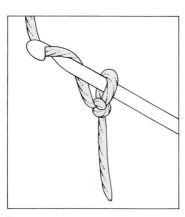

a

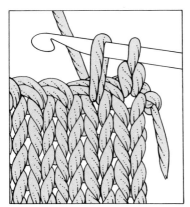

a

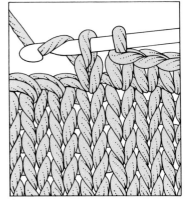

b

Double crochet
This stitch (abbreviated dc) can be worked on a completed knitted fabric to provide a neat, firm edge, perhaps in a contrasting colour.
1 Fasten the yarn to the RH corner of the work. Insert the hook into the first stitch from front to back, and draw through a loop.
2 Take the yarn around the hook

and draw this loop through the first loop.
3 Insert the hook into the next stitch and draw through a loop (a). Two loop are now on the hook.
4 Take the yarn around the hook (b) and draw it through both loops. One double crochet has been completed. Repeat steps 3 and 4 as required.
To turn a corner, work 3 double crochet into the corner stitch.

EMBROIDERY ON KNITTING

Embroidery stitches can be used to add motifs to a piece of plain knitting or to enhance or accentuate a stitch pattern.

By far the most commonly used embroidery technique in knitting is Swiss darning. This is worked on a stocking stitch fabric and gives the appearance of having been knitted in. Motifs for Swiss darning are normally given in chart form, with one square of the chart representing each stitch. A cross-stitch motif can also be used.

Embroidery on knitting is always worked with a tapestry needle to avoid splitting the yarn. Either a knitting yarn or embroidery thread can be used; the only criterion is that the thread should be appropriate in weight and texture for the background and to the technique used. It is important to stitch with an easy tension to preserve the elasticity of the fabric. Practise first on a spare swatch of the knitting.

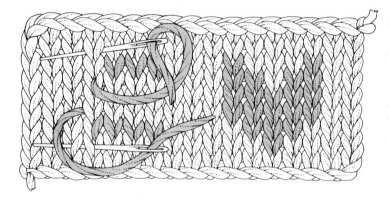

Swiss darning

Use a single strand of yarn, the same weight and type as that used for the knitting. Begin at the bottom RH corner of the motif, and fasten the yarn with one or two stitches under the area to be covered with the embroidery. Bring the needle up through the base of the first stitch to be embroidered.

1 Take the needle up to the right, along over the stitch, then under it from right to left, bringing it out as shown in the upper left of the drawing.

2 Take the needle down at the centre of the stitch, where it emerged, and then one stitch to the left, as shown in the lower left of the drawing. Repeat steps 1 and 2 to cover this and all subsequent stitches. Take care not to pull the stitches tightly.

a

Cross stitch

This stitch, too, is well suited to a stocking stitch fabric. The yarn used should be somewhat thinner than that used for the knitting. Depending on the scale of the work, it is best to work over groups of four stitches. Fasten the yarn on the wrong side.

1 Bring the needle up at the lower RH corner of the area to

b

be covered with the stitch, and take it down at the upper LH.

2 Bring it up at the lower LH corner and take it down at the upper RH corner. This completes the stitch (a).

When working cross stitch it is important that all the lower stitches slant in one direction and all the top stitches in another. For this reason, it is better to work in rows, in two stages (b).

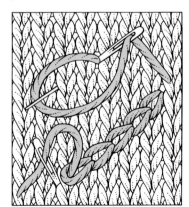

a

b

Chain stitch

This versatile stitch can be used to work lines in any direction. By varying the thickness of yarn and the spacing of stitches, you can produce quite different effects. Bring the needle up to the right side of the work, form the thread into a small loop, and take the needle back down into the fabric and up inside the loop (a, top). Continue forming loops in this way along the line of stitching. Fasten the last loop by taking the needle down into the fabric just outside the loop (a, bottom).

Individual chain stitches can be worked in a circle to suggest the petals of a flower (b); in this form the stitch is called 'lazy daisy'. They can also be scattered over the surface.

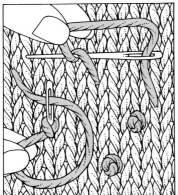

French knots

Several French knots can be grouped to suggest the centre of a flower or scattered over a small area for textural interest. It is usually better to choose a yarn at least as thick as that used for the knitting, so that the knots will stand out prominently on the surface. Attractive effects can be produced by using a contrasting fuzzy yarn or, for a dressy sweater, a glitter yarn.

1 Bring the needle up at the point for the knot. Holding the yarn taut, wrap it once around the needle, close to the place where it emerged, then take the needle to the wrong side, just beside the starting point. The trick in working a French knot is to take the needle through quickly, so that the thread does not have a chance to unwind.

For a larger knot, take the thread twice around the needle. However, more than two loops produce a somewhat untidy knot; so if it needs to be still larger, try a thicker thread.

a

Buttonhole stitch

Also known as blanket stitch, because it is sometimes used to edge blankets, this is a very useful stitch as well as a decorative one. The stitches can be spaced as shown or close together. The vertical legs can be of different lengths, producing an interesting random effect.

1 Work from left to right. Take the needle to the right, to the desired width of the stitch, then insert it above this point at the desired depth.

2 Loop the thread around to the right and bring the needle up over it on the lower stitching line. This completes the stitch (a). Continue working to the right in this way.

Buttonhole stitch can also be worked in circles (b) to produce stylized flower shapes.

b

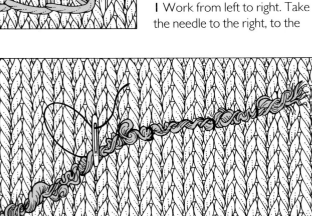

Couching

This stitch can be used to decorate a knitted fabric with threads that would be difficult or impossible to sew through the fabric. Use a fine sewing thread for the stitching.

1 Lay the main thread on the surface of the knitting, leaving a short end free. Bring the stitching thread to the right side, a little beyond the point where the couched thread will be fastened. Take it over the couched thread and back into the fabric.

2 Make another stitch about 1 cm/ ½" farther along the stitching line. Continue in this way. After the last stitch, fasten the working thread on the wrong side.

3 Use a large tapestry needle to take each end of the couched thread to the wrong side. Using fine thread, sew the ends in place.

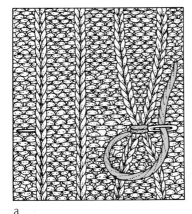
a

Smocking

As an alternative to knitting in smocking (see page 55), you can embroider the smocking on a knitted fabric. A relatively lightweight yarn should be used for the knitting. The yarn used for the smocking can be the knitting yarn or an embroidery thread. Work the fabric in a K1, P3 rib.

1 Secure the smocking thread at the lower RH corner, to the left of the second rib.

b

2 Take it back over the first rib and up again at the starting point, drawing the two ribs together.

3 Work 2 more backstitches over the ribs, then take the thread under the work and bring it up to the left of the fourth rib (a).

4 Join the third and fourth ribs in the same way. Work to the end. Work the next row above the first, joining different ribs (b).

EDGINGS

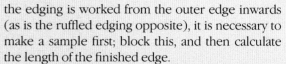

A knitted edging can provide the perfect finishing touch for many garments and accessories, baby clothes, shawls, bedspreads or the lower edge of a dressy sweater.

It is important to make sure that the finished edging is the right length to fit the edge to which it is attached. In the case of an edging worked sideways, the best approach is to follow the hint given for button/buttonhole bands on page 211. If the edging is worked from the outer edge inwards (as is the ruffled edging opposite), it is necessary to make a sample first; block this, and then calculate the length of the finished edge.

The edging may be sewn on with slipstitch, using sewing thread. One that is worked inwards may be grafted to a knitted edge (see page 90). Knit the last row, rather than casting off, making sure that the number of stitches matches that on the other edge.

LEAF EDGING

This edging is worked sideways.
Cast on 8 sts.
Row 1 (RS) K5, yf, K1, yf, K2.
Row 2 P6, K into front and back of next st, K3.
Row 3 K4, P1, K2, yf, K1, yf, K3.
Row 4 P8, K into front and back of next st, K4.
Row 5 K4, P2, K3, yf, K1, yf, K4.
Row 6 P10, K into front and back of next st, K5.
Row 7 K4, P3, K4, yf, K1, yf, K5.
Row 8 P12, K into front and back of next st, K6.
Row 9 K4, P4, sl 1, K1, psso, K7, K2 tog, K1.
Row 10 P10, K into front and back of next st, K7.
Row 11 K4, P5, sl 1, K1, psso, K5, K2 tog, K1.
Row 12 P8, K into front and back of next st, K2, P1, K5.
Row 13 K4, P1, K1, P4, sl 1, K1, psso, K3, K2 tog, K1.
Row 14 P6, K into front and back of next st, K3, P1, K5.
Row 15 K4, P1, K1, P5, sl 1, K1, psso, K1, K2 tog, K1.
Row 16 P4, K into front and back of next st, K4, P1, K5.
Row 17 K4, P1, K1, P6, sl 1, K2 tog, psso, K1.
Row 18 P2 tog, cast off 5 sts using P2 tog to cast off first st, P3, K4.

FAGGOT & SCALLOP EDGING

This edging is worked sideways.
Cast on 13 sts.
Row 1 K7, yf, sl 1, K1, psso, yf, K4.
Row 2 K2, P10, K2.
Row 3 K6, (yf, sl 1, K1, psso) twice, yf, K4.
Row 4 K2, P11, K2.
Row 5 K5, (yf, sl 1, Kl, psso) 3 times, yf, K4.
Row 6 K2, P12, K2.
Row 7 K4, (yf, sl 1, Kl, psso) 4 times, yf, K4.
Row 8 K2, P13, K2.
Row 9 K3, (yf, sl 1, Kl, psso) 5 times, yf, K4.
Row 10 K2, P14, K2.
Row 11 K4, (yf, sl 1, Kl, psso) 5 times, K2 tog, K2.
Row 12 K2, P13, K2.
Row 13 K5, (yf, sl 1, Kl, psso) 4 times, K2 tog, K2.
Row 14 K2, P12, K2.
Row 15 K6, (yf, sl 1, Kl, psso) 3 times, K2 tog, K2.
Row 16 K2, P11, K2.
Row 17 K7, (yf, sl 1, Kl, psso) twice, K2 tog, K2.
Row 18 K2, P10, K2.
Row 19 K8, yf, sl 1, Kl, psso, K2 tog, K2.
Row 20 K2, P9, K2.

SEASHORE EDGING

This edging is worked sideways.
Cast on 13 sts.
Row 1 Sl 1, K3, yf, K5, yf, K2 tog, yf, K2.
Row 2 K2, P11, K2.
Row 3 Sl 1, K4, sl 1, K2 tog, psso, K2, (yf, K2 tog) twice, K1.
Row 4 K2, P9, K2.
Row 5 Sl 1, K3, sl 1, K1, psso, K2, (yf, K2 tog) twice, K1.
Row 6 K2, P8, K2.
Row 7 Sl 1, K2, sl 1, K1, psso, K2, (yf, K2 tog) twice, K1.
Row 8 K2, P7, K2.
Row 9 Sl 1, K1, sl 1, K1, psso, K2, (yf, K2 tog) twice, K1.
Row 10 K2, P6, K2.
Row 11 Sl 1, sl 1, K1, psso, K2, yf, K1, yf, K2 tog, yf, K2.
Row 12 K2, P7, K2.
Row 13 Sl 1, (K3, yf) twice, K2 tog, yf, K2.
Row 14 K2, P9, K2

GODMOTHER'S EDGING

This edging is worked sideways.
Cast on 20 sts.
Row 1 Knit.
Row 2 Sl 1, K3, (yf, K2 tog) 7 times, yf, K2.
Rows 3, 5, 7, and 9 K to end.
Row 4 Sl 1, K6, (yf, K2 tog) 6 times, yf, K2.
Row 6 Sl 1, K9, (yf, K2 tog) 5 times, yf, K2.
Row 8 Sl 1, K12, (yf, K2 tog) 4 times, yf, K2.
Row 10 Sl 1, K23.
Row 11 Cast off 4 sts, K19.
Rep rows 2–10.

RUFFLED EDGING

This edging is worked from the outer edge inward.
Multiple of 10 plus 3 extra.
Rows 1 and 3 (WS) K3, *P7, K3; rep from *.
Row 2 P3, *K7, P3; rep from *.
Row 4 P3, *K2, sl 2, K1, p2sso, K2, P3; rep from *.
Rows 5 and 7 K3, *P5, K3; rep from *.
Row 6 P3, K5, P3; rep from *.
Row 8 P3, *K1, sl 2, K1, p2sso, K1, P3; rep from *.
Rows 9 and 11 K3, *P3, K3; rep from *.
Row 10 P3, *K3, P3; rep from *.
Row 12 P3, *sl 2, K1, p2sso, P3; rep from *.
Rows 13 and 15 K3, *P1, K3; rep from *.
Rows 14 and 16 P3, *K1, P3; rep from *.
Rows 17 and 18 Knit.
Cast off.

Special Techniques

The skills covered in this chapter include some that you may need only occasionally, such as inserting a zip fastener or working a knitted-in hem, as well as skills that will give your knitting a professional touch; these include such refinements as a bias cast-off for slanting shoulder seams, an invisible cast-on edge, how to join knitted edges by grafting, rather than sewing them together and several different kinds of hems and pockets.

As you gain experience and confidence as a knitter, you will often find that you can improve on the techniques specified in a commercial pattern. For example, you might wish to knit a patch pocket on picked-up stitches, rather than sewing it on. Practise these special techniques and keep the samples for reference later.

ADVANCED CASTING ON

The two methods of casting on shown here are well worth learning. They are often called 'invisible' casting-on methods because they employ a separate length of yarn which is later removed.

Method I is used on a single rib fabric; when the foundation yarn is removed, the edge that remains appears to consist only of ribbing, although the first four rows are actually produced by a slipstitch technique. The smooth edge is flexible and attractive, and worth the small amount of extra work involved.

In Method II the edge that remains consists of loose stitches which can either be picked up and knitted (for a lacy edging perhaps) or grafted to another edge for an invisible join.

The edge produced by the invisible cast-on (Method I, bottom) is flexible, attractive and hard-wearing.

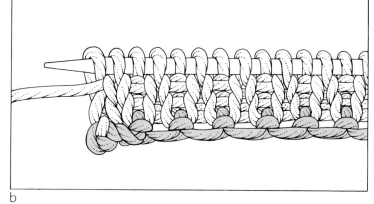

a

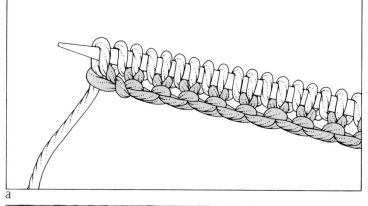

b

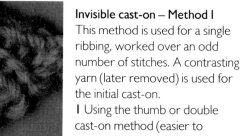

Invisible cast-on – Method I
This method is used for a single ribbing, worked over an odd number of stitches. A contrasting yarn (later removed) is used for the initial cast-on.

I Using the thumb or double cast-on method (easier to remove than the cable method), cast onto the needle half the number of stitches that will be required, rounding the result up to the next number. Thus, if 53 stitches will be needed, you should cast on 27 (rounded up from 26½).

2 Join on the main yarn and cut off the contrasting yarn. Work the first 5 rows as follows:
Row I (inc row): K1, ✳ yf, K1, rep from ✳ to end. The correct number of sts should now be on the needle (a).
Row 2: K1, ✳ wyf sl I purlwise, K1, rep from ✳ to end.
Row 3: wyf sl 1, ✳ K1, wyf sl 1, rep from ✳ to end.
Row 4: As row 2.
Row 5: As row 3 (b).
Now work in K1 P1 rib for the required depth. Unpick the contrasting yarn.

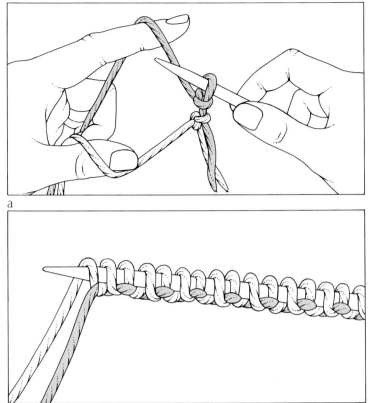

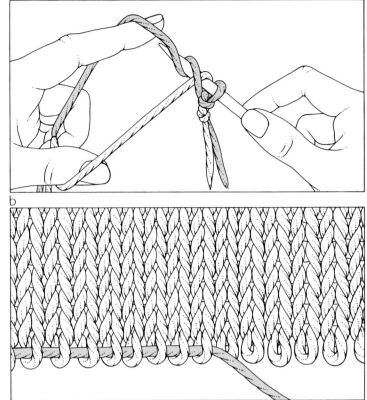

Invisible cast-on – Method II

A contrasting yarn, of any colour, is used in this method; it is removed later.

1 Make a slip knot in the main yarn (called A) and place it on the needle. Tie the contrasting yarn (called B) to the main yarn, and hold the two yarns in the left hand as shown (a).

2 Take yarn A over the needle from front to back.

3 Take yarn B over the needle from back to front. The yarns are now crossed on top of the needle (b).

4 Take yarn A over the needle again from front to back, and pull both yarns around the far side of the needle, thus bringing them below it. You will soon master this technique if you recite to yourself, 'front to back, back to front, front to back and down'. The contrasting yarn should lie in a more-or-less straight line along the lower edge of the cast-on stitches (c).

When the required number of stitches have been cast on, tie the contrasting yarn to the main yarn at the end, and cut it off. Leave this yarn in place until the knitting is completed, then remove it (d) and pick up the stitches as instructed by the pattern for further knitting or grafting.

Multiple increase

Some patterns will require you to cast on a number of stitches at a side edge in order to work some shaping – for example to add a sleeve on a T-shaped garment. Any convenient cast-on method can be used for this; however, if you are using a two-strand method, such as the double cast-on, you will need to tie an extra strand onto the work.

If the increase is to be made at the left-hand edge of the garment (that is, the left edge with the work facing you), the extra stitches are cast on immediately after completing a right-side row, so that the first row worked on them will be a wrong-side row. If the increase is to come at the right-hand edge, the stitches are cast on after completing a wrong-side row.

ADVANCED CASTING OFF

Here are four different ways of casting off to add to your repertoire of knitting techniques.

The suspended cast-off is a very useful method, as it is more flexible than the basic method (page 19). It can be used on ribbing (although the edge is somewhat more conspicuous than a rib cast-off) or wherever elasticity is important.

The bias cast-off is not really a cast-off method *per se*, but a special way of shaping an edge that would otherwise be cast off on alternate rows, in stages, producing a stepped effect.

The double cast-off can be used to join a shoulder seam or any other straight edges having the same number of stitches. It makes the perfect finishing touch to a bias cast-off.

The invisible cast-off is the trickiest of these methods; however, it is ideal on a piece of single ribbing – where an inconspicuous finish is desired.

a

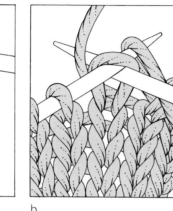

b

c

Suspended cast-off

1 Work the first 2 stitches. ✿Lift the first stitch over the second, as usual, but leave the lifted stitch on the LH needle (a).
2 Still leaving the first 2 stitches in place, work the third stitch (b).
3 Drop the second and third stitches off the LH needle. Two loops are now on the RH needle. Repeat (c) from ✿ until 2 stitches remain; knit these together.

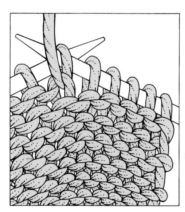

a

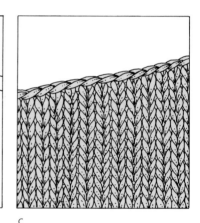

b

c

Bias cast-off

A pattern will normally instruct you to cast off in stages and will give the exact number of stitches to be cast off on each shaping row. The process will typically take 5 rows. You can easily convert the instructions for a bias cast-off, as described below. The illustrations here show a cast-off on the LH edge.
1 Work up to the last row before the shoulder shaping, ending at the neck edge with a wrong-side row.
2 Work across the stitches up to those to be cast off. Turn, leaving these stitches unworked. Slip the first stitch purlwise (a).
3 Work across to the end (neck edge).
4 Turn and work across the stitches up to the next group to be cast off. Repeat step 3. Continue in this way until only the last group of stitches remains to be worked. With the right side facing, cast off all the stitches (b). The cast-off edge (c) slopes smoothly. To cast off a RH edge, work as above, reversing the terms 'right side' and 'wrong side'.

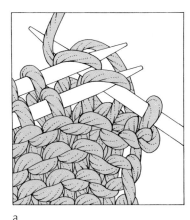

a

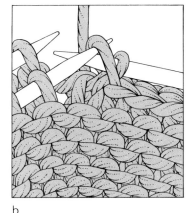

b

Double cast-off

This is a combined cast-off and seam. The edges to be joined must have exactly the same number of stitches.

Work the two pieces of knitting up to the last row before casting off; leave the stitches on a spare needle. Before working the cast-off, arrange the two pieces on the needles so that when they are placed together with right sides facing the needles will point towards the right.

1 Holding the two pieces together, with right sides facing, insert a third needle knitwise through the first stitch on both pieces, and knit the two together.
2 Work the next 2 stitches together in the same way (a).
3 Using one of the two needles in the left hand (either will do), lift the first stitch over the second, as for the basic cast-off (b).
Repeat steps 1–3 until all the stitches have been cast off.

The invisible cast-off produces an edge that is ideal for a polo neck – or wherever smooth, flexible ribbing is especially important.

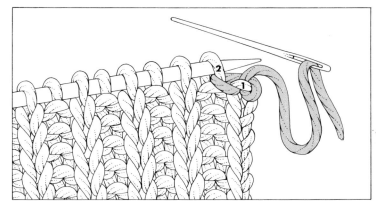

a

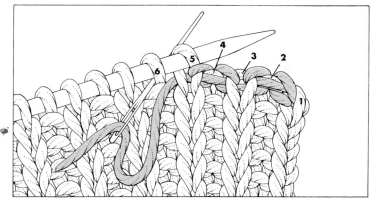

b

Invisible cast-off

This ingenious method of casting off a single rib fabric may seem dauntingly complex at first; but if you persevere you will be delighted with the results. It makes a highly professional finish on a ribbed collar or neckband.

To practise, cast on an odd number of stitches – at least 25 – and work in K1 P1 rib for about 4cm/1½", ending with a wrong-side row. Cut off the thread, allowing 3 times the width of the knitting, and thread the end into a tapestry needle. In the illustrations this is shown in a contrasting colour for clarity. The knit stitches have been given odd numbers, the purl stitches even ones.

Each stitch is worked into twice: the first time in a direction contrary to its construction; the second time in the same direction. Only then is it slipped off the needle.

1 To begin, insert the tapestry needle purlwise into stitch 1, then knitwise into stitch 2. Leave these stitches on the needle.
2 Work knitwise into stitch 1 and slip it off the needle (a).
3 Work purlwise into stitch 3.
4 Work purlwise into stitch 2 and slip it off the needle.
5 Take the tapestry needle behind stitch 3 and to the front between stitches 3 and 4. Work knitwise into stitch 4.
Repeat steps 2–5, working into stitches 3, 5, 4 and 6 (b). Continue in this way to the end of the row.

RAFTING

Grafting is a method of sewing two knitted edges together stitch by stitch, so that the join, if carefully worked, is invisible. The sewing stitches duplicate the structure of the knitting.

This technique is often used to join a front and back section at the shoulder. The edges need not be straight, as shown; they could be shaped, as shown on page 88.

To work the grafting, you can either place the pieces on a flat surface, as shown in these illustrations, or hold them together with wrong sides facing and the needles close together in your hand.

Grafting can also be used to join an edge that has been cast on using the invisible method II (page 87).

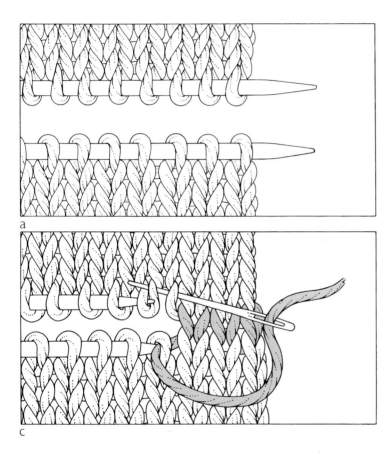

a

c

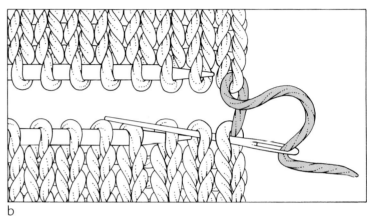

b

Grafting stocking stitch

End one piece of knitting with a knit row and the other with a purl row, so that when the work is positioned as shown the needles will both point to the right (a).
1 Thread a tapestry needle with matching yarn, 3 times the width.
2 Insert the needle purlwise through the first stitch on the lower edge, then purlwise through the opposite stitch on the upper edge. Take it knitwise through the first stitch again, then purlwise through the second stitch on the same edge (b).
3 ✭ Insert the needle knitwise into the stitch on the upper edge where the yarn emerges, then purlwise into the next stitch to the left (c). Insert it knitwise into the stitch just below, then purlwise into the next stitch to the left. Repeat from ✭ to end.

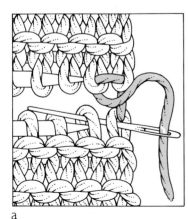

a

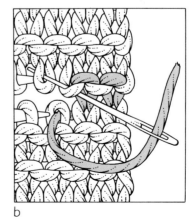

b

Grafting garter stitch

Although most often used on stocking stitch, grafting also lends itself to other simple stitch patterns, such as garter stitch.

End one piece on a right-side row, the other on a wrong-side row, so that the lower piece will have a ridge close to the needle and the other piece will have the ridge one row away.
1 Take the needle purlwise through the first stitch on the lower edge, purlwise through the first upper stitch and knitwise through the next upper stitch.
2 ✭Insert the needle knitwise again through the first lower stitch, then purlwise through the second lower stitch (a). Insert the needle purlwise through the upper stitch, then knitwise through the next upper stitch (b). Repeat from ✭ to end.

Hems, Facings & Waistbands

Although hems are less often used on knitted garments than ribbing or decorative borders such as garter or moss stitch, they are needed wherever a reasonably firm edge that lies flat is required: at the lower edge of a skirt, for example, or on the lower and front opening edges of a tailored jacket. A vertical hem is normally called a facing.

It is sometimes possible – when working a skirt, for example – to work from the top downwards,

ending with the hem. The hem edge stitches can be cast off, or left on the needle and sewn to the main fabric using the stitch-by-stitch method (page 92).

Similar to a hem is a knitted waistband. This is often worked in single ribbing and used on garments for babies or toddlers, as the extra-snug fit compensates for the lack of a natural waistline. A less bulky alternative to a knitted waistband is one worked in herringbone stitch.

Sewn-in hem with slipstitch foldline

This hem is preferred for garments worked in textured stitch patterns or heavyweight yarn.

1 Work the hem in stocking stitch, using smaller needles, as for the ridge fold hem, ending with a wrong-side row.
2 On the next (right-side) row, work as follows: ✱K1, wyf sl 1,

rep from ✱ to last st, K1.
3 Change to larger needles and work the main part of the garment in pattern.

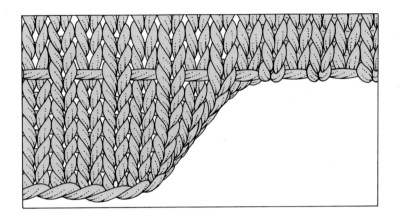

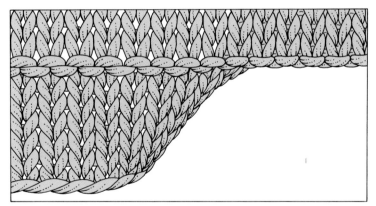

Sewn-in hem with ridge foldline

This hem is best suited to a garment worked in stocking stitch. Use a cast-on method with a fairly flat edge. If you plan to use the stitch-by-stitch sewing method (page 92) for attaching the hem, use the invisible cast-on method II (page 87). For the hem itself, use needles one or two sizes smaller than those specified for the main fabric. This

helps it it to lie smoothly when turned up.
1 Work in stocking stitch for the required depth of the hem, ending with a wrong-side row.
2 On the next (right-side) row, purl, rather than knitting, to produce a ridge on the fabric. This will serve as the foldline.
3 Change to the larger needles and continue in stocking stitch for the main part of the garment.

Sewn-in hem with picot foldline

This is a pretty edge often found on baby clothes and delicate or dressy garments. It is best worked in a fine yarn.

1 Cast on an odd number of stitches, and work in stocking stitch, using smaller needles, until the hem is the desired depth, ending with a wrong-side row.
2 On the next (right-side) row, work as follows: ✱K2 tog, yf, rep

from ✱ to last st, K1.
3 Change to larger needles, and continue in pattern. When the work is complete, turn up the hem along the line of eyelets to produce the picot effect.

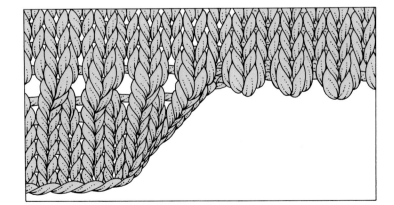

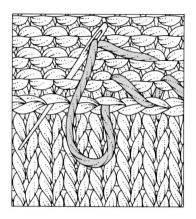

Whipstitch

This stitch is suitable for a garment worked in a light- or medium-weight yarn. Work through a single purled loop of the main fabric, then through a loop on the hem edge as shown.

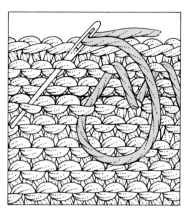

Blind hemming stitch

This method is suitable for a heavyweight fabric. You may need to separate the yarn and use one or two plies to reduce bulk.

First tack the hem in place, about 1 cm/³⁄₈″ below the edge. Turn the garment as shown, with the hem fold away from you. Work the stitches between the hem edge and the main fabric so that the hem edge is free.

Stitch-by-stitch method

This method can be used on an edge that has been cast on using the invisible method II or on the edge of a section that has been worked from the top down. In the first case, remove the foundation yarn gradually as you work the hem; in the second, leave the needle in the work, removing it as you stitch.

1 Fasten the sewing yarn at the

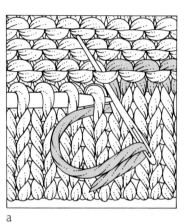

a

RH edge, and insert the needle purlwise through the first stitch on the lower edge. Take it through the corresponding stitch in the main fabric, then knitwise through the first lower stitch.

2 Insert the needle knitwise through the next stitch on the lower edge, then purlwise (a) into the next stitch above. Continue working in this way (b) to the end.

b

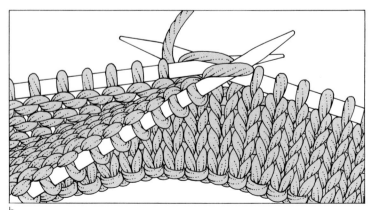

a

b

Knitted-in hem

This is an ingenious way of turning up a hem, but it must be worked carefully if it is not to look bulky. Before knitting the garment itself, work a small sample and adjust the hem needle size and the number of rows if necessary. The needles used for the hem should be two or three sizes smaller than those used for the main fabric.

1 Cast on the required number of stitches and work the hem allowance as for a sewn-in hem.

2 Work a ridge or slipstitch foldline, and continue with the larger needles until the main part of the garment is the same depth as the hem allowance, ending with a wrong-side row. Leave the stitches on the needle.

3 Using a spare needle and working on the right side, pick up and knit stitches along the cast-on edge (a). Work into the farther loop of each stitch – the one that

will be closer to the garment. Fasten off the extra yarn.

4 Turn up the hem along the ridge; using the main yarn and working on the right side of the garment, knit one stitch from the garment together with one stitch from the hem all along the row (b). The picked-up stitches from the hem are now securely knitted into the main fabric.

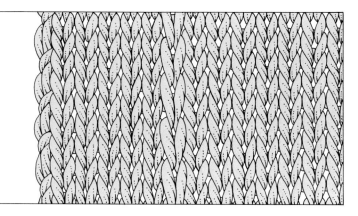

Vertical facing

A vertical facing may be required on the front edge of a Chanel-style jacket, for example. The facing itself should be worked in stocking stitch, whatever the main fabric is worked in. The illustration shows a left front edge; for a right front edge the process is reversed.

1 On a right-side row, work in pattern to the foldline; slip the next stitch purlwise; continue in stocking stitch to the end of the row.

2 On a wrong-side row, work in stocking stitch up to and including the slipped stitch; continue in pattern to the end.

When the section is complete, turn the facing to the wrong side along the foldline and stitch it in place.

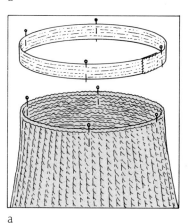

Mitred hem and facing

For a neat finish on the front and lower edges of a jacket, work a hem and facing with a mitred corner. First calculate, from the garment tension, the number of stitches to cast on for the hem. Find the number of stitches in 2.5cm/1″, and subtract this from the number required for the full width of the section.

1 Cast on the reduced number of

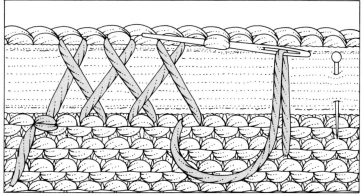

b

stitches and work the hem in stocking stitch, increasing 1 stitch at the front edge on every alternate row until the total number are on the needle.

2 Work the turning ridge, then continue increasing, working a slipstitch foldline (above). When the facing is the same depth as the hem, work straight (a).

3 Oversew the diagonal edges neatly together (b).

a

b

Herringbone casing

1 Join the elastic to form a ring, first making sure that it fits the waist smoothly without stretching.

2 Divide the elastic into 4 equal sections and mark them with pins. Similarly mark the 4 quarters of the skirt edge (a).

3 Pin the elastic to the wrong side of the waist edge, matching the corresponding points.

4 Fasten the knitting yarn to the fabric with two backstitches, just below the elastic. Take it up over the elastic and to the right, and insert the needle through the edge of the knitting from right to left as shown. Take it down to the right and insert it again from the left. Continue in this way all around the waistband (b); fasten off securely.

For a stronger version of the herringbone-stitched casing, work in crocheted chain stitch (page 81) diagonally over the elastic.

Knitted waistband

1 Work a ridge foldline as shown on page 91, then knit the waistband in K1, P1 rib until it is the required depth.

2 Sew the waistband in place, leaving about 5cm/2″ unstitched.

3 Thread elastic through the casing, and pin the ends together with a safety pin. Check the fit. Sew the ends together firmly, then complete the stitching on the casing edge.

OCKETS

The three most popular styles of pocket are the patch pocket, the horizontal inside pocket and the vertical inside pocket. There are various methods of working these different types; you can often substitute a method you prefer for the one in a pattern.

Patch pockets are usually most successful in a textured stitch pattern, which provides contrast. A stocking stitch patch pocket can have a homemade look if it is not sewn on very carefully. If a stocking stitch pocket is required, a neat way of attaching it is with Swiss darning. Another option is to work a modified patch pocket on stitches picked up from the main fabric. Working a garter stitch selvedge along the two sides will provide a neat finish.

A patch pocket can be attached with one of the side edges left unstitched, instead of the top edge, to make a vertical patch pocket.

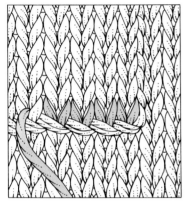

a

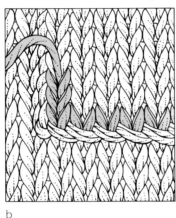

b

Swiss-darned patch pocket

1 Work the patch to the desired size and cast off. Block or press it as appropriate, and darn in the ends on the wrong side.
2 Pin the pocket to the garment. Fasten the yarn (shown here in a contrasting colour for clarity) at the lower RH corner on the wrong side of the main fabric, and bring it up in the centre of the first stitch in from the edge as shown. Work Swiss darning (see page 82) over all the stitches across the lower edge of the pocket (a).
3 Continue up the LH side of the pocket as shown (b). Fasten off.
4 Swiss-darn the RH edge of the pocket in the same way.

Patch pocket on picked-up stitches

This style of pocket, too, is worked after the main section has been completed.
1 Fasten the yarn on the wrong side of the work just above the ribbing, at the position of the lower RH corner of the pocket. Using a crochet hook, pick up the required number of stitches for the pocket and place them on the needle (a).
2 Beginning with a purl row, work in stocking stitch to the required depth for the pocket (b). Cast off evenly.
3 Sew the side edges of the pocket in place, either with Swiss darning or with oversewing.

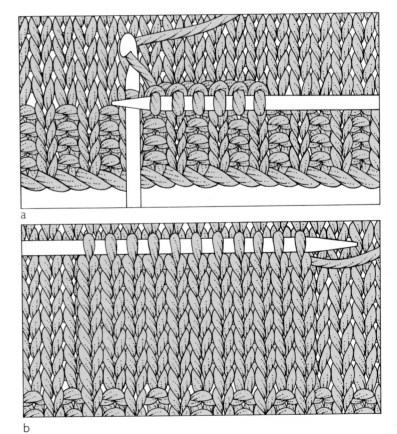

a

b

Oversewing a patch pocket

1 Lay the pocket on the main section, and insert a pin diagonally at each corner, through the background fabric only. Remove the pocket, and check that the pins are aligned on the same vertical and horizontal rows.
2 Take two fine double-pointed needles and insert them in the fabric between the pins, picking up alternate stitches (a).
3 Place the pocket between the needles, and oversew it to the picked-up stitches, working into the alternating stitches along the pocket edge (b). When both sides have been sewn, oversew the lower edge in place, again working through alternate stitches.

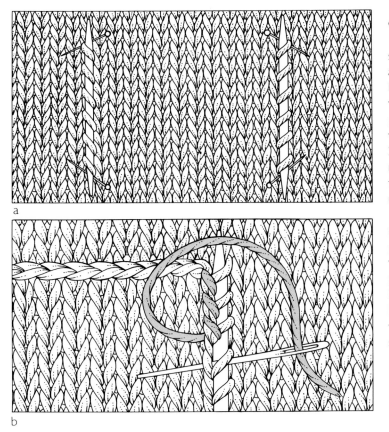

a

b

Horizontal inside pocket

A pattern will often instruct you to place a horizontal pocket by leaving the stitches for the border on a spare needle, joining in the pocket lining and then picking up the opening stitches and working the border. The following method incorporates the border stitches in the fabric, producing a slightly neater finish.
1 First work the pocket lining, casting on 2 more stitches than are allowed for the opening. Work the lining to the required depth, ending with a knit row and decreasing 1 stitch at each end of the previous purl row. Leave the stitches on a spare needle (a).
2 Work the main fabric up to the position for the pocket border. Continue knitting, working the border in the chosen pattern.
3 When the border is the required depth, cast off these stitches on a right-side row; work to the end (b).
4 On the next row, purl across to the beginning of the pocket opening, then purl across the stitches of the pocket lining (c) and continue to the end of the row.
5 When the section is complete, oversew the pocket lining edges in place on the wrong side.

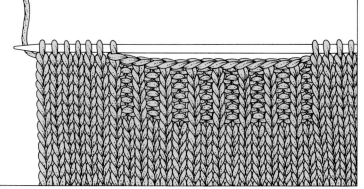

a

b

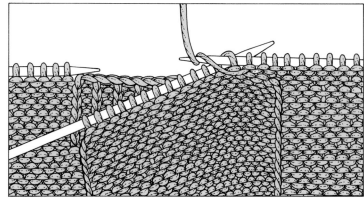

c

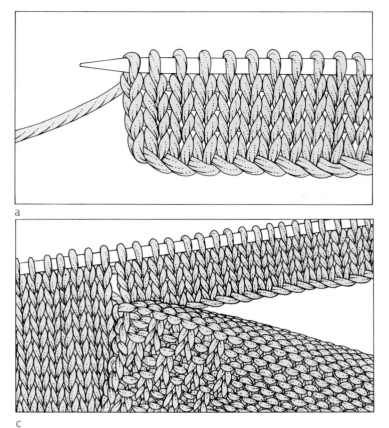

a

b

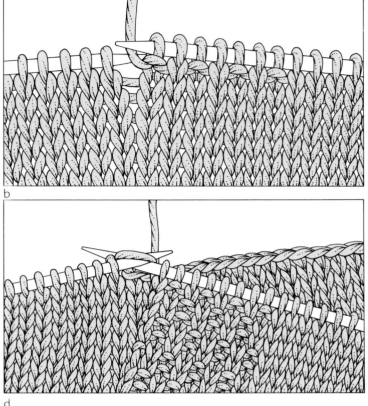

c

d

Vertical pocket with borders included

The opening for a vertical pocket is worked in two stages, first one side and then the other. When the second side is as deep as the first, the two sides are rejoined. A pocket lining is incorporated in the outer side section of the fabric.

The border of a vertical pocket can either be knitted along with the top part of the pocket or worked later on picked-up

stitches as shown below. The illustrations show a pocket in the right side of a garment. For the left side, reverse the instructions.

1 Work a few rows of stocking stitch for the lower part of the pocket lining. End with a right-side row, and place the stitches on a spare needle (a).

2 Work the main section up to the level for the pocket opening, ending with a wrong-side row. On the next row, work across to the inner edge of the border,

then work in the border pattern across the specified number of stitches (b). Slip the remaining stitches for the outer side section onto a spare needle.

3 Continue working on the top section of the pocket until it is the required depth, ending with a right-side row. Slip these stitches onto a spare needle; do not break off the yarn.

4 Now pick up the pocket lining; place it alongside the outer side section, join on new yarn if

necessary, and knit to the end of the row (c).

5 Continue working across the outer side section and pocket lining until this piece is one row shorter than the top section, thus ending with a wrong-side row.

6 On the next row, cast off the pocket lining stitches. Rejoin the two sections of the main fabric (d) and knit to the end of the row.

7 When the section is complete, sew the pocket lining to the main fabric with whipstitch.

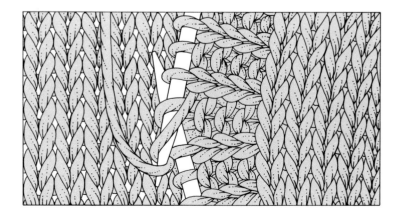

Vertical pocket with border added

Work this pocket as for the one with a knitted border, but do not work the border stitches. (The division should thus be placed slightly closer to the centre front.) When the section is completed, pick up stitches along the edge of the top section of the pocket and work in the chosen pattern. Sew the edges to the main fabric.

ℱASTENINGS

Fastenings can be problematical in a knitted garment, simply because the fabric is soft and stretchy and is inclined to pull away from a zip or buttons. The following techniques will help you to give your work a professional finish.

When inserting a zip, it is important to provide a firm edge for the zip opening. If the knitting is in a heavyweight yarn, this is best done by working a selvedge; on lightweight knitting, use crochet.

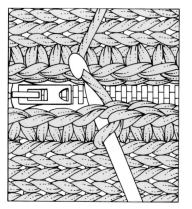

Crocheted zip opening

1 Before sewing in the zip, work a row of double crochet (page 81) along the opening edges.

2 Tack and stitch the zip in place as described for a selvedge opening, working the backstitch along the outer edge of the crochet.

3 Open the zip and work slip stitches (page 81) into the double crochet.

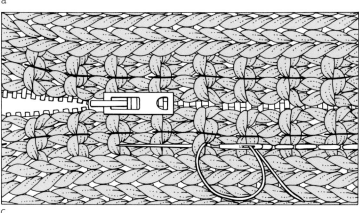

a

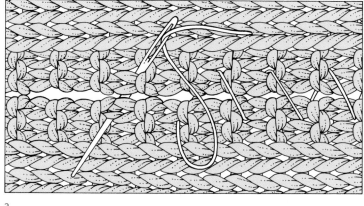

c

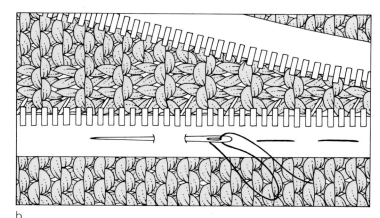

b

Inserting a zip – selvedge opening

When working the garment, add 2 stitches to the opening edges, and work a double garter stitch selvedge (page 27). Block or press the completed sections.

1 Place the adjacent sections right side up, and tack them together using an oversewing stitch and a tapestry needle (a).

2 Turn the work wrong side upwards. Open the zip and place it over the opening with the teeth exactly centred. Using an ordinary sewing needle, tack the zip tape to the knitting down one side (b). Close the zip; continue tacking up the other side.

3 Working from the right side and using strong sewing thread such as buttonhole twist, sew the zip in place with backstitch. Start at the top and work down one side and up the other (c).

a

b

Ribbon-faced buttonhole band

To prevent the button and buttonhole bands of a cardigan from sagging, sew a length of ribbon (grosgrain is the usual choice, but any firm ribbon will do) to the underside of the bands.

1 Cut the ribbon about 3cm/1 ¼" longer than the band. Turn under one end and tack it to the knitting; trim the other end if necessary, and turn it under.

2 Slipstitch the ribbon in place as shown (a).

To finish the buttonholes, turn the buttonhole band right side up, and cut a slit in the ribbon under each buttonhole, taking care not to cut into the knitting. Using yarn or matching perlé cotton and a chenille needle (a large-eyed, sharp-pointed embroidery needle), work buttonhole stitch (b) around the buttonholes.

RIBBON PATTERNS

Among the most intriguing of knitting stitch patterns are those in which smooth, ribbon-like bands of stocking stitch form zigzag, plaited or woven effects. A simple basketweave pattern is shown on page 21. Here are some patterns offering more of a challenge and a more dramatic effect.

The zigzag ribbon pattern is relatively simple, but creates a wonderful *trompe l'oeil* texture. Double wing openwork combines the ribbon-like motif with the delicacy of lace. Ribbon lattice is a striking pattern which has considerable impact when worked in a large piece. But the 'star turn' for any knitter is surely the *entrelacs* pattern (a French word meaning 'interlaced'). It is certainly complex – but worth the effort!

ZIGZAG RIBBON PATTERN

multiple of 11 plus 2
Row 1 (RS) K1, *P1, K10; rep from * to last st, K1.
Row 2 K1, *P9, K2; rep from * to last st, K1.
Row 3 K1, *P3, K8; rep from * to last st, K1.
Row 4 K1, *P7, K4; rep from * to last st, K1.
Row 5 K1, *P5, K6; rep from * to last st, K1.
Rows 6 and 7 As Row 5.
Row 8 As Row 4.
Row 9 As Row 3.
Row 10 As Row 2.
Row 11 As Row 1.
Row 12 K1, *K1, P10; rep from * to last st, K1.
Row 13 K1, *K9, P2; rep from * to last st, K1.
Row 14 K1, *K3, P8; rep from * to last st, K1.
Row 15 K1, *K7, P4; rep from * to last st, K1.
Row 16 K1, *K5, P6; rep from * to last st, K1.
Rows 17 and 18 As Row 16.
Row 19 As Row 15.
Row 20 As Row 14.
Row 21 As Row 13. **Row 22** As Row 12.

DOUBLE WING OPENWORK

multiple of 16
Row 1 (RS) Knit.
Row 2 *K4, P8, K4; rep from *.
Row 3 *P3, K2 tog, K3, yf and around needle twice, K3, ssk, P3; rep from *.
Row 4 K3, P4, purl into front and back of extra loop, P4, K3; rep from *.
Row 5 *P2, K2 tog, K3, yf, K2, yf, K3, ssk, P2; rep from *.
Row 6 *K2, P12, K2; rep from *.
Row 7 *P1, K2 tog, K3, yf, K4, yf, K3, ssk, P1; rep from *.
Row 8 *K1, P14, K1; rep from *.
Row 9 *K2 tog, K3, yf, K6, yf, K3, ssk; rep from *.
Row 10 Purl.

ENTRELACS PATTERN

multiple of 6

Note Colour A = green, Colour B = yellow, Colour C = grey.

Join in and break off yarns where necessary.

Foundation Row (base triangles) With B, ✳P2, turn and K2, turn and P3, turn and K3, turn and P4, turn and K4, turn and P5, turn and K5, turn and P6; rep from ✳. Cont in stripe sequence of 1 row in C, 1 row in A, and 1 row in B, as follows:

Row 1 (RS) K2, turn and P2, turn and inc in first st, sl 1, K1, psso, turn and P3, turn and inc in first st, K1, sl 1, K1, psso, turn and P4, turn and inc in first st, K2, sl 1, K1, psso, turn and P5, turn and inc in first st, K3, sl 1, K1, psso (edge triangle complete), then cont as follows: ✳K up 6 sts down side edge of same section of previous row; working across these sts and next 6 sts on LH needle, cont as follows: (turn and P6, turn and K5, sl 1, K1, psso) 6 times; rep from ✳ to last section, K up 6 sts down side edge of last section, turn and P2 tog, P4, turn and K5, turn and P2 tog, P3, turn and K4, turn and P2 tog, P2, turn and K3, turn and P2 tog, P1, turn and K2, turn and P2, tog. Fasten off.

Row 2 ✳With WS facing, pick up and P6 sts down side edge of first section of previous row and working across these sts, and next 6 sts on LH needle, cont as follows: (turn and K6, turn and P5, P2 tog) 6 times; rep from ✳.

Keeping stripe sequence correct, rep rows 1 and 2 for the required depth, ending with row 1.

Next row (finishing row): ✳with WS facing, pick up and P6 sts down side edge of first section of previous row. Working across these sts and next 6 sts on LH needle, cont as follows: turn and K6, turn and P2 tog, P3, P2 tog, turn and K5, turn and P2 tog, P2, P2 tog, turn and K4, turn and P2 tog, P1, P3 tog, turn and K3, turn and P2 tog, P3 tog, turn and K2, turn and P2 tog. Fasten off; rep from ✳.

RIBBON LATTICE PATTERN

multiple of 18 plus 1 extra

Note 'Kfb': K into front and back of st.

Row 1 (RS) ✳K3, K2 tog, K4, (K1, yf, K1) into next st, K4, sl 1, K1, psso, K2; rep from ✳ to last st, K1.
Row 2 K1, ✳K2, P6, K1, P6, K3; rep from ✳.
Row 3 ✳K2, K2 tog, K5, yf, K1, yf, K5, sl 1, K1, psso, K1; rep from ✳ to last st, K1.
Row 4 K1, ✳K1, P6, K3, P6, K2; rep from ✳.
Row 5 ✳K1, K2 tog, K5, yf, K3, yf, K5, sl 1, K1, psso; rep from ✳ to last st, K1.
Row 6 K1, ✳P6, K5, P6, K1; rep from ✳.
Row 7 K2 tog, ✳K5, (yf, K5) twice, sl 1, K2 tog, psso; rep from ✳, ending last rep sl 1, K1, psso instead of sl 1, K2 tog, psso.

(continued on next page)

Row 8 P1, ✴P5, K7, P6; rep from ✴.
Row 9 Kfb, ✴sl 1, K1, psso, K3, yf, K7, yf, K3, K2 tog, (K1, yf, K1) into next st; rep from ✴, ending last rep Kfb instead of (K1, yf, K1) into next st.
Row 10 P1, ✴P5, K9, P6; rep from ✴.
Row 11 Kfb, ✴K1, sl 1, K1, psso, K13, K2 tog, K1, (K1, yf, K1) into next st; rep from ✴, ending last rep Kfb instead of (K1, yf, K1) into next st.
Row 12 P1, ✴P2, P2 tog, P1, K9, P1, P2 tog tbl, P3; rep from ✴.
Row 13 Kfb, ✴K2, sl 1, K1, psso, K9, K2 tog, K2, (K1, yf, K1) into next st; rep from ✴, ending last rep Kfb instead of (K1, yf, K1) into next st.
Row 14 P1, ✴P4, K9, P5; rep from ✴.
Row 15 Kfb, ✴K3, sl 1, K1, psso, K7, K2 tog, K3, (K1, yf, K1) into next st; rep from ✴, ending last rep Kfb instead of (K1, yf, K1) into next st.
Row 16 As Row 8.
Row 17 Kfb, ✴K4, sl 1, K1, psso, K5, K2 tog, K4, (K1, yf, K1) into next st; rep from ✴, ending last rep kfb instead of (K1, yf, K1) into next st.
Row 18 As Row 6.

Row 19 K1, ✴yf, K5, sl 1, K1, psso, K3, K2 tog, K5, yf, K1; rep from ✴.
Row 20 As Row 4.
Row 21 K1, ✴K1, yf, K5, sl 1, K1, psso, K1, K2 tog, K5, yf, K2; rep from ✴ to end.
Row 22 As Row 2.
Row 23 K1, ✴K2, yf, K5, sl 1, K2 tog, psso, K5, yf, K3; rep from ✴.
Row 24 K1, ✴K3, P11, K4, rep from ✴.
Row 25 K1, ✴K3, yf, K3, K2 tog, (K1, yf, K1) into next st, sl 1, K1, psso, K3, yf, K4; rep from ✴.
Row 26 K1, ✴K4, P11, K5; rep from ✴.
Row 27 K1, ✴K6, K2 tog, K1, (K1, yf, K1) into next st, K1, sl 1, K1, psso, K7; rep from ✴.
Row 28 K1, ✴K4, P1, P2 tog tbl, P5, P2 tog, P1, K5; rep from ✴.
Row 29 K1, ✴K4, K2 tog, K2, (K1, yf, K1) into next st, K2, sl 1, K1, psso, K5; rep from ✴.
Row 30 K1, ✴K4, P9, K5; rep from ✴.
Row 31 K1, ✴K3, K2 tog, K3, (K1, yf, K1) into next st, K3, sl 1, K1, psso, K4; rep from ✴.
Row 32 As Row 24.

CANDLE FLAMES

This lovely pattern (shown on page 7) is another one to tempt the experienced knitter. It would be an excellent choice for a glamorous sweater.

multiple of 12 plus 2 extra
Note In this pattern the number of sts varies from row to row. Accurate count of sts may be made on row 12 or 24.

Row 1 ✴P2, yon, K1, yrn, P2, K2, K2 tog, K3; rep from ✴ to last 2 sts, P2.
Row 2 ✴K2, P6, K2, P3; rep from ✴ to last 2 sts, K2.
Row 3 ✴P2, K1, (yf, K1) twice, P2, K2, K2 tog, K2; rep from ✴ to last 2 sts, P2.
Row 4 ✴(K2, P5) twice; rep from ✴ to last 2 sts, K2.
Row 5 ✴P2, K2, yf, K1, yf, K2, P2, K2, K2 tog, K1; rep from ✴ to last 2 sts, P2.
Row 6 ✴K2, P4, K2, P7; rep from ✴ to last 2 sts, K2.
Row 7 ✴P2, K3, yf, K1, yf, K3, P2, K2, K2 tog; rep from ✴ to last 2 sts, P2.
Row 8 ✴K2, P3, K2, P9; rep from ✴ to last 2 sts, K2.
Row 9 ✴P2, K2, K2 tog, K5, P2, K1, K2 tog; rep from ✴ to last 2 sts, P2.

Row 10 ✴K2, P2, K2, P8; rep from ✴ to last 2 sts, K2.
Row 11 ✴P2, K2, K2 tog, K4, P2, K2 tog; rep from ✴ to last 2 sts, P2.
Row 12 ✴K2, P1, K2, P7; rep from ✴ to last 2 sts, K2.
Row 13 ✴P2, K2, K2 tog, K3, P2, yon, K1, yrn; rep from ✴ to last 2 sts, P2.
Row 14 ✴K2, P3, K2, P6; rep from ✴ to last 2 sts, K2.
Row 15 ✴P2, K2, K2 tog, K2, P2, (K1, yf) twice, K1; rep from ✴ to last 2 sts, P2.
Row 16 ✴(K2, P5) twice; rep from ✴ to last 2 sts, K2.
Row 17 ✴P2, K2, K2 tog, K1, P2, K2, yf, K1, yf, K2; rep from ✴ to last 2 sts, P2.
Row 18 ✴K2, P7, K2, P4; rep from ✴ to last 2 sts, K2.
Row 19 ✴P2, K2, K2 tog, P2, K3, yf, K1, yf, K3; rep from ✴ to last 2 sts, P2.
Row 20 ✴K2, P9, K2, P3; rep from ✴ to last 2 sts, K2.
Row 21 ✴P2, K1, K2 tog, P2, K2, K2 tog, K5; rep from ✴ to last 2 sts, P2.
Row 22 ✴K2, P8, K2, P2; rep from ✴ to last 2 sts, K2.
Row 23 ✴P2, K2 tog, P2, K2, K2 tog, K4; rep from ✴ to last 2 sts, P2.
Row 24 ✴K2, P7, K2, P1; rep from ✴ to last 2 sts, K2.

8 The Patterns

On the following pages you will find a selection of patterns in which to use your knitting skills. As you will see, some of the designs are very simple while others are more complex. However, they will all be within your grasp once you have mastered the techniques in the preceding chapters.

Coral

Cleverly interlocking stitches in rose and white form a pattern as subtle as lacy branches of coral.

MEASUREMENTS

To fit bust 86–91(97–102:107–112)cm/34–36(38–40:42–44)"
Actual measurements 102(112:124)cm/40(44:48¾)"
Length from shoulders 55(60:66)cm/21½(23½:26)"
Sleeve seam 40.5(43:46)cm/16(17:18)"
Instructions are given for the smallest size first, with figures for larger sizes in ( ).

MATERIALS

500(550:600)g/20(22:24)oz of a double knitting yarn in main colour A
400(450:450)g/16(18:18)oz in contrasting colour B
A pair each of 3¼mm and 4mm knitting needles (or sizes to obtain correct tension)

Remember to check your tension.

TENSION

25 sts and 26 rows to 10cm/4" measured over patt worked on larger needles

INSTRUCTIONS

BACK

Using smaller needles and A, cast on 111(121:133) sts.
Row 1: K1, *P1, K1, rep from * to end.
Row 2: P1, *K1, P1, rep from * to end.
Rep these 2 rows for 7cm/2¾", ending with a first row.
Inc row: Rib 3, *inc in next st, rib 6(5:5), rep from * to last 3(4:4) sts, inc in next st, rib to end: 127(141:155) sts.
Change to larger needles.
Join on and cut off colours as required and carry yarn not in use loosely across back of work.
Reading odd-numbered rows from right to left and even-numbered rows from left to right, work from chart as indicated until 118(132:146) patt rows have been completed.

Shape neck

Next row: Patt 53(60:67) sts, cast off next 21 sts, patt across rem 53(60:67) sts.
Work on first set of sts as follows:
Work 1 row.
Cast off 5(5:6) sts at beg of next row, 4(5:6) sts at beg of foll alternate row, then 4(5:5) sts at beg of foll alternate row.
Work 1 row.
Cast off.
Return to rem sts.
With RS facing, rejoin yarn and patt to end of row.

Complete to match first side of neck, reversing all shaping.

FRONT

Work as given for back until 62(70:76) patt rows have been completed.

Divide for neck

Keeping patt correct, patt across 63(77:77) sts, K2 tog and mark this st, patt to end.
Work on first set of 63(70:77) sts as follows:
Work 1 row.
Dec 1 st at neck edge on next and every foll alternate row to 51(58:65) sts, then every foll 3rd row until 40(45:50) sts rem.
Work straight until front measures same as back to shoulder.
Cast off.
Return to rem sts.
With RS facing, rejoin yarn and patt to end.
Complete to match first side of neck, reversing all shaping.

SLEEVES

Using smaller needles and A, cast on 53(57:61) sts.
Work 7cm/2¾" in rib as given for back, ending with a first row.
Inc row: Rib 4(4:3), *inc in next st, rib 8(6:5), rep from * to last 4 sts, inc in next st, rib to end: 59(65:71) sts.
Change to larger needles.
Work in patt from chart as indicated for sleeves, *at the same time* inc and work into patt 1 st at each end of every 3rd row until there are 121(131:141) sts.
Work a further 13(13:15) rows in patt without shaping.
Cast off.

19 (20, 22) cm

BACK & FRONT

48 (53, 59) cm

51 (56, 62) cm

48 (52, 56) cm

SLEEVE

40.5 (43, 46) cm

24 (26, 28) cm

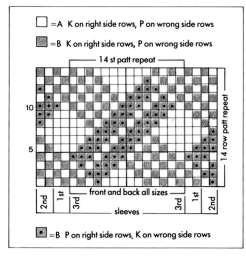

☐ =A K on right side rows, P on wrong side rows

▦ =B K on right side rows, P on wrong side rows

14 st patt repeat

14 row patt repeat

10

5

2nd 1st 3rd front and back all sizes 3rd 1st 2nd

sleeves

▨ =B P on right side rows, K on wrong side rows

NECKBAND

Join right shoulder seam. With RS facing, using smaller needles and A, pick up and K64(70:78) sts down left side of neck, 1 st from marked st at centre, 64(70:78) sts up right side of neck and 55(59:63) sts across back neck: 184(200:220) sts.

Row 1: P1, ☆K1, P1, rep from ☆ to 2 sts before marked st, K2 tog, P marked st, K2 tog, ☆☆P1, K1, rep from ☆☆ to end.

Row 2: Rib to 2 sts before marked st, P2 tog, K1, P2 tog, rib to end.

Rep these 2 rows for 5cm/2".

Cast off loosely, dec each side of marked st as before.

TO MAKE UP

Press or block as appropriate for yarn used.

Join left shoulder and neckband seam.

Fold sleeves in half lengthwise, and with fold at top of sleeves placed to shoulder seams, sew in sleeves.

Join side and sleeve seams.

Liquorice

Stylish casual wear for a latter-day Jack of Diamonds — an updated black and white check classic.

MEASUREMENTS

To fit bust 81(86:91:97:102)cm/32(34:36:38:40)"
Actual measurements 86(90:96:100:106)cm/34(35½:38:39¼:42)"
Length from shoulders 53cm/21"
Sleeve seam 42cm/16½"
Instructions are given for the smallest size first with figures for larger sizes in ( ).

MATERIALS

Sweater
300(350:350:400:400)g/12(14:14:16:16)oz of a double knitting yarn in main colour A
250(250:250:300:300)g/10(10:10:12:12)oz in contrasting colour B

Tie
50g/2oz of same yarn in either A or B
A pair each of 3¼mm and 4mm knitting needles (or sizes to obtain correct tension).

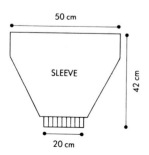

Remember to check your tension.

TENSION

24 sts and 30 rows to 10cm/4" measured over patt worked on larger needles

INSTRUCTIONS

BACK

Using smaller needles and A, cast on 103(109:115:121:127) sts.
Row 1: Sl 1, K1, *P1, K1, rep from * to last st, K1.
Row 2: Sl 1, *P1, K1, rep from * to end.
Rep first and 2nd rows 4 more times.
Change to larger needles.
Join on and cut off colours as necessary and carry colour not in use loosely across back of work.
Reading odd-numbered (K) rows from right to left and even-numbered (P) rows from left to right, cont in st st in patt from chart until back measures 53cm/21" from beg, ending with a WS row.
Shape shoulders
Cast off 12(13:14:15:16) sts at beg of next 4 rows and 13(14:15:16:17) sts at beg of foll 2 rows.
Cast off rem 29 sts.

FRONT

Work as given for back until front measures 46cm/18" from beg, ending with a WS row.
Shape neck
Next row: Sl 1, patt 44(47:50:53:56) sts, cast off next

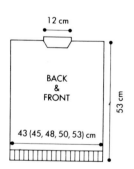

13 sts, patt to last st, K1.
Work on first set of sts as follows:
Next row: Sl 1, patt to last st, K1.
Keeping patt correct, dec 1 st at neck edge until 37(40:43:46:49) sts rem.
Work straight until front measures same as back to shoulder, ending at armhole edge.
Shape shoulder
Row 1: Cast off 12(13:14:15:16) sts, patt to last st, K1.
Row 2: Sl 1, patt to end.
Rows 3 and 4: As first and 2nd.
Cast off rem 13(14:15:16:17) sts.
With WS facing, rejoin yarn to rem sts, K1, patt to last st, K1.
Now complete 2nd side of neck to match first, reversing shaping.

SLEEVES

Using smaller needles and A, cast on 49 sts.
Row 1: Sl 1, K1, *P1, K1, rep from * to last st, K1.
Row 2: Sl 1, *P1, K1, rep from * to end.
Rep first and 2nd rows 10 more times, then the first row again.
Inc row: Sl 1, [P1, K1] twice, P1, *inc in next st, P1, K1, P1, rep from * to last 3 sts, K1, P1, K1: 59 sts.
Change to larger needles.
Working patt as given for back, work from chart where indicated for sleeve, *at the same time* inc and work into patt 1 st at each end of 3rd and every foll 4th row until there are 139 sts. Work straight until 94 rows of patt have been completed. Cast off.

COLLAR

Using smaller needles and A, cast on 135 sts.
Work 2 rows in rib as given for back until collar measures 10cm/4" from beg, ending with a 2nd row.
Cast off 17 sts in rib at beg of next 2 rows and 18 sts at beg of next 4 rows.
Cast off rem 29 sts in rib.

TIE

Using smaller needles and A or B, cast on 11 sts.
Row 1: Sl 1, K1, *P1, K1, rep from * to last st, K1.
The first row forms the patt.
Cont in patt until tie measures 132cm/52" from beg, ending with a WS row.
Cast off in patt.

TO MAKE UP

Press or block as appropriate for yarn used.
Join shoulder seams. Place markers 25cm/10" down
from shoulders on back and front to denote beg of
armholes. Sew in sleeves between markers. Join side
and sleeve seams. Sew shaped edge of collar to neck
edge of sweater.

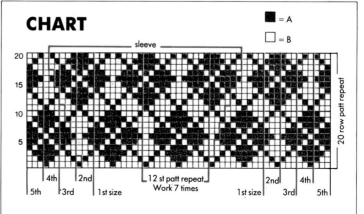

CHART

■ = A
□ = B

sleeve

20 row patt repeat

12 st patt repeat
Work 7 times

5th 4th 3rd 2nd 1st size 1st size 2nd 3rd 4th 5th

Ideal for the novice knitter, this bright and breezy sleeveless pullover is knitted with one extra-large and one medium-sized needle used together.

MEASUREMENTS
To fit bust 81(86:91:97)cm/32(34:36:38)"
Actual measurements 100(106:112:118)cm/ 39¼(41¾:44:46½)"
Length from shoulders 53cm/21"
Instructions are given for smallest size first with figures for larger sizes in ( ).

MATERIALS
300(300:300:350)g/12(12:12:14)oz of a double knitting yarn
A pair of 6mm knitting needles
One 20mm and one 6½mm knitting needle (or sizes to obtain correct tension)

Remember to check your tension.

TENSION
7 sts to 10cm/4" measured over g st worked on one extra-large and one medium-sized needle

NOTE
Use 2 strands of yarn together throughout.

INSTRUCTIONS
BACK AND FRONT (alike)
Using smaller needles and using yarn double, cast on 59(63:67:71) sts.
Work 19 rows in g st.
Dec row: Sl 1, K4, [K2 tog] 24(26:28:30) times, K6: 35(37:39:41) sts.
Change to one medium-sized needle and 1 extra-large needle.
Cont in g st as follows:
Row 1: Using 1 medium-sized needle, sl 1, K to end.
Row 2: Using 1 extra-large needle, sl 1, K to end.
These 2 rows form patt.
Cont in patt until work measures 53cm/21" from beg, ending with a wrong-side row.
Cast off.

ARMBANDS
Join shoulder seams leaving 28cm/11" open at centre for neck.
Place markers 25(28:28:28)cm/10(11:11:11)" down from shoulders to denote beg of armhole.
With right side facing and using smaller needles, pick up and K55(63:63:63) sts evenly between markers.
Work 6 rows g st.
Cast off.

TO MAKE UP
Do not press. Block pieces to correct size if necessary. Join side and armband seams.

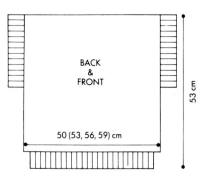

BACK & FRONT

53 cm

50 (53, 56, 59) cm

Potpourri

A softly feminine interpretation of Fair Isle Knitting in delicate shades of pink and mauve.

MEASUREMENTS
To fit bust 81(86:91:97)cm/32(34:36:38)"
Actual measurements 87(96:99:103)cm/
34(37¾:39:40½)"
Length from shoulders 64.5(66:68.5:70)cm/
25½(26:27:27½)"
Sleeve seam 45.5(47:48:48)cm/18(18½:19:19)"
Instructions are given for smallest size first with figures for larger sizes in ( ).

MATERIALS
300(350:350:400)g/12(14:14:16)oz of a Shetland double knitting yarn in main colour A
150(150:150:150)g/6(6:6:6)oz in contrasting colour B
50(50:100:100)g/2(2:4:4)oz in contrasting colour C
A pair each of 3¼mm and 4mm knitting needles (or sizes to obtain correct tension)
3 buttons

Remember to check your tension.

TENSION
25 sts and 29 rows to 10cm/4" measured over patt worked on larger needles

NOTE
If the figure '0' is given, this means that there are no stitches to be knitted in that colour for your size on this section of the row; move on to the next part of the row which relates to the size you are knitting.

INSTRUCTIONS
LEFT FRONT
Using smaller needles and A, cast on 47(51:55:55) sts.
Row 1: K2, *P2, K2, rep from * to last st, P1.
Row 2: K1, *P2, K2, rep from * to last 2 sts, P2.
** Rep the last 2 rows for 5.5(7.5:5.5:7.5)cm/
2¼(2¾:2¼:2¾)", ending with a first row.
First and 4th sizes only
Inc row: Rib 2(3), inc in next st, *rib 20(11), inc in next st, rep from * to last 2(3) sts, rib to end: 50(60) sts.
2nd and 3rd sizes only
Inc row: Inc in first st, rib to last 2 sts, inc in next st, rib 1: 53(57) sts.
All sizes
Change to larger needles. **
Cont in patt as follows:
Join in and cut off colours as necessary.
Row 1: K1(0:0:1)A, *K1B, 3A, rep from * to last 1(1:1:3) sts, K1B, 0(0:0:2)A.

Row 2: P0(0:0:1)A, 1(1:1:2)B, *P1B, 1A, 2B, rep from * to last 1(0:0:1) st, P1(0:0:1)B.
Row 3: With B, K to end.
Row 4: With B, P to end.
Row 5: K1(0:0:1)B, *K1C, 3B, rep from * to last 1(1:1:3) sts, K1C, 0(0:0:2)B.
Row 6: P0(0:0:1)B, 1(1:1:2)C, *P1C, 1B, 2C, rep from * to last 1(0:0:1) st, P1(0:0:1)C.
Row 7: With C, K to end.
Row 8: With C, P to end.
Row 9: K1(0:0:1)C, *K1A, 3C, rep from * to last 1(1:1:3) sts, K1A, 0(0:0:2)C.
Row 10: P0(0:0:1)C, 1(1:1:2)A, *P1A, 1C, 2A, rep from * to last 1(0:0:1) st, P1(0:0:1)A.
Row 11: With A, K to end.
Row 12: With A, P to end.
Rows 13–24: As rows 1–12.
Row 25: K1(0:0:1)A, *K2A, 1B, 1A, rep from * to last 1(1:1:3) sts, K1(1:1:3)A.
Row 26: With A, P to end.
Row 27: With A, K to end.
Row 28 and 29: As rows 26 and 27.
Row 30: P1(1:1:3)A, *P1A, 1B, 2A, rep from * to last 1(0:0:1) st, P1(0:0:1)A.
Row 31 With A, K to end.
Row 32: With A, P to end.
Rows 33 and 34: As rows 31 and 32.
Rows 35–42: As rows 25–32.
These 42 rows form patt.
Shape front
*** Keeping patt correct, dec 1 st at end (beg for right front) of next and every foll 6th row until 41(44:48:51) sts rem.
Work 5 rows straight, so ending with a 12th patt row.
Mark end (beg for right front) of last row with a contrasting thread to denote beg of armhole.
Cont in patt, dec 1 st at front edge on 3rd(first:first:first) and every foll 8th(6th:6th:6th) row until 34(40:45:44) sts rem.
2nd, 3rd and 4th sizes only
Dec 1 st at front edge on every foll 8th row until (36:39:41) sts rem.
All sizes
Cont without shaping until armhole measures 25.5(25.5:29:29)cm/10(10:11.5:11.5)" from marker, ending with a 42nd(42nd:12th:12th) patt row.
Shape shoulder
Cast off rem sts. ***

RIGHT FRONT
Using smaller needles and A cast on 47(51:55:55) sts.

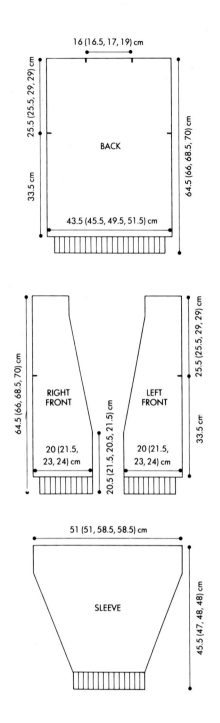

16 (16.5, 17, 19) cm

25.5 (25.5, 29, 29) cm

BACK

33.5 cm

64.5 (66, 68.5, 70) cm

43.5 (45.5, 49.5, 51.5) cm

RIGHT FRONT

LEFT FRONT

64.5 (66, 68.5, 70) cm

25.5 (25.5, 29, 29) cm

33.5 cm

20 (21.5, 23, 24) cm

20 (21.5, 23, 24) cm

20.5 (21.5, 20.5, 21.5) cm

51 (51, 58.5, 58.5) cm

SLEEVE

45.5 (47, 48, 48) cm

Row 1: P1, *K2, P2, rep from * to last 2 sts, K2.
Row 2: P2, *K2, P2, rep from * to last st, K1.
Now work as given for left front from ** to **.
Cont in patt as follows:
Row 1: K0(0:0:2)A, *K1B, 3A, rep from * to last 2(1:1:2) sts, K1B, 1(0:0:1)A.
Row 2: P2(1:1:2)B, *P1B, 1A, 2B, rep from * to last 0(0:0:2) sts, then for **4th size only** P1B, 1A.
Row 3: With B, K to end.
Row 4: With B, P to end.
Row 5: K0(0:0:2)B, *K1C, 3B, rep from * to last 2(1:1:2) sts, K1C, 1(0:0:1)B.
Row 6: P2(1:1:2)C, *P1C, 1B, 2C, rep from * to last 0(0:0:2) sts, then for **4th size only** P1C, 1B.
Row 7: With C, K to end.
Row 8: With C, P to end.
Row 9: K0(0:0:2)C, *P1A, 3C, rep from * to last 2(1:1:2) sts, K1A, 1(0:0:1)C.
Row 10: P2(1:1:2)A, *P1A, 1C, 2A, rep from * to last 0(0:0:2) sts, then for **4th size only** P1A, 1C.
Row 11: With A, K to end.
Row 12: With A, P to end.
Rows 13–24: As rows 1–12.
Row 25: K0(0:0:2)A, *K2A, 1B, 1A, rep from * to last 2(1:1:2) sts, K2(1:1:2)A.
Row 26: With A, P to end.
Row 27: With A, K to end.
Rows 28 and 29: As rows 26 and 27.
Row 30: P2(1:1:2)A, *P1A, 1B, 2A, rep from * to last 0(0:0:2) sts, P0(0:0:2)A.
Row 31: With A, K to end.
Row 32: With A, P to end.
Rows 33 and 34: As rows 31 and 32.
Rows 35–42: As rows 25–32.
These 42 rows form the patt.
Complete to match left front from *** to *** noting the exceptions in brackets.

BACK

Using smaller needles and A, cast on 102(106:114:118) sts.
Row 1: K2, *P2, K2, rep from * to end.
Row 2: P2, *K2, P2, rep from * to end.
Rep last 2 rows for 5.5(7:5.5:7)cm/2¼(2¾:2¼:2¾)", ending with a first row.
Inc row: Rib 8(1:5:6), inc in next st, *rib 20(16:16:12), inc in next st, rep from * to last 9(2:6:7) sts, rib to end: 107(113:121:127) sts.
Change to larger needles.
Cont in patt as follows:
Row 1: K1(0:0:1)A, *K1B, 3A, rep from * to last 2(1:1:2) sts, K1B, 1(0:0:1)A.
Row 2: P2(1:1:2)B, *P1B, 1A, 2B, rep from * to last 1(0:0:1) st, P1(0:0:1)B.

Row 3: With B, K to end.
Row 4: With B, P to end.
Row 5: K1(0:0:1)B, *K1C, 3B, rep from * to last 2(1:1:2) sts, K1C, 1(0:0:1)B.
Row 6: P2(1:1:2)C, *P1C, 1B, 2C, rep from * to last 1(0:0:1) st, P1(0:0:1)C.
Row 7: With C, K to end.
Row 8: With C, P to end.
Row 9: K1(0:0:1)C, *K1A, 3C, rep from * to last 2(1:1:2) sts, K1A, 1(0:0:1)C.
Row 10: P2(1:1:2)A, *P1A, 1C, 2A, rep from * to last 1(0:0:1) st, P1(0:0:1)A.
Row 11: With A, K to end.
Row 12: With A, P to end.
Rows 13–24: As rows 1–12.
Row 25: K1(0:0:1)A, *K2A, 1B, 1A, rep from * to last 2(1:1:2) sts, K2(1:1:2)A.
Row 26: With A, P to end.
Row 27: With A, K to end.
Row 28 and 29: As rows 26 and 27.
Row 30: P2(1:1:2)A, *P1A, 1B, 2A, rep from * to last 1(0:0:1) st, P1(0:0:1)A.
Row 31: With A, K to end.
Row 32: With A, P to end.
Rows 33 and 34: As rows 31 and 32.
Rows 35–42: As rows 25–32.
These 42 rows form the patt.
Cont in patt until back measures same as fronts to armhole markers.
Mark each end of last row with a contrasting thread to denote beg of armholes.
Cont in patt until back measures same as fronts to shoulders, ending on same patt row.

Shape shoulders
Next Row: Cast off 34(36:39:41) sts, K until there are 39(41:43:45) sts on needle, cast off rem 34(36:39:41) sts.
Leave rem sts on a holder.

SLEEVES

Using smaller needles and A cast on 42(42:46:46) sts.
Work 5.5(7:4.5:4.5)cm/2¼(2¾:1¾:1¾)″ in rib as given for back, ending with a first row.
Inc row: Rib 4(2:4:2), inc in next st, * rib 1, inc in next st, rep from * to last 5(3:5:3) sts, rib to end: 59(61:65:67) sts.

Change to larger needles.
Beg with a 25th(25th:13th:13th) patt row, cont in 42 row patt as given for back *at the same time* inc and work into patt 1 st at each end of 3rd and every foll alternate row until there are 95(93:113:111) sts, then every foll 4th row until there are 125(125:143:143) sts.
Cont without shaping until sleeve measures 45.5(47:48:48)cm/18(18 ½:19:19)″ ending with a 12th patt row.
Cast off loosely.

BUTTON BORDER

Join shoulder seams.
Mark centre st at back neck with a contrasting thread.
With RS facing and using smaller needles and A, K across 20(21:22:23)sts from back neck holder starting at marker, pick up and K114(114:124:124) sts evenly down left front edge to beg of front shaping, then 52(55:52:55) sts down to lower edge: 186(190:198:202) sts.
Beg with a 2nd row, work 9 rows in rib as given for back.
Cast off in rib.

BUTTONHOLE BORDER

With RS facing and using smaller needles and A pick up and K52(55:52:55) sts up right front from lower edge to beg of neck shaping, 114(114:124:124) sts evenly up neck to shoulder, then K across rem 20(21:22:23) sts from back neck holder to marked st: 186(190:198:202) sts.
Beg with a 2nd row, work 3 rows rib as given for back.
Buttonhole row: Rib 4, cast off 2 sts, *rib 18(20:18:20) sts including st on needle, cast off 2 sts, rep from * once more, rib to end.
Next row: Rib to end, casting on 2 sts over those cast off in previous row.
Work 4 more rows in rib.
Cast off in rib.

TO MAKE UP

Press or block as appropriate for yarn used.
Join borders of centre back neck.
Sew in sleeves between markers, then join side and sleeve seams. Sew on buttons.

Lead the pack in this medium-weight striped jersey, worked in simple stocking stitch with crunchy moss-stitch edgings.

MEASUREMENTS

To fit bust 81(86:91:96cm/32(34:36:38)"
Actual measurements 86(92:100:108)cm/
34(36:39¼:42)"
Length from shoulders 54(55:55:56)cm/
21¼(21½:21½:22)"
Sleeve seam 46(48:48:48)cm/18(19:19:19)"
Instructions are given for smallest size first, with figures for larger sizes in ( ).

MATERIALS

300(350:350:400)g/12(14:14:16)oz of an Aran-weight yarn in main colour A
250(250:250:300)g/10(10:10:12)oz in contrasting colour B
A pair each of 4mm, 4½mm and 5mm knitting needles (or sizes to obtain correct tension)

TENSION

17 sts and 24 rows to 10cm/4" measured over st st worked on largest needles.

INSTRUCTIONS

BACK

Using smallest needles and A, cast on 64(68:72:76) sts.
Row 1: ✲K1, P1, rep from ✲ to end.
Row 2: ✲P1, K1, rep from ✲ to end.
Rep these 2 rows for 4(5:5:6)cm/1½(2:2:2¼)" to form moss st.
Inc row K4(4:6:3), [inc in next st, K6(5:4:4) sts] 8(10:12:14) times, inc in next st, K3(3:5:2): 73(79:85:91) sts.
P 1 row.
Change to largest needles.
Cont in st st, working in stripes of 24 rows B and 24 rows A until back measures 54(55:55:56)cm/
21¼(21½:21½:22)" from beg, ending with a P row.
Shape shoulders
Cast off 25(27:29:31) sts at beg of next 2 rows.
Leave rem 23(25:27:29) sts on a holder.

FRONT

Work as given for back until front measures 12 rows less than back to shoulders.
Shape neck
Next row: Work across 31(33:35:37) sts, turn and

leave rem sts on a spare needle.
Work on first set of sts as follows:
Work 1 row.
Dec 1 st at neck edge on next 6 rows: 25(27:29:31) sts.
Cont without shaping until front measures same as back to shoulder, ending with a P row.
Cast off. Return to sts on spare needle.
With right side facing, sl first 11(13:15:17) sts onto a holder, rejoin yarn and K to end: 31(33:35:37) sts.
Now complete to match first side of neck.

SLEEVES

Using smallest needles and A, cast on 34(34:38:38) sts.
Work 3(4:4:4)cm/1¼(1½:1½:1½)" in moss st as given for back.
Inc row: K3, [inc in next st, K1] 14(14:16:16) times, inc in next st, K2: 49(49:55:55) sts.
P 1 row.
Change to largest needles.
Using A, cont in st st until sleeve measures 6(8:8:8)cm/
2½(3¼:3¼:3¼)" from beg, ending with a P row.
Now working in stripes of 24 rows B and 24 rows A, inc 1 st at each end of next and every foll 6th row until there are 75(79:81:85) sts.
Cont without shaping until sleeve measures 46(48:48:48)cm/18½(19¼:19¼:19¼)" from beg, ending with a P row.
Cast off.

COLLAR

Join left shoulder seam.
Using smallest needles, A, and with right side facing, K23(25:27:29) sts from back neck holder, pick up and K17 sts down left side of front neck, K across 11(13:15:17) sts from front neck holder, then pick up and K17 sts up right side of front neck: 68(72:76:80) sts.
Work in moss st as given for back for 3cm/1¼".
Change to medium-sized needles and work a further 10(10:12:12) cm/4(4:4¾:4¾)" moss st.
Cast off loosely in patt.

TO MAKE UP

Press or block, as appropriate for yarn used, avoiding moss st.
Join right shoulder seam.
Fold sleeves in half lengthwise, and placing fold at top of sleeves to shoulder seam, sew sleeves into place.
Join side and sleeve seams.
Join 3cm/1¼" of collar seam at neck edge, then fold collar over to right side.

Remember to check your tension.

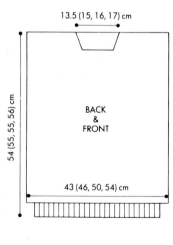

Rocket

A dazzling and versatile jumper in double knitting for any occasion. Wear it to brighten up a Saturday morning, or to make a party go with a bang.

MEASUREMENTS

To fit bust 81(86:91:97)cm/32(34:36:38)"
Actual measurements 92(96:102:106)cm/36(38:40:42)"
Length from shoulders 57cm/22½"
Sleeve seam 46cm/18"
Instructions are given for the smallest size first, with figures for larger sizes in ( ).

MATERIALS

300(300:300:300)g/12(12:12:12)oz of a double knitting yarn in main colour A
100(100:100:100)g/4(4:4:4)oz in each of contrasting colours B and E
50(50:100:100)g/2(2:4:4)oz in contrasting colour C
50(50:50:100)g/2(2:2:4)oz in contrasting colour D
A pair each of 3¼mm and 4mm knitting needles (or sizes to obtain correct tension)

Remember to check your tension.

TENSION

22 sts to 10cm/4" measured over st st worked on larger needles

INSTRUCTIONS

BACK

Using smaller needles and A, cast on 89(95:99:105) sts.
Row 1: Sl 1, K1, *P1, K1, rep from * to last st, K1.
Row 2: Sl 1, *P1, K1, rep from * to end.
Rep first and 2nd rows 10 more times, then the first row again.
Inc row: Sl 1, P7(6:6:9), *[inc in next st, P5(7:6:6) sts] 12(10:12:12) times, inc in next st, P8(7:7:10): 102(106:112:118) sts **.
Change to larger needles.
Cont to work in patt from chart as follows:
Join on and break off yarns as necessary.
Use separate small balls of yarn for each area of colour and twist yarns tog on WS when changing colour to avoid making a hole.
Cont working in st st reading odd-numbered (K) rows from right to left and even-numbered (P) rows from left to right.
Work from chart A until row 126 has been completed.
Shape shoulders
Using appropriate colours, cast off 31(33:36:39) sts, patt across 40 sts (including st on needle), cast off rem sts.
Place rem sts on a holder.

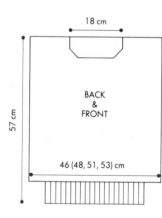

BACK & FRONT
18 cm
57 cm
46 (48, 51, 53) cm

SLEEVE
46 cm
46 cm

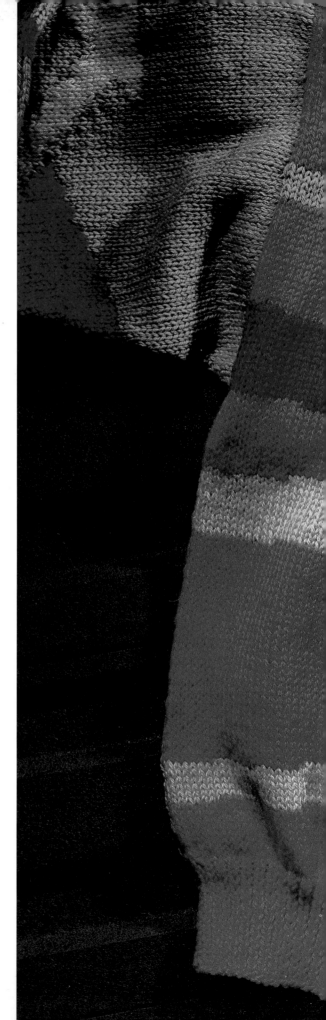

CHART A

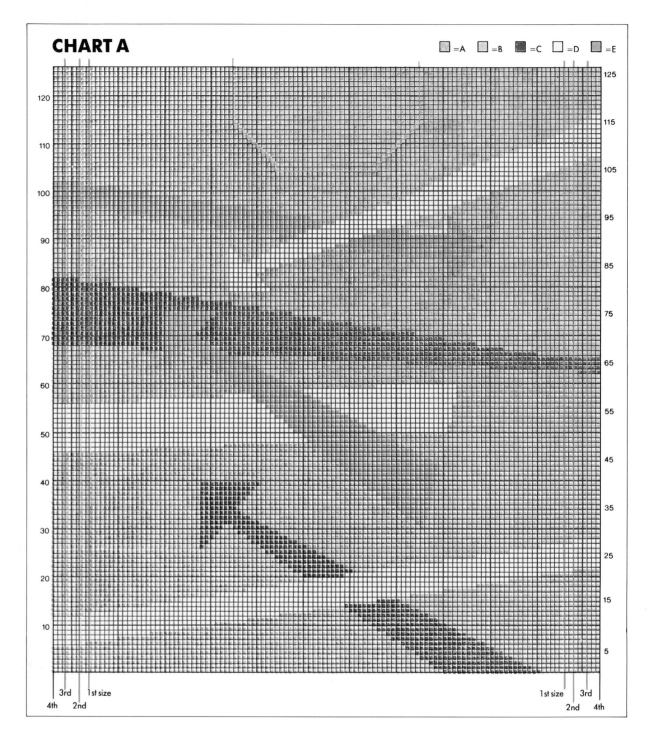

A = A B = B C = C D = D E = E

FRONT

Work as given for back to ✩✩.

Change to larger needles.

Cont to work from chart A as given for back until row 104 has been completed.

Shape neck

Neck row: Keeping patt correct, work across 40(42:45:48) sts, turn and leave rem sts on a spare needle.

Work on first set of sts as follows:

Patt 1 row.

Dec 1 st at neck edge on next 9 rows: 31(33:36:39) sts.

Cont without shaping until front measures same as back to shoulders.

Cast off.

Return to sts on spare needle.

Sl first 22 sts onto a holder.

Rejoin yarn to rem sts and patt 2 rows.

CHART B

A = A B = B C = C D = D E = E

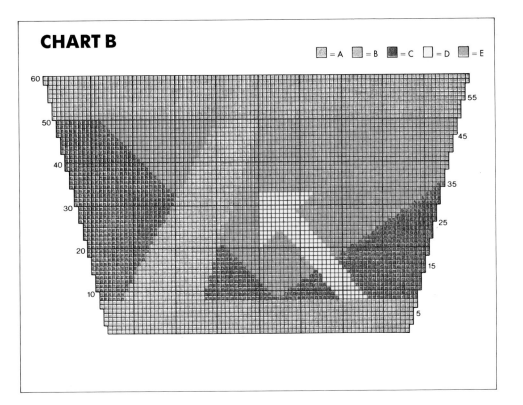

Now complete to match first side of neck.

SLEEVES

Using smaller needles and A, cast on 45(45:47:47) sts.
Row 1: Sl 1, K1, ☆P1, K1, rep from ☆ to last st, K1.
Row 2: Sl 1, ☆P1, K1, rep from ☆ to end.
Rep first and 2nd rows 10 more times, then first row again.
Inc row: Sl 1, P3(3:2:2), [inc in next st, P2(2:3:3) sts] 12(12:10:10) times, inc in next st, P3(3:2:2), K1: 58 sts.
Change to larger needles.
Cont in st st but inc 1 st at each end of 5th and every foll 6th row until there are 72 sts, ending with a P row.
Cont to inc 1 st at each end of every foll 4th row, work in patt from chart B as given for chart A until row 60 has been completed: 102 sts.
Cast off.

COLLAR

Join right shoulder seam.
With RS facing, using smaller needles and A, pick up and K17 sts down left side of front neck, K across front neck sts from holder, pick up and K18 sts up right side of front neck, then K across sts from back neck holder: 97 sts.
Row 1: Sl 1, ☆P1, K1, rep from ☆ to end.

Row 2: Sl 1, K1, ☆P1, K1, rep from ☆ to last st, K1.
Rep first and 2nd rows twice more.
Next row: Sl 1, [P1, K1] 33 times, P1, inc in next st, [P1, K1] 14 times: 98 sts.
Divide for collar
Next row: Sl 1, [K1, P1] 13 times, K1, turn and leave rem sts on a spare needle.
Work on first set of sts as follows:
Next row: Sl 1, K1, ☆P1, K1, rep from ☆ to end.
Rep last row 22 more times.
Cast off loosely in rib.
Return to sts on spare needle.
With RS facing, rejoin yarn to rem 70 sts.
Cont as follows:
Next row: K1, ☆P1, K1, rep from ☆ to last st, K1.
Next row: Sl 1, ☆P1, K1, rep from ☆ to last st, K1.
Rep last row 22 more times.
Cast off loosely in rib.

TO MAKE UP

Press or block as appropriate for yarn used.
Join left shoulder and collar seam.
Place markers 23cm/9" below shoulder seams on back and front to denote beg of armholes.
Sew in sleeves between markers, then join side and sleeve seams.

La Stampa

A simple but stylish two-tone effect, as eye-catching as the morning's headlines.

MEASUREMENTS

To fit bust 81(86:91:97)cm/32(34:36:38)"
Actual measurements 92(96:102:106)cm/
36(37¾:40:41¾)"
Length from shoulders 56cm/22"
Sleeve seam 44cm/17"
Instructions are given for smallest size first, with figures for larger sizes in ( ).

MATERIALS

300(300:300:300)g/12(12:12:12)oz of a double knitting yarn in main colour A
250(250:250:300)g/10(10:10:12)oz in contrasting colour B
A pair each of 3¼mm and 4mm knitting needles (or sizes to obtain correct tension)

TENSION

22 sts to 10cm/4" measured over st st worked on larger needles

INSTRUCTIONS

BACK

Using smaller needles and A, cast on 89(95:99:105) sts.
Row 1: Sl 1, K1, ✫P1, K1, rep from ✫ to last st, K1.
Row 2: Sl 1, ✫P1, K1, rep from ✫ to end.
Rep first and 2nd rows 10 more times, then the first row again.

First and 4th sizes only
Inc row: Sl 1, ✫P7, P twice into next st, rep from ✫ 9(11) times, P7, K1: 99(117) sts. ✫✫✫

2nd and 3rd sizes only
Inc row: Sl 1, ✫P(8:7), P twice into next st✫, rep from ✫ to ✫ (2:4) times, ✫✫P(7:5), P twice into next st✫✫, rep from ✫✫ to ✫✫ (4:2) times, rep from ✫ to ✫ (2:4) times, P(8:7), K1: (105:111) sts. ✫✫✫

All sizes
Change to larger needles.
Joining on and breaking off colours as necessary and twisting yarns tog at back of work when changing colour in the middle of a row to avoid making a hole, cont as follows:
Reading odd-numbered rows from right to left and even-numbered rows from left to right, work in patt from chart A until row 70 has been completed.
Rep rows 1 to 70 of chart once more.

Shape shoulders
Next row: Cast off 35(38:41:44) sts in patt, patt across

29 sts (including st on needle), cast off rem sts in patt. Leave rem 29 sts on a holder.

FRONT

Work as given for back to ✫✫✫.
Change to larger needles.
Work in patt from chart B until row 70 has been completed.
Cont in patt from chart B, work until row 40 has been completed.

Shape neck
Next row: Sl 1, patt 41(44:47:50) sts, turn.
Next row: Sl 1, patt to last st, K1.
Working on these sts for first side of neck, cont as follows:
Dec 1 st at neck edge on next 7 rows: 35(38:41:44) sts.
Cont without shaping until work measures same as back, ending with row 70 of chart.
Cast off.
Return to rem 57(60:63:66) sts.
With RS facing, sl first 15 sts onto a holder, rejoin B to neck and cont as follows:
Next row: K1, patt to last st, K1.
Next row: Sl 1, patt to last st, K1.
Complete to match first side of neck.

SLEEVES

Using smaller needles and A, cast on 45(45:45:47) sts.
Row 1: Sl 1, K1, ✫P1, K1, rep from ✫ to last st, K1.
Row 2: Sl 1, ✫P1, K1, rep from ✫ to end.
Rep first and 2nd rows 11 more times, inc 1 st at each end of last row: 47(47:47:49) sts.
Change to larger needles.
Cont in patt as follows:
Working in patt from chart C, inc and work into patt 1 st at each end of 3rd and every foll 4th row until there are 75(75:75:79) sts, then every foll alternate row until there are 95(95:95:99) sts.
Cont without shaping until row 104 has been completed. Cast off.

NECKBAND

Join right shoulder seam.
With RS facing, using smaller needles and B, pick up and K19 sts evenly down left side of neck, K across 15 sts from holder, pick up and K20 sts up right side of neck then K across 29 sts from back neck holder: 83 sts.
Row 1: Sl 1, ✫P1, K1, rep from ✫ to end.
Row 2: Sl 1, K1, ✫P1, K1, rep from ✫ to last st, K1.
Rep first and 2nd rows 10 more times, then first row again. Cast off loosely in rib.

Remember to check your tension.

13 cm

BACK
&
FRONT

56 cm

46 (48, 51, 53) cm

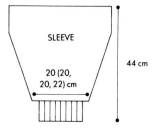

SLEEVE

20 (20,
20, 22) cm

44 cm

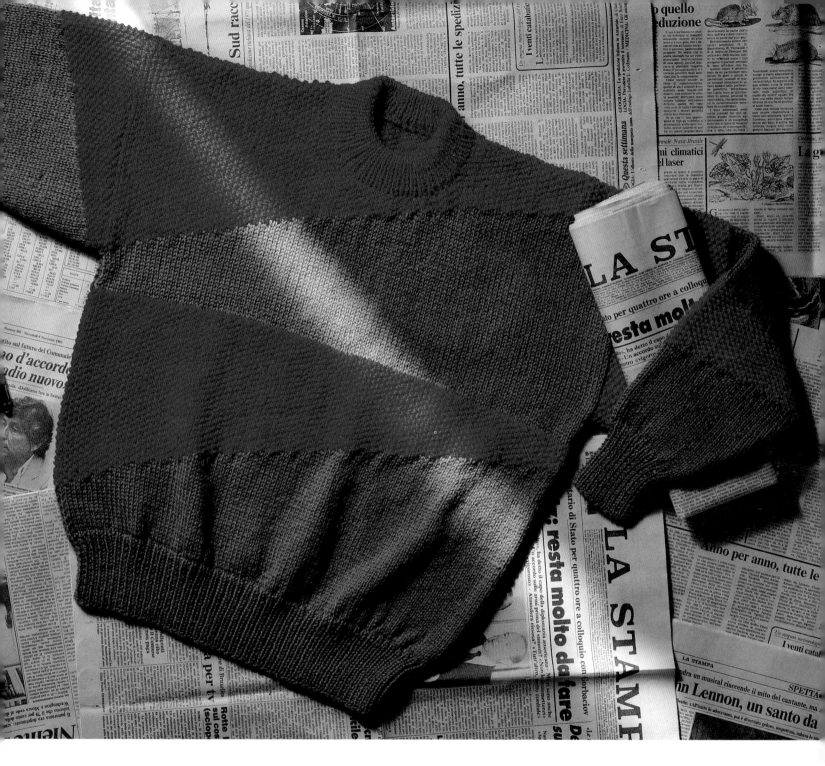

TO MAKE UP

Press or block as appropriate for yarn used, avoiding
textured areas when pressing. Join left shoulder and
neckband seam.
Place markers 22(22:22:23)cm/8¾(8¾:8¾:9)" down
from shoulders to denote armholes.
Sew in sleeves between markers.
Join side and sleeve seams. Fold neckband in half to WS
and slipstitch in place.

CHART A

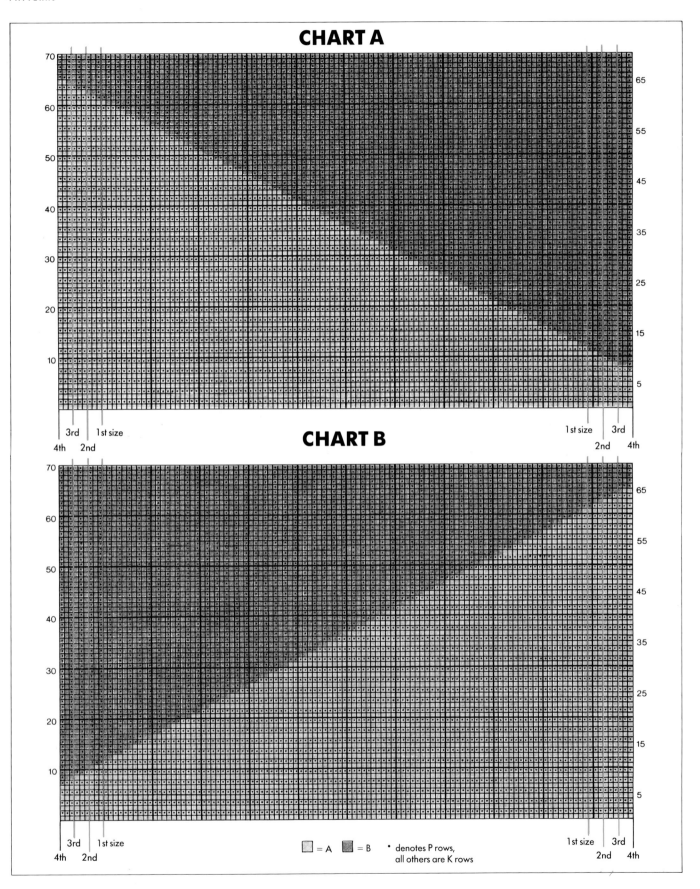

CHART B

□ = A   ▨ = B   • denotes P rows,
all others are K rows

CHART C

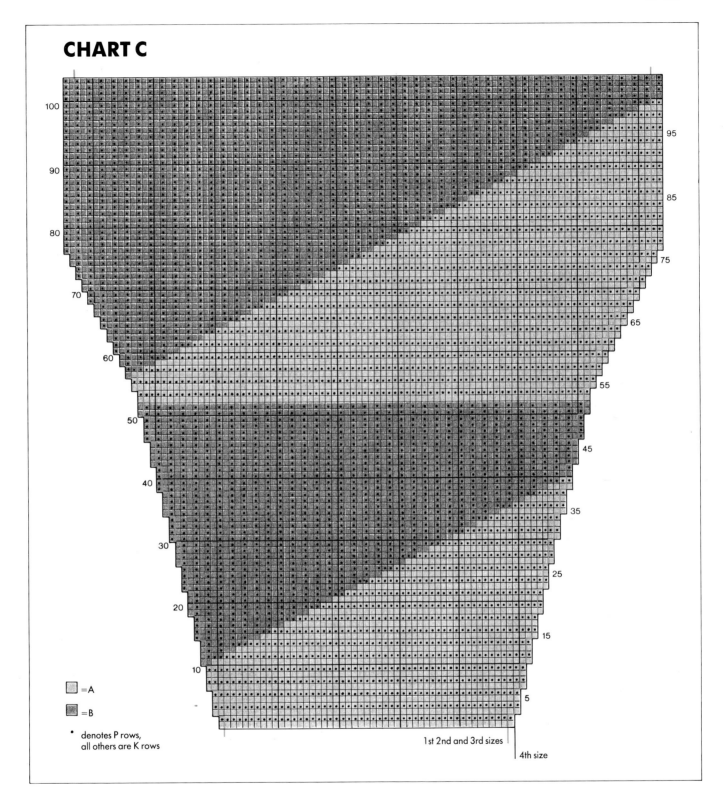

=A

=B

• denotes P rows,
all others are K rows

1st 2nd and 3rd sizes

4th size

Pioneer

A rugged double-breasted jacket in sturdy tweed double knitting, ideal for cold winter days.

MEASUREMENTS

To fit bust 86–91(97–101)cm/34–36(38–40)"
Actual measurements 114(124)cm/45(49)"
Length from shoulders 68(72)cm/26¾(28¼)"
Sleeve seam 41(43)cm/16(17)"
Instructions are given for smallest size first with figures for larger sizes in ( ).

MATERIALS

500(550)g/20(22)oz of a double knitting yarn in main colour A
300(350)g/12(14)oz in contrasting colour B
A pair each of 3¼mm and 4mm knitting needles (or size to obtain correct tension)
8 buttons

TENSION

24 sts and 26 rows to 10cm/4" measured over patt worked on larger needles

SPECIAL ABBREVIATION

M3 (Make 3) – Insert needle into st below next st on LH needle and K1 in the usual way, but do not let st above fall off needle, K1 into next st on needle in usual way letting st drop off needle, then K again into st below st just worked.

INSTRUCTIONS

BACK

Using smaller needles and A, cast on 133(145) sts.
Row 1: K1 tbl, *P1, K1 tbl, rep from * to end.
Row 2: P1, *K1 tbl, P1, rep from * to end.
Rep these 2 rows for 4cm/1½", ending with a 2nd row.
Inc row: Rib 3(1), [rib 14(16), M1] 8 times, rib 18(16): 141(153) sts.
Change to larger needles.
Next row: P to end.
Cont in patt as follows:
Row 1 (RS): With B, K1, skpo, *K1, M3, K1, sl 1, K2 tog, psso, rep from * ending last rep skpo, K1.
Row 2: With B, P to end.
Row 3: With A work as for first row.
Row 4: With A, P to end.
These 4 rows form patt.
Cont in patt until work measures 67(71)cm/26½(28)" from beg, ending with a 4th row.
Shape neck
Next row: Patt 45(51) sts, K2, turn and leave rem sts

on a spare needle.
Next row: P2 tog, patt to end.
Next row: Patt 44(50) sts, K2 tog.
Next row: Patt to end.
Cast off.
Return to sts on spare needle.
With RS facing, sl first 47 sts onto a holder, rejoin yarn and work 2nd side of neck to match first side, reversing all shaping.

POCKET LININGS (make 2)

Using larger needles and A, cast on 30 sts.
Work 12cm/4¾" in st st, ending with a P row.
Leave sts on a holder.

RIGHT FRONT

Using smaller needles and A, cast on 88(94) sts.
Row 1: *K1 tbl, P1, rep from * to end.
Rep this row for 2cm/¾", ending with a WS row.
Buttonhole row: Rib 6, cast off 2 sts, rib 25, cast off 2 sts, rib 53(59).
Next row: Rib to end, casting on 2 sts over those cast off in previous row.
Cont in rib until work measures 4cm/1½" from beg, ending with a WS row.
Next row: Rib 41 sts, leave these sts on a holder for front panel, rib 1(2), [rib 9(10), M1] 4 times, rib 10(11): 51(57) sts.
Change to larger needles.
Next row: P to end.
Cont in patt as given for back until front measures 18cm/7" from beg, ending with a 2nd row.
Place pocket
Next row: Patt 1 st, sl next 30 sts onto a holder, patt across sts of first pocket lining, patt to end of row.
Cont without shaping until front measures 58(62)cm/22¾(24¼)" from beg, ending with a 2nd or 4th patt row.
Shape front edge
Keeping patt correct, cont as follows:
Row 1: Work 2 tog, K4, patt to end.
Row 2 and every alternate row: P to last 2 sts, P2 tog.
Row 3: K4, patt to end.
Row 5: K3, patt to end.
Row 7: K2, patt to end.
Row 9: K2 tog, skpo, patt to end: 45(51) sts.
Cont without shaping until front measures same as back to shoulders.
Cast off.
Using smaller needles and with WS facing, join A to 41 sts on holder, cast on 1 st and rib to end.

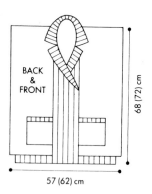

BACK & FRONT

68 (72) cm

57 (62) cm

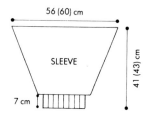

56 (60) cm

SLEEVE

41 (43) cm

7 cm

Remember to check your tension.

Cont in rib until panel measures 13(14.5)cm/5(5¾)"
from cast-on edge, ending with a WS row.
Next row: Rib 6, cast off 2 sts, rib 25, cast off 2 sts, rib
7.
Next row: Rib to end, casting on 2 sts over those cast
off in previous row.
Cont working in rib, making buttonholes as before
when work measures 24(27)cm/9½(10½)" and
35(39.5)cm/13¾(15½)".
Cont without shaping in rib until panel, slightly
stretched, fits up front edge to start of neck shaping.
Cast off in rib.

LEFT FRONT

Using smaller needles and A, cast on 88(94) sts.
Row 1: ✩P1, K1 tbl, rep from ✩ to end.
Complete to match right front, omitting buttonholes
and reversing all shaping.

SLEEVES

Using smaller needles and A, cast on 42(48) sts.
Row 1: ✩K1 tbl, P1, rep from ✩ to end.
Rep this row for 14cm/5½", ending with a WS row.
Inc row: K4, [K1, M1] 33(39) times, K5.
Change to larger needles.
Cont in patt as given for back *at the same time* inc and
work into patt 1 st at each end of 5th and every foll 4th
row until there are 99(111) sts. NOTE: Work extra sts
in st st until there are enough to work into patt rep.
Cont without shaping until sleeve measures 48(50)cm/
19(19¾)" from beg, ending with a 2nd or 4th row.
Cast off loosely.

COLLAR

Join shoulder seams.
With RS facing, using smaller needles and A, pick up
and K29 sts up right front neck from beg of shaping, 3
sts down right back neck, K across 47 sts from back
neck holder, pick up and K3 sts up left back neck and
29 sts down left front neck to beg of shaping: 111 sts.
Row 1: P1, ✩K1 tbl, P1, rep from ✩ to end.
Row 2: K1 tbl, ✩P1, K1 tbl, rep from ✩ to end.
Rep these 2 rows for 16cm/6¼".
Cast off in rib.

POCKET TOPS

With RS facing, using smaller needles and A, K across 30
sts from sts on holder for pocket lining.
Work 5 rows in K1 tbl, P1 rib.
Cast off in rib.

TO MAKE UP

Block each piece separately if required, but do not press.
Place markers 28(30)cm/11(12)" down from shoulders
on back and fronts to denote beg of armholes. Sew in
sleeves between markers. Join side and sleeve seams,
reversing seam for turn back cuff.
Sew front panels to front edge, join top of panel to
collar for 5cm/2".
Sew down pocket tops and slipstitch pocket linings into
position.
Sew on buttons to correspond with buttonholes.

Chequers

A geometric design with a subtly interlocking zigzag motif for the mathematically minded and those who like to concentrate while knitting.

MEASUREMENTS

To fit bust 86–91(97–102:107–112)cm/34–36(38–40:42–44)″
Actual measurements 102(112:122)cm/40(44:48)″
Length from shoulders 50(54:57.5)cm/19½(21¼:22½)″
Sleeve seam 45(47.5:49)cm/17¾(18¾:19¼)″
Instructions are given for smallest size first, with figures for larger sizes in ( ).

MATERIALS

300(350:400)g/12(14:16)oz of a double knitting yarn in main colour A
150(200:200)g/6(8:8)oz in each of contrasting colours B, C and D
A pair each of 3¼mm and 4mm knitting needles (or sizes to obtain correct tension)
5 buttons

TENSION

25 sts and 26 rows to 10cm/4″ measured over patt worked on larger needles

INSTRUCTIONS

BACK

Using smaller needles and A, cast on 116(126:136) sts. Work 5cm/2″in K1, P1 rib, ending with a RS row.
Inc row: Rib 3, ✲inc in next st, rib 10(9:7), rep from ✲ to last 3(4:5) sts, inc in next st, rib to end: 127(139:153) sts.
Change to larger needles. Cont working in st st in patt from chart as follows:
Join on and cut off colours as required and carry yarn not in use loosely across back of work. Reading odd-numbered (K) rows from right to left and even-numbered (P) rows from left to right, work from chart A until 124(134:144) patt rows have been completed.
Shape Neck
Next row: Keeping patt correct, work across 57(62:69) sts, cast off next 13(15:15) sts, patt to end.
Working on first set of sts, patt 1 row.
Cast off 6(6:7) sts at beg of next and foll alternate row.
Work 1 row.
Cast off rem 45(50:55) sts.
Return to rem sts, rejoin yarn and complete to match first side, reversing all shaping.

LEFT FRONT

Using smaller needles and A, cast on 58(63:68) sts. Work 5cm/2″in K1, P1 rib, ending with a RS row.
Inc row: Rib 4(4:2), ✲inc in next st, rib 9(8:8), rep from ✲ to last 4(5:3) sts, inc in next st, rib to end: 64(70:76) sts.
Change to larger needles.
Cont working in patt from chart A as given for back until 71(75:81) patt rows have been completed, so ending with an RS row.
Shape front neck
Keeping patt correct, dec 1 st at beg of next and foll 9 alternate rows, then dec 1 st at neck edge on every foll 3rd row until 45(50:55) sts rem.
Work straight until front measures same as back to shoulders, endings with a WS row.
Cast off.

RIGHT FRONT

Work as given for left front but read odd numbered rows from left to right and even numbered rows from right to left and ending with a WS row before beg neck shaping.

SLEEVES

Using smaller needles and A, cast on 54(60:66) sts. Work 5cm/2″in K1, P1 rib, ending with a RS row.
Inc row: Rib 2(3:4), ✲inc in next st, rib 6(5:4), rep from ✲ to last 3(3.5) sts, inc in next st, rib to end: 62(70:78) sts.
Change to larger needles. Working in patt from chart B, inc and work into patt 1 st at each end of every foll 3rd row until there are 126(136:146) sts, ending with a RS row.
Work a further 4(11:18) rows in patt. Cast off.

BUTTON AND BUTTONHOLE BORDER AND COLLAR

Join shoulder seams.
Using smaller needles and A, cast on 15 sts.
Row 1: K1, ✲P1, K1, rep from ✲ to end.
Row 2: P1, ✲K1, P1, rep from ✲ to end.
Rep these 2 rows until border, slightly stretched, fits up left front to beg of neck shaping.
Shape collar
Inc 1 st at neck edge at beg of next and every foll alternate row until there are 65 sts. Cont without shaping for a further 13cm/5″.
Dec 1 st at neck edge on next and every foll alternate row until 15 sts rem.
Before cont with buttonhole border, mark positions for 5 buttons on button border, the first one 2cm/¾″ from

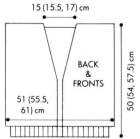

15 (15.5, 17) cm

BACK & FRONTS

51 (55.5, 61) cm

50 (54, 57.5) cm

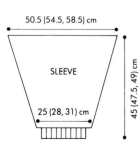

50.5 (54.5, 58.5) cm

SLEEVE

25 (28, 31) cm

45 (47.5, 49) cm

cast-on edge, the top one 2cm/¾" below beg of collar shaping and the others spaced evenly in between.
Cont in rib for buttonhole border, working buttonholes to correspond with markers as follows:

Buttonhole row: Rib 6, cast off 3 sts, rib to end.
Next row: Rib to end, casting on 3 sts above those cast off in previous row.
After the last buttonhole, complete to match button border, ending with a WS row.
Cast off in rib.

TO MAKE UP
Press or block as appropriate for yarn used. Sew borders and collar in place. Fold sleeves in half lengthwise, and placing folds at top of sleeves to shoulder seams, sew in place. Join side and sleeve seams. Sew on buttons.

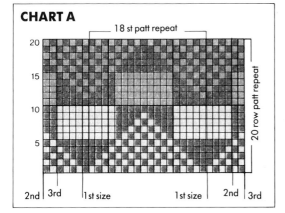

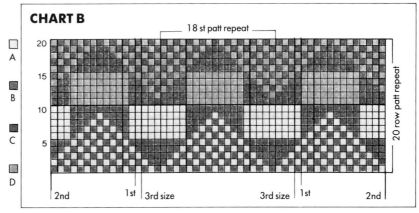

Tapestry

This intricate-looking woven-effect waistcoat is not at all complex to make if you follow the charts carefully.

MEASUREMENTS
To fit bust 86–91(97–101)cm/34–36(38–40)″
Actual measurements 108(116)cm/42½(45)″
Length from shoulders 50(53)cm/19¾(21)″
Instructions are given for smallest size first, with figures for larger size in ( ).

MATERIALS
150(200)g/6(8)oz of a double knitting yarn in main colour A
100(100)g/4(4)oz in contrasting colour B
50(100)g/2(4)oz in each of contrasting colours C and D
A pair each of 3¼mm and 4mm knitting needles (or sizes to obtain correct tension)
4 buttons

Remember to check your tension.

TENSION
23 sts and 24 rows to 10cm/4″ measured over patt worked on larger needles

INSTRUCTIONS
BACK
Using smaller needles and A, cast on 117(127) sts.
Row 1: (Right side) K1 tbl, ✻P1, K1 tbl, rep from ✻ to end.
Row 2: P1, ✻K1 tbl, P1, rep from ✻ to end.
Rep these 2 rows 3 more times, then the first row once again.
Inc row: P3(4), [P14 (15), M1] 7 times, P16(18): 124 (134) sts.
Change to larger needles.
Joining on and cutting off colours as necessary and working right-side (K) rows from right to left and wrong-side (P) rows from left to right, work in patt from chart, casting off and dec sts as indicated.

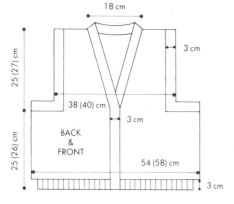

18 cm

3 cm

25 (27) cm

38 (40) cm

3 cm

25 (26) cm

BACK & FRONT

54 (58) cm

3 cm

LEFT FRONT

Using smaller needles and A, cast on 59(63) sts.
Rep the 2 rib rows as given for back 4 times, then the first row once again.
Inc row: P1, [P14(12), M1] 3(4) times, P16(14): 62(67) sts.
Change to larger needles.
Work from chart as given for back but working only up to dividing line for fronts as indicated and working front neck shaping as shown on chart.

RIGHT FRONT

Work as for left front, reversing shaping as on chart.

BUTTONHOLE BAND

Join shoulder seams.
With right side facing, using smaller needles and A, pick up and K52(62) sts along right front from cast-on edge to beg of neck shaping, 68 sts up front neck shaping to shoulder and 20 sts from shoulder to centre back neck: 140(150) sts.
Next row: ☆K1 tbl, P1, rep from ☆ to end.
Rep this row twice more.
Buttonhole row: Rib 5, [cast off 2 sts, rib 13(16) sts] 3 times, cast off 2 sts, rib to end.
Next row: Rib to end, casting on 2 sts over those cast off in previous row.
Work 4 more rows in rib. Cast off loosely in rib.

BUTTON BAND

Work as given for buttonhole band, omitting buttonholes and beg first rib row with P1, K1 tbl.

ARMBANDS

With right side facing, using smaller needles and A, pick up 23(25) sts along underarm edge, 1 st from corner and mark this st, pick up and K131(139) sts evenly along armhole edge to next corner, pick up 1 st from corner and mark this st, then 23(25) sts along underarm edge: 179(191) sts.
Row 1: [P1, K1 tbl] 10(11) times, P1, P2 tog, K1, P2 tog tbl, [P1, K1 tbl] 63(67) times, P1, P2 tog, K1, P2 tog tbl, [P1, K1 tbl] 10(11) times, P1.
Row 2: [K1 tbl, P1] 10(11) times, skpo, P1, K2 tog, [P1, K1 tbl] 62(66) times, P1, skpo, P1, K2 tog, [P1, K1 tbl] 10(11) times.
Cont dec 1 st each side of marked st as given, work a further 7 rows in rib.
Cast off loosely in rib, dec each side of marked st.

TO MAKE UP

Press or block as appropriate for yarn used.
Join button and buttonhole bands at centre back neck.
Join side and armband seams. Sew on buttons.

CHART

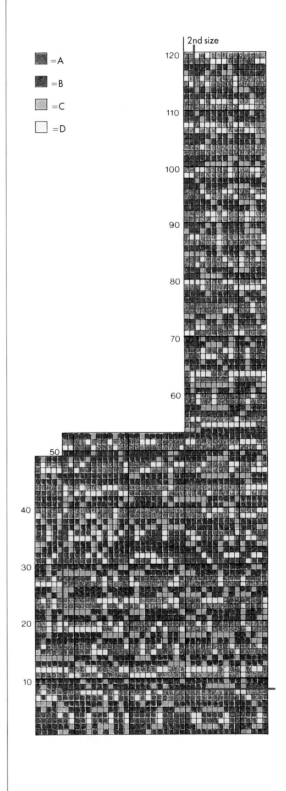

■ =A
■ =B
□ =C
□ =D

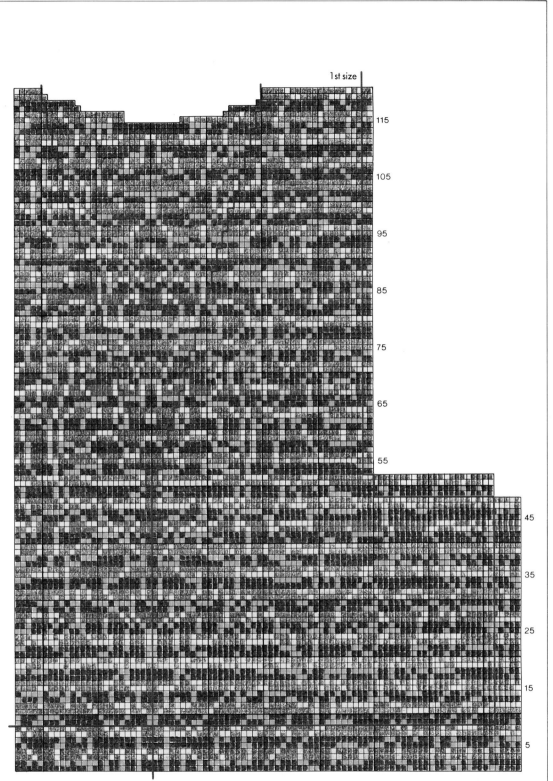

1st size

115

105

95

85

75

65

55

45

35

25

15

5

Division for left and right fronts

Canute

A thick seafaring sweater knitted in a traditional stitch, combining ribs and bobbles for an attractive heavily textured effect.

MEASUREMENTS

To fit bust 81(86:91:97)cm/32(34:36:38)"
Actual measurements 90(94:100:106)cm/
35½(37:39¼:41¾)"
Length from shoulders 63.5(63.5:66:66)cm/
25(25:26:26)"
Sleeve seam 44.5(44.5:45.5:45.5)cm/17½(17½:18:18)"
Instructions are given for smallest size first with figures for larger sizes in ( ).

MATERIALS

950(1000:1050:1100)g/38(40:42:44)oz of a chunky knitting yarn
A pair each of 5½mm and 6½mm knitting needles (or sizes to obtain correct tension)

TENSION

15 sts and 21 rows to 10cm/4" measured over patt worked on larger needles

SPECIAL ABBREVIATION

MB (Make bobble) – [K1, yf, K1, yf, K1] all into next st, turn and P5, turn and K2 tog, K3 tog, pass first st over 2nd st and off needle.

INSTRUCTIONS

BACK

Using smaller needles cast on 62(66:70:74) sts.
Row 1: K2, ✿P2, K2, rep from ✿ to end.
Row 2: P2, ✿K2, P2, rep from ✿ to end.
Rep these 2 rows for 7.5cm/3", ending with a 2nd row.
Inc row: Rib 6(6:6:8), ✿inc in next st, rib 11(12:13:13), rep from ✿ to last 8(8:8:10) sts, inc in next st, rib to end: 67(71:75:79) sts.
Change to larger needles.
Cont in patt as follows:
Row 1: (Wrong side) K3(5:7:9), ✿P1, K1, P1, K3, P2, K15, P2, K3, P1, K1, rep from ✿ once more, P1, K3(5:7:9).
Row 2: P3(5:7:9), K1, ✿K2 tog, P3, K1, yrn, P8, MB, P8, yon, K1, P3, sl 1, K1, psso, K1, rep from ✿ once more, P3(5:7:9).
Row 3: K3(5:7:9), P2, ✿K3, P2, K8, P1, K8, P2, K3✿, P3, rep from ✿ to ✿ once more, P2, K3(5:7:9).
Row 4: P3(5:7:9), K2, ✿P2 tog, P1, K1, yrn, P5, MB, P3, K1, P3, MB, P5, yon, K1, P1, P2 tog✿, K3, rep from ✿ to

Remember to check your tension.

☆ once more, K2, P3(5:7:9).

Row 5: K3(5:7:9), P2, ☆K2, P2, K5, P1, [K3, P1] twice, K5, P2, K2☆, P3, rep from ☆ to ☆ once more, P2, K3(5:7:9).

Row 6: P3(5:7:9), K2, ☆P2 tog, K1, yrn, P2, MB, [P3, K1] 3 times, P3, MB, P2, yon, K1, P2 tog☆, K3, rep from ☆ to ☆ once more, K2, P3(5:7:9).

Row 7: K3(5:7:9), P2, ☆K1, P2, K2, P1, [K3, P1] 4 times, K2, P2, K1☆, P3, rep from ☆ to ☆ once more, P2, K3(5:7:9).

Row 8: P3(5:7:9), K2, ☆K2 tog, yrn, [P3, K1] 5 times, P3, yon, sl 1, K1, psso☆, K3, rep from ☆ to ☆ once more, K2, P3(5:7:9).

Row 9: K3(5:7:9), P4, ☆[K3, P1] 5 times, K3☆, P7, rep from ☆ to ☆ once more, P4, K3(5:7:9).

Row 10: P3(5:7:9), K1, ☆K2 tog, yrn, P4, yon, K1, P3, K1, P1, P2 tog, K1, P2 tog, P1, K1, P3, K1, yrn, P4, yon, sl 1, K1, psso, K1, rep from ☆ to last 3(5:7:9) sts, P3(5:7:9).

Row 11: K3(5:7:9), P3, ☆K4, P2, K3, [P1, K2] twice, P1, K3, P2, K4☆, P5, rep from ☆ to ☆ once more, P3, K3(5:7:9).

Row 12: P3(5:7:9), K2 tog, ☆yrn, P6, yon, K1, P3, [K1, P2 tog] twice, K1, P3, K1, yrn, P6, yon☆, sl 1, K2 tog, psso, rep from ☆ to ☆ once more, sl 1, K1, psso, P3(5:7:9).

Row 13: K11(13:15:17), ☆P2, K3, [P1, K1] twice, P1, K3, P2☆, K15, rep from ☆ to ☆ once more, K11(13:15:17).

Row 14: P3(5:7:9), ☆MB, P8, yon, K1, P3, sl 1, K1, psso, K1, K2 tog, P3, K1, yrn, P8, rep from ☆ once more, MB, P3(5:7:9).

Row 15: K3(5:7:9), ☆P1, K8, P2, K3, P3, K3, P2, K8, rep from ☆ once more, P1, K3(5:7:9).

Row 16: P3(5:7:9), K1, ☆P3, MB, P5, yon, K1, P1, P2 tog, K3, P2 tog, P1, K1, yrn, P5, MB, P3, K1, rep from ☆ once more, P3(5:7:9).

Row 17: K3(5:7:9), ☆P1, K3, P1, K5, P2, K2, P3, K2, P2, K5, P1, K3, rep from ☆ once more, P1, K3(5:7:9).

Row 18: P3(5:7:9), K1, ☆P3, K1, P3, MB, P2, yon, K1, P2 tog, K3, P2 tog, K1, yrn, P2, MB, [P3, K1] twice, rep from ☆ once more, P3(5:7:9).

Row 19: K3(5:7:9), ☆[P1, K3] twice, P1, K2, P2, K1, P3, K1, P2, K2, [P1, K3] twice, rep from ☆ once more, P1, K3(5:7:9).

Row 20: P3(5:7:9), K1, ☆[P3, K1] twice, P3, yon, sl 1, K1, psso, K3, K2 tog, yrn, [P3, K1] 3 times, rep from ☆ once more, P3(5:7:9).

Row 21: K3(5:7:9), ☆[P1, K3] 3 times, P7, [K3, P1] twice, K3, rep from ☆ once more, P1, K3(5:7:9).

Row 22: P3(5:7:9), K1, ☆P2 tog, P1, K1, P3, K1, yrn, P4, yon, sl 1, K1, psso, K1, K2 tog, yrn, P4, yon, K1, P3, K1, P1, P2 tog, K1, rep from ☆ once more, P3(5:7:9).

Row 23: K3(5:7:9), ☆P1, K2, P1, K3, P2, K4, P5, K4, P2, K3, P1, K2, rep from ☆ once more, P1, K3(5:7:9).

Row 24: P3(5:7:9), K1, ☆P2 tog, K1, P3, K1, yrn, P6, yon, sl 1, K2 tog, psso, yrn, P6, yon, K1, P3, K1, P2 tog, K1, rep from ☆ once more, P3(5:7:9).

These 24 rows form the patt.

Cont in patt until back measures 63.5(63.5:66:66)cm/ 25(25:26:26)″ from beg, ending with a wrong-side row.

Shape shoulders and back neck

Next row: Cast off 9(10:11:12) sts, work in patt until there are 11(12:12:13) sts on needle, turn and leave rem sts on a spare needle.

Next row: K2 tog, patt to end.

Cast off rem 10(11:11:12) sts.

Return to sts on spare needle.

With right side facing, sl centre 27(27:29:29) sts onto a holder, rejoin yarn and patt to end.

Next row: Cast off 9(10:11:12) sts, patt to last 2 sts, K2 tog.

Cast off rem 10(11:11:12) sts.

FRONT

Work as given for back until front measures 57(57:58.5:58.5)cm/22½(22½:23:23)″ from beg, ending with a wrong-side row.

Shape neck

Next row: Patt across 24(26:28:30) sts, turn and leave rem sts on a spare needle.

Work on first set of sts as follows:

☆☆ Keeping patt correct, dec 1 st at neck edge on every row until 19(21:22:24) sts rem.

Cont without shaping until front measures same as back to shoulder, ending at armhole edge.

Shape shoulder

Cast off 9(10:11:12) sts at beg of next row.

Work 1 row. Cast off. ☆☆

Return to sts on spare needle.

With right side facing, sl first 19 sts onto a holder, rejoin yarn to next st and patt to end.

Now work as given for first side of neck from ☆☆ to ☆☆.

SLEEVES

Using smaller needles cast on 26 sts.

Work 6.5 cm/2½″ in rib as given for back, ending with a 2nd row.

Inc row: Rib 2, ☆inc in next st, rep from ☆ to last st, rib 1: 49 sts.

Change to larger needles.

Cont in patt as follows:

Row 1: K17, P2, K3, [P1, K1] twice, P1, K3, P2, K17.

Row 2: P9, MB, P8, yon, K1, P3, sl 1, K1, psso, K1, K2 tog, P3, K1, yrn, P8, MB, P9.

Row 3: K9, P1, K8, P2, K3, P3, K3, P2, K8, P1, K9.

Row 4: P5, MB, P3, K1, P3, MB, P5, yon, K1, P1, P2 tog, K3, P2 tog, P1, K1, yrn, P5, MB, P3, K1, P3, MB, P5.

Row 5: K5, P1, [K3, P1] twice, K5, P2, K2, P3, K2, P2, K5, [P1, K3] twice, P1, K5.

Row 6: P1, MB, [P3, K1] 3 times, P3, MB, P2, yon, K1, P2 tog, K3, P2 tog, K1, yrn, P2, MB, P3, [K1, P3] 3 times, MB, P1.

Row 7: K1, P1, [K3, P1] 4 times, K2, P2, K1, P3, K1, P2, K2, [P1, K3] 4 times, P1, K1.

Row 8: Inc in first st, [K1, P3] 5 times, yon, sl 1, K1, psso, K3, K2 tog, yrn, [P3, K1] 5 times, inc in last st.

Row 9: K2, [P1, K3] 5 times, P7, [K3, P1] 5 times, K2.

Row 10: P2, ✿yon, K1, P3, K1, P1, P2 tog, K1, P2 tog, P1, K1, P3, K1, yrn✿, P4, yon, sl 1, K1, psso, K1, K2 tog, yrn, P4, rep from ✿ to ✿ once more, P2.

Row 11: K2, P2, K3, [P1, K2] twice, P1, K3, P2, K4, P5, K4, P2, K3, P1, [K2, P1] twice, K3, P2, K2.

Row 12: P3, ✿yon, K1, P3, [K1, P2 tog] twice, K1, P3, K1, yrn✿, P6, yon, sl 1, K2 tog, psso, yrn, P6, rep from ✿ to ✿ once more, P3.

Row 13: K3, P2, K3, [P1, K1] twice, P1, K3, P2, K15, P2, K3, P1, [K1, P1] twice, K3, P2, K3.

Row 14: P4, ✿yon, K1, P3, sl 1, K1, psso, K1, K2 tog, P3, K1, yrn✿, P8, MB, P8, rep from ✿ to ✿ once more, P4.

Row 15: K4, P2, K3, P3, K3, P2, K8, P1, K8, P2, K3, P3, K3, P2, K4.

Row 16: Inc in first st, P4, ✿yon, K1, P1, P2 tog, K3, P2 tog, P1, K1, yrn✿, P5, MB, P3, K1, P3, MB, P5, rep from ✿ to ✿ once more, P4, inc in last st.

Row 17: K6, P2, K2, P3, K2, P2, K5, [P1, K3] twice, P1, K5, P2, K2, P3, K2, P2, K6.

Row 18: P7, yon, K1, P2 tog, K3, P2 tog, K1, yrn, P2, MB, [P3, K1] 3 times, P3, MB, P2, yon, K1, P2 tog, K3, P2 tog, K1, yrn, P7.

Row 19: K7, P2, K1, P3, K1, P2, K2, [P1, K3] 4 times, P1, K2, P2, K1, P3, K1, P2, K7.

Row 20: P8, yon, sl 1, K1, psso, K3, K2 tog, yrn, [P3, K1] 5 times, P3, yon, sl 1, K1, psso, K3, K2 tog, yrn, P8.

Row 21: K8, P7, [K3, P1] twice, K3, [P1, K3] 3 times, P7, K8.

Row 22: P9, yon, sl 1, K1, psso, K1, K2 tog, yrn, P4, yon, K1, P3, K1, P1, P2 tog, K1, P2 tog, P1, K1, P3, K1, yrn, P4, yon, sl 1, K1, psso, K1, K2 tog, yrn, P9.

Row 23: K9, P5, K4, P2, K3, [P1, K2] twice, P1, K3, P2, K4, P5, K9.

Row 24: Inc in first st, P9, yon, sl 1, K2 tog, psso, yrn, P6, yon, K1, P3, K1, [P2 tog, K1] twice, P3, K1, yrn, P6, yon, sl 1, K2 tog, psso, yrn, P9, inc in last st.

Cont in patt, inc and working into rev st st, 1 st at each end of every foll 8th row until there are 63(63:67:67) sts.

Work straight until sleeve measures 44.5(44.5:45.5:45.5)cm/17 ½(17½:18:18)″ from beg, ending with a wrong-side row.

Cast off loosely.

NECKBAND

Join right shoulder seam.

With right side facing and using smaller needles, pick up and K12(12:13:13) sts down left side of front neck, K across 19 sts from holder, pick up and K12(12:13:13) sts up right side of front neck, 2 sts down right back neck, K across 27(27:29:29) sts from back neck holder, pick up and K2 sts up left back neck: 74(74:78:78) sts.

Beg with a 2nd row, work 5 rows in rib as given for back.

Cast off loosely in rib.

TO MAKE UP

Block, if necessary, but do not press.

Join left shoulder and neckband seam.

Place markers 21(21:22:22)cm/8¼(8¼:8½:8½)″ down from shoulders on back and front to denote beg of armholes.

Sew in sleeves between markers, then join side and sleeve seams.

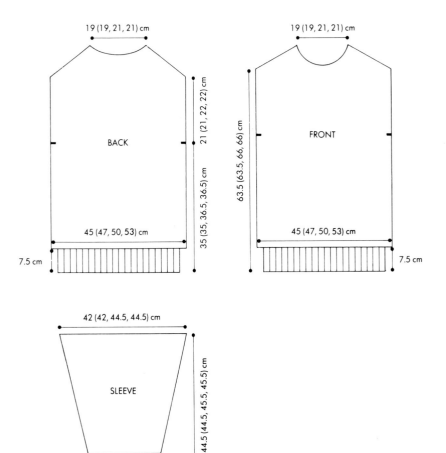

A bonny jumper with an heraldic look, knitted in thick, chunky yarn.

MEASUREMENTS

To fit bust 81(86:91:97)cm/32(34:36:38)"
Actual measurements 92(98:108:112)cm/
36(38½:42½:44)"
Length from shoulders 54(55:56:57)cm/
21¼(21½:22:22½)"
Sleeve seam 41(44:44:45)cm/16(17¼:17¼:17¾)"
Instructions are given for smallest size first, with figures for larger sizes in ( ).

MATERIALS

400(400:400:500)g/16(16:16:18)oz of a chunky knitting yarn in main colour A
200(200:200:250)g/8(8:8:10)oz in contrasting colour B
100(100:100:150)g/4(4:4:6)oz in contrasting colour C
100g/4oz in each of contrasting colours D and E
50g/2oz in contrasting colour F
A pair each of 5mm and 6½mm knitting needles (or sizes to obtain correct tension)

Remember to check your tension.

TENSION

16 sts and 18 rows to 10cm/4" measured over patt worked on larger needles.

NOTE

When the figure '0' is given this means that there are no stitches to be worked on this section of the row for your size; move on to the next part of the row that relates to the size you are knitting.

SPECIAL ABBREVIATION

MB (make bobble) – (P1, K1, P1) into next st, turn and P3, turn and K3 tog.

INSTRUCTIONS

BACK AND FRONT (alike)

Using smaller needles and A, cast on 55(59:63:67) sts.
Row 1 (RS): K1, *P1, K1, rep from * to end.
Row 2: P1, *K1, P1, rep from * to end.
Rep these 2 rows for 9cm/3½", ending with a first row.
Inc row: Rib 9(2:9:11), M1, [rib 2(3:2:2), M1]
18(18:22:22) times, rib to end: 74(78:86:90) sts.
Change to larger needles.
Join on and break off colours as necessary. Use small balls of colour for each pattern square, twisting yarns at back of work when changing colour to avoid leaving a hole.
Reading odd-numbered (K) rows from right to left and even-numbered (P) rows from left to right, work from chart as follows:
Row 1 (RS): K0(2:0:2) in A, work first 2(2:14:14) sts from chart as indicated for appropriate size, rep 24-st patt repeat 3 times, then K0(2:0:2) in A.
Row 2: P0(2:0:2) in A, rep 24-st patt repeat 3 times, work next 2(2:14:14) sts from chart as indicated on 2nd row, then P0(2:0:2) A.
Cont in patt from chart, rep the 32 rows of patt until work measures 49(50:51:52)cm/19¼(19½:20:20½)" from beg, ending with a wrong-side row.
Shape neck
Next row: Patt 27(28:31:32), turn and leave rem sts on a spare needle.
Work on first set of sts as follows:
Keeping patt correct, dec 1 st at neck edge until 22(23:26:27) sts rem.
Work 4 rows straight, so ending at armhole edge.
Shape shoulder
Cast off 7(8:9:9) sts at beg of next and foll alternate row.
Work 1 row. Cast off.
Return to sts on spare needle.
With right side facing, slip first 20(22:24:26) sts onto a holder, rejoin yarn and patt to end.
Now complete 2nd side of neck to match first, reversing all shaping.

SLEEVES

Using smaller needles and A, cast on 27(27:29:29) sts.
Work 7cm/3" in rib as given for back, ending with a first row.

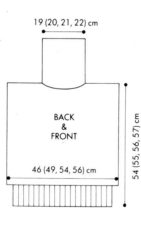

19 (20, 21, 22) cm

BACK
&
FRONT

46 (49, 54, 56) cm

54 (55, 56, 57) cm

30 (35, 36, 37) cm

SLEEVE

22 (24, 24, 25) cm

41 (44, 44, 45) cm

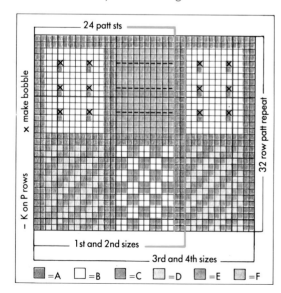

24 patt sts

x make bobble

– K on P rows

32 row patt repeat

1st and 2nd sizes

3rd and 4th sizes

■ =A □ =B ▨ =C □ =D ▨ =E ▨ =F

Inc row: Rib 1(3:2:4), M1, [rib 3(2:3:2), M1] 8(10:8:10) times, rib to end: 36(38:38:40) sts.
Change to larger needles.
Beg with a K row, work in st st, inc 1 st at each end of 12th(7th:9th:11th) and every foll 9th(7th:6th:6th) row until there are 48(56:58:60) sts.
Cont without shaping until sleeve measures 41(44:44:45)cm/16(17¼:17¼:17¾)" from beg, ending with a wrong-side row. Cast off.

POLO COLLAR

Join right shoulder seam.
With RS facing, using smaller needles and B, pick up and K10 sts down left side of neck, K across 20(22:24:26) sts from holder, pick up and K10 sts up right side of neck and 10 sts down right back neck, dec 1 st at centre, K across 20(22:24:26) sts from holder, then pick up and K10 sts up left side of neck: 79(83:87:91) sts.
Beg with a 2nd row, work in rib as given for back for 18(18:19:19)cm/7(7:7½:7½)".
Cast off loosely in rib.

TO MAKE UP

Press or block as appropriate for yarn used; but do not press textured areas.
Join left shoulder and polo collar seam.
Fold sleeves in half lengthwise; placing folds at top of sleeves to shoulder seams, sew in place.
Join side and sleeve seams.

Waves

A warm Aran-knit for blustery days worked in plain stocking stitch and broken cables. Wear it for cool spring rambles in the countryside.

MEASUREMENTS

To fit bust 81–91(96–107)cm/32–36(38–40)"
Actual measurements 96(112)cm/38(44)"
Length from shoulders 61(63)cm/24(24¾)"
Sleeve seam 41(43)cm/16(17)"
Instructions are given for smaller size first, with instructions for larger size in ( ).

MATERIALS

250(300)g/10(12)oz of an Aran-weight yarn in main colour A
350(400)g/14(16)oz in contrasting colour B
150(150)g/6(6)oz of contrasting colour C
50(50)g/2(2)oz of an Aran-weight tweed yarn in contrasting colour D
A pair each of 4½mm and 5½mm knitting needles (or size to obtain correct tension)
A cable needle

TENSION

21 sts and 23 rows to 10cm/4" measured over patt worked on larger needles

SPECIAL ABBREVIATION

C8F – Cable 8 forward as follows: sl next 4 sts onto cable needle and hold at front of work, K4, then K4 from cable needle.

INSTRUCTIONS

BACK

Using smaller needles and A, cast on 80(90) sts.
Work 6(8)cm/2¼(3)" in K1, P1 rib.
Inc row: K2(4), [inc in next st, K3(2) sts]
19(27) times, inc in next st, K1(4): 100(118) sts.
P1 row.
Change to larger needles.
Cont in patt as follows:
Row 1: With B, K1, ✳C8F, turn and P8, turn, K18, rep from ✳ to last 9 sts, C8F, turn and P8, turn, K9.
Row 2: With B, P to end.
Row 3: With B, K to end.
Rows 4 and 5: As rows 2 and 3.
Row 6: As row 2.
Rows 7–18: Rep rows 1–6 twice.
Row 19: As first row.
Row 20: As row 2.
Row 21: With C, K to end.

Row 22: With C, P to end.
Row 23: With D, K to end.
Row 24: With D, P to end.
Row 25: With A, K10, ✳C8F, turn and P8, turn, K18, rep from ✳ to end.
Row 26: With A, P to end.
Row 27: With A, K to end.
Row 28: As row 26.
Row 29: As row 27.
Row 30: As row 26.
Rows 31–42: Rep rows 25–30 twice.
Row 43: As row 25.
Row 44: As row 26.
Rows 47 and 48: As rows 21 and 22.
These 48 rows form the patt. Rep them once more then the first–20th rows again.
Shape shoulders
Cast off 31(40) sts at beg of next 2 rows.
Leave rem 38 sts on a holder.

FRONT

Work as given for back until front measures 53(55)cm/21(21¾)" from beg, ending with a WS row.
Shape neck
Next row: Patt across 37(46) sts, turn and leave rem sts on a spare needle.
Work on first set of sts as follows:
Patt 1 row.
Keeping patt correct, dec 1 st at neck edge on next and every foll alternate row until 31(40) sts rem.
Work straight until front measures same as back to shoulder, ending with a WS row.
Cast off.
Return to sts on spare needle.
Sl centre 26 sts onto a holder.
Rejoin yarn and patt to end.
Patt 1 row.
Now complete to match first side of neck.

SLEEVES

Using smaller needles and C, cast on 50 sts.
Work 6(8)cm/2¼(3)" in K1, P1 rib.
Inc row: K twice into every st to end: 100 sts.
Change to larger needles.
Beg with row 45, work in patt for 72 rows, so ending with a 20th row.
Next row: P in B.
Cast off loosely.

NECKBAND

Join left shoulder seam.

Remember to check your tension.

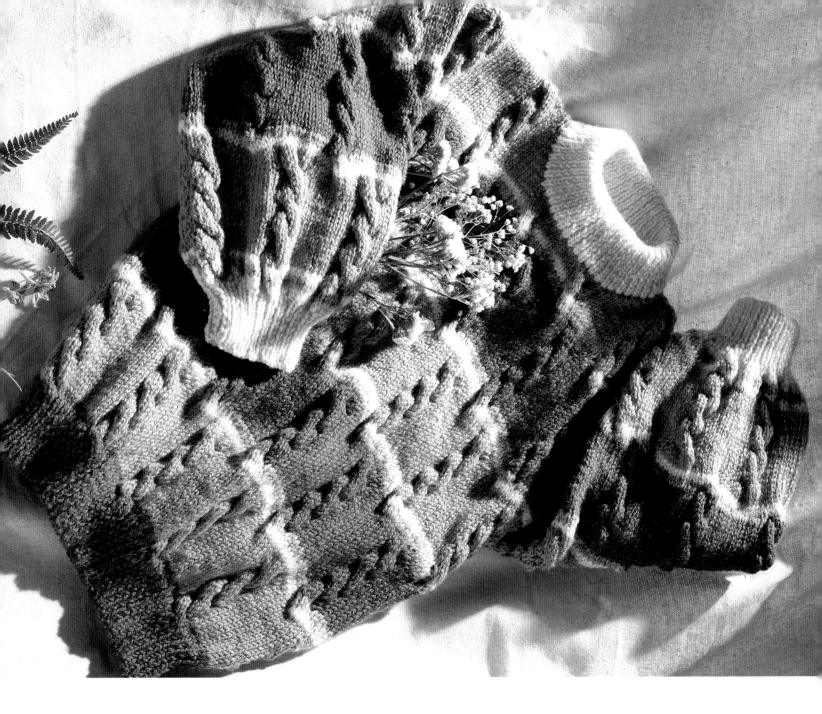

Using smaller needles and C, K across 38 sts from back
neck holder, pick up and K16 sts down left side of neck,
K across 26 sts from front neck holder, pick up and K16
sts up right side of neck: 96 sts.
Work 10cm/4" in K1, P1 rib.
Cast off loosely in rib.

TO MAKE UP

Block each piece separately if necessary, but do not press.
Join right shoulder and neckband seam. Fold neckband
in half to WS and slipstitch in place.
Fold sleeves in half lengthwise, and placing folds at top
of sleeves to shoulder seams, sew in place.
Join side and sleeve seams.

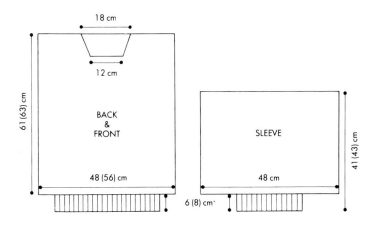

18 cm

12 cm

61 (63) cm

BACK
&
FRONT

48 (56) cm

SLEEVE

41 (43) cm

6 (8) cm

48 cm

137

Norwegian style

Three colours contrast in the traditional Scandinavian decoration on this stylish cardigan.

MEASUREMENTS

To fit bust 86(91:97)cm/34(36:38)"
Actual measurements 91(95.5:100)cm/36(37½:39¼)"
Length from shoulders 60(60:61.5)cm/
23½(23½:24½)"
Sleeve seam 42cm/16½"
Instructions are given for smallest size first, with figures for larger sizes in ( ).

MATERIALS

350(350:400)g/14(14:16)oz of a double knitting yarn in main colour A
200(200:250)g/8(8:10)oz in contrasting colour B
100(100:150)g/4(4:6)oz in contrasting colour C
A pair each of 3¼mm and 4mm knitting needles (or sizes to obtain correct tension)
9 buttons

Remember to check your tension.

TENSION

26 sts and 29 rows to 10cm/4" measured over patt worked on larger needles

INSTRUCTIONS

BACK

Using smaller needles and B, cast on 93(99:105) sts.
Row 1: K1, *P1, K1, rep from * to end.
Row 2: P1, *K1, P1, rep from * to end.
Work 19 more rows in rib as set.
Inc row: Rib 4(7:10) inc in next st, *rib 3, inc in next st, rep from * to last 4(7:10) sts, rib 4(7:10): 115(121:127) sts.
Change to larger needles.
Beg with a K row cont working in st st throughout, joining in and breaking off colours as required and working border patt as follows:
★★★★ Row 1: Work in C to end.
Row 2: 3(0:3)C, *1B, 5C, rep from * to last 4(1:4) sts, 1B, 3(0:3)C.
Row 3: 2(0:2)C, 3(2:3)B, *3C, 3B, rep from * to last 2(5:2) sts, 2(3:2)C, 0(2:0)B.
Row 4: 1C, *2B, 1C, rep from * to end.
Row 5: 2(0:2)B, 3(2:3)C, *3B, 3C, rep from * to last 2(5:2) sts, 2(3:2)B, 0(2:0)C.
Row 6: 0(3:0)C, *1B, 5C, rep from * to last 1(4:1) sts, 1B, 0(3:0)C.
Row 7: Work in C to end.
Row 8: Work in A to end.
Row 9: 1(0:3)A *1B, 3A, rep from * to last 2(1:0) sts,

1B, 1A(1B:0).
Row 10: P2A(2B,3A:2A,2B,2A), *1B, 1A, 1B, 3A, 3B, 3A, rep from * to last 5(8:11) sts, 1B, 1A, 1B, then 2A(3B,2A:3B,2A,3B).
Row 11: K0(3B:1A,5B), *3A, 1B, 3A, 5B, rep from * to last 7(10:1) sts, 3A,1B,3A(3A,1B,3A,3B:1A).
Row 12: As row 10.
Row 13: As row 9.
These 13 rows complete lower border patt.
Cont working in st st in main patt as follows:
Row 1: With A, P to end.
Row 2: With A, K to end.
Row 3: P3(0:3)A, *1B, 5A, rep from * to last 4(1:4) sts, 1B, 3(0:3)A.
Row 4: With A, K to end.
Row 5: With A, P to end.
Row 6: K0(3:0)A, *1B, 5A, rep from * to last 1(4:1) sts, 1B, 0(3:0)A. ★★★★
These 6 rows form main patt.
Work 77 more rows in patt as set.
Rep 9th – 12th lower border patt rows once more.

Shape armholes

Row 1: (13th lower border patt row): Keeping patt correct, cast off 6 sts at beg of row, patt to end.
Row 2: With A only, cast off 6 sts, work to end: 103(109:115) sts.
Work 2 rows straight with A.
★★★★★ Cont working yoke patt in st st as follows:
Rows 1 and 2: 0(3:0)A, *1C, 5A, rep from * to last 1(4:1) sts, 1C, 0(3:0)A.
Row 3: Work in C to end.
Row 4: 3(0:3)C, *1B, 5C, rep from * to last 4(1:4) sts, 1B, 3(0:3)C.
Row 5: 3C(2B,4C:2C,3B,4C), *2B, 3C, 2B, 4C, 3B, 4C, rep from * to last 10(13:16) sts, 2B, 3C, 2B, then 3C(4C,2B:4C,3B,2C).
Row 6: 3C(1B,5C:3C,1B,5C), *3B, 1C, 3B, 5C, 1B, 5C, rep from * to last 10(13:16) sts, 3B, 1C, 3B, then 3C(5C,1B:5C,1B,3C).
Row 7: 2B(2C,3B:2B,3C,3B), *2C, 2B, 1C, 2B, 2C, 3B, 3C, 3B, rep from * to last 11(14:17) sts, 2C, 2B, 1C, 2B, 2C, then 2B(3B,2C:3B,3C,2B).
Row 8: 0(3C:1B,5C), *3B, 2C, 1B, 1C, 1B, 2C, 3B, 5C, rep from * to last 13(16:19) sts, 3B, 2C, 1B, 1C, 1B, 2C, then 3B(3B,3C:3B,5C,1B).
Row 9: 1C(1B,3C:3B,1C,3B), *3B, 2C, 1B, 2C, 3B, 3C, 1B, 3C, rep from * to last 12(15:18) sts, 3B, 2C, 1B, 2C, 3B, then 1C(3C,1B:3C,1B,3C).
Row 10: 5(0:2)C, 3(2:3)B, *6C, 3B, rep from * to last 5(8:2) sts, 5C(6C,2B:2C).
Rows 11–17: Work from 9th row back to 3rd.

Rows 18 and 19: As first and 2nd.

Rows 20 and 21: 3(0:3)A, ☆1C, 5A, rep from ☆ to last 4(1:4) sts, 1C, 3(0:3)A. ☆☆☆☆☆

Row 22: 3(0:3)C, ☆1B, 5A, rep from ☆ to last 4(1:4) sts, 1B, 3(0:3)C.

Row 23: 2C(2B,3C:2C), ☆3B, 3C, rep from ☆ to last 5(2:5) sts, 3(2:3)B, 2(0:2)C.

Row 24: 1C, ☆2B, 1C, rep from ☆ to end.

Row 25: 2B(2C,3B:2B), ☆3C, 3B, rep from ☆ to last 5(2:5) sts, 3(2:3)C, 2(0:2)B.

Row 26: 1B, ☆2C, 1B, rep from ☆ to end.

Cont working in patt as set from 23rd to 26th rows. Work 16(16:20) more rows.

Shape shoulders

Cast off 9(9:10) sts at beg of next 4 rows and 8(9:9) sts at beg of foll 4 rows: 35(37:39) sts.

Leave sts on a spare needle.

LEFT FRONT

Using smaller needles and B, cast on 47(49:51) sts.

Work 21 rows in rib as given for back.

Inc row: Rib 3(2:1), inc in next st, ☆rib 3, inc in next st, rep from ☆ to last 3(2:1) sts, rib 3(2:1): 58(61:64) sts.

Change to larger needles.

Cont working in st st as given for back, working lower border patt as follows:

☆☆ **Row 1:** With C to end.

Row 2: ☆1B, 5C, rep from ☆ to last 4(1:4) sts, 1B, 3(0:3)C.

Row 3: 2C(2B,3C:2C), ☆3B, 3C, rep from ☆ to last 2 sts, 2B.

Row 4: 1C, ☆2B, 1C, rep from ☆ to end.

Row 5: 2B(2C,3B:2B), ☆3C, 3B, rep from ☆ to last 2 sts, 2C.

Row 6: 3C, ☆1B, 5C, rep from ☆ to last 1(4:1) sts, 1B, 0(3:0)C.

Row 7: With C to end.

Row 8: With A to end.

Row 9: 1A(1B,3A:3A,1B,3A), 1B, ☆3A, 1B, rep from ☆ to end.

Row 10: 2B, ☆3A, 1B, 1A, 1B, 3A, 3B, rep from ☆ to last 8(11:14) sts, 3A, 1B, 1A, 1B, then 2A(3A,2B:3A,3B,2A).

Row 11: 3A(3B,3A:1A,5B,3A), ☆1B, 3A, 5B, 3A, rep from ☆ to last 7 sts, 1B, 3A, 3B.

Row 12: As 10th.

Row 13: As 9th.

These 13 rows complete border patt.

Cont working in main patt in st st as follows:

Rows 1 and 2: With A to end.

Row 3: 1B, ☆5A, 1B, rep from ☆ to last 3(0:3) sts, 3(0:3)A.

Rows 4 and 5: With A to end.

Row 6: 0(3:0)A, ☆1B, 5A, rep from ☆ to last 4 sts, 1B, 3A.

These 6 rows form main patt.

Cont in patt until work measures same as back to end of main patt, then work 9th–12th rows of lower border patt once.

Shape armhole

Next row: (13th border patt): Cast off 6 sts, patt to end: 52(55:58) sts.

With A, work 3 rows straight.

Cont working in yoke patt as follows:

Row 1: 0(3:0)A, ☆1C, 5A, rep from ☆ to last 4 sts, 1C, 3A.

Row 2: 3A, ☆1C, 5A, rep from ☆ to last 1(4:1) sts, 1C, 0(3:0)A.

Row 3: With C to end.

Row 4: ☆1B, 5C, rep from ☆ to last 4(1:4) sts, 1B, 3(0:3)C.

Row 5: 3C(2B,4C:2C,3B,4C), ☆2B, 3C, 2B, 4C, 3B, 4C, rep from ☆ to last 13 sts, 2B, 3C, 2B, 4C, 2B.

Row 6: ☆1B, 5C, 3B, 1C, 3B, 5C, rep from ☆ to last 10(13:16) sts, 3B, 1C, 3B, then 3C(5C,1B:5C,1B,3C).

☆☆☆ Cont in yoke patt as set to match back, work 25(25:29) more rows.

Shape neck

Keeping patt correct, cast off 8(9:10) sts at beg of next row. Dec 1 st at neck edge on foll 10 rows: 34(36:38) sts.

Shape shoulder

Cast off 9(9:10) sts at beg (side edge) on next and foll alternate row, then 8(9:9) sts at beg of foll alternate row: 8(9:9) sts.

Work 1 row. Cast off.

RIGHT FRONT

Work as given for left front to ☆☆.

Row 1: With C to end.

Row 2: 3(0:3)C, 1B, ☆5C, 1B, rep from ☆ to end.

Row 3: 2B, ☆3C, 3B, rep from ☆ to last 2(5:2) sts, 2C(3C,2B:2C).

Row 4: 1C, ☆2B, 1C, rep from ☆ to end.

Row 5: 2C, ☆3B, 3C, rep from ☆ to last 2(5:2) sts, 2B(3B,2C:2B).

Row 6: 1B(3C,1B:1B), ☆5C, 1B, rep from ☆ to last 3 sts, 3C.

Row 7: With C to end.

Row 8: With A to end.

Row 9: ☆1B, 3A, rep from ☆ to last 2(1:0) sts, 1B, 1A(1B:0).

Row 10: 2A(2B,3A:2A,3B,3A), ☆1B, 1A, 1B, 3A, 3B, 3A, rep from ☆ to last 8 sts, 1B, 1A, 1B, 3A, 2B.

Row 11: 3B, ☆3A, 1B, 3A, 5B, rep from ☆ to last 7(10:13) sts, 3A, 1B, then 3A(3A,3B:3A,5B,1A).

Row 12: As 10th row.

Row 13: As 9th row.

Cont in main patt in st st as follows:

Rows 1 and 2: With A to end.

Row 3: 3(0:3)A, ☆1B, 5A, rep from ☆ to last st, 1B.

Rows 4 and 5: With A to end.

Row 6: 3A, 1B, ☆5A, 1B, rep from ☆ to last 0(3:0) sts, 0(3:0)A.

Cont in main patt as set, work a further 77 rows then 9th – 13th rows of lower border patt.

Shape armhole

Next row: With A, cast off 6 sts, work to end: 52(55:58) sts.

With A, work 2 rows straight.

Cont working yoke patt as follows:

Row 1: 3A, ☆1C, 5A, rep from ☆ to last 1(4:1) sts, 1C, 0(3:0)A.

Row 2: 0(3:0)A, ☆1C, 5A, rep from ☆ to last 4 sts, 1C, 3A.

Row 3: With C to end.

Row 4: 3C(1B,5C:3C,1B,5C), 1B, ☆5C, 1B, rep from ☆ to end.

Row 5: 2B, ☆4C, 2B, 3C, 2B, 4C, 3B, rep from ☆ to last 14(17:20) sts, 4C, 2B, 3C, 2B, then 3C(4C,2B:4C,3B,2C).

Row 6: 3C(1B,5C:3C,1B,5C), ☆3B, 1C, 3B, 5C, 1B, 5C, rep from ☆ once more, 3B, 1C, 3B, 5C, 1B.

Complete as given for left front, working from ☆☆☆ to end, but working one extra row before working neck shaping.

SLEEVES

Using smaller needles and B, cast on 45(45:49) sts.

Work 21 rows in rib as given for back.

Inc row: Rib 8(8:9), inc 1 st in each of next 28(28:30) sts, rib to end: 73(73:79) sts.

Change to larger needles.

Cont in patt as given for back, working from ☆☆☆☆ to ☆☆☆☆, but foll figures for 2nd(2nd:3rd) size.

Keeping main patt correct and working extra sts into patt, inc 1 st at each end of 2nd and every foll 6th row until there are 91(91:97) sts.

Patt 12 rows straight.

Cont in top patt as follows:

Row 1: 2(2:1)A, ☆1B, 3C, rep from ☆ to last 1(1:0) st, 1(1:0)B.

Row 2: 2B(2B:2A,3B), ☆3A, 1B, 1A, 1B, 3A, 3B, rep from ☆ to last 5(5:8) sts, 3A, 1B, then 1A(1A:1A,1B,2A).

Row 3: 1B(1B:3A,1B), 3A, ☆5B, 3A, 1B, 3A, rep from ☆ to last 3(3:6) sts, 3B(3B:5B,1A).

Row 4: As 2nd.

Row 5: As first.

With A, work 3 rows straight.

Cont in patt as given for back, working from ☆☆☆☆☆ to ☆☆☆☆☆, foll figures for 2nd(2nd:3rd) size and marking each end of 13th row to indicate end of sleeve seam. Cast off.

NECKBAND

Join shoulder seams.

Using smaller needles, B, and with RS facing, pick up and K 27(28:29) sts around right front neck edge, K across 35(37:39) back neck sts, pick up and K 27(28:29) sts around left front neck: 89(93:97) sts.

Work 8 rows in rib as given for back.

Cast off in rib.

BUTTONHOLE BAND

Using smaller needles, B, and with RS facing, pick up and K 153(153:157) sts evenly along right front edge, including row ends of neckband.

Work 3 rows in rib as given for back.

Make buttonholes

Row 1: Rib 4(4:6), ☆cast off 2, rib 15, rep from ☆ 7 more times, cast off 2, rib to end.

Row 2: Rib to end, casting on 2 sts over those cast off in previous row.

Rib 3 rows. Cast off in rib.

BUTTON BAND

Work as given for buttonhole band, omitting buttonholes.

TO MAKE UP

Press or block as appropriate for yarn used.

Set in sleeves, sewing row ends above markers to sts cast off at underarms.

Join side and sleeve seams. Sew on buttons to correspond with buttonholes.

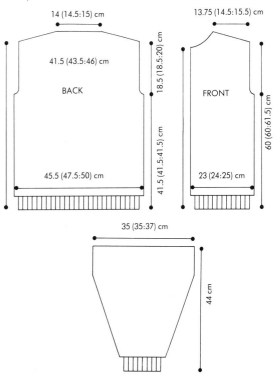

Three-colour Zigzags

The design on the shoulders and the unusual line of the sleeves are special features on this pretty sweater.

MEASUREMENTS

To fit bust 86(91:97)cm/34(36:38)"
Actual measurements 90.5(95:100)cm/
35½(37½:39½)"
Length from shoulders 56(57:57.5)cm/22(22½:22¾)"
Sleeve seam 51cm/20"
Instructions are given for smallest size first with figures for larger sizes in ( ).

MATERIALS

250(250:300)g/10(10:12)oz of a double knitting yarn in main colour A
100(150:150)g/4(6:6)oz in contrasting colour B
50(50:50)g/2(2:2)oz in contrasting colour C
A pair each of 3¼mm and 4mm knitting needles (or sizes to obtain correct tension)
A 3.50mm crochet hook
2 buttons

Remember to check your tension.

TENSION

25 sts and 30 rows to 10cm/4" measured over st st worked on larger needles

INSTRUCTIONS

BACK

Using smaller needles and B, cast on 112(116:124) sts.
Work 26 rows in K2, P2 rib inc 1(3:1) sts evenly across last row: 113(119:125) sts.
Break off B. Join in A. ☆☆
Change to larger needles.
Beg with a K row cont working in st st until back measures
35cm/13¼" from beg, ending with a WS row.
Shape armholes
Cast off 8 sts at beg of next 2 rows: 97(103:109) sts.
Work 24(26:28) rows straight.
Cont in st st in colour patt, breaking off and joining in colours as required, as follows:
Row 1: 1C(9A,1C:1C), 11A, ☆1C, 11A, rep from ☆ to last 1(10:1) sts, 1C(1C,9A:1C).
Row 2: 2C(8A,3C:2C), ☆9A, 3C, rep from ☆ to last 11(8:11) sts, 9A, 2C(8A:9A:2C).
Row 3: 3C(7A,5C:3C), ☆7A, 5C, rep from ☆ to last 10(7:10) sts, 7A,3C(7A:7A,3C).
Row 4: 1B(1C,5A,3C,1B:1B), ☆3C, 5A, 3C, 1B, rep from ☆ to last 0(9:0) sts, 0(3C,5A,1C:0).
Row 5: 2B(2C,3A,3C,3B:2B), ☆3C, 3A, 3C, 3B, rep from ☆ to last 11(8:11) sts,

3C,3A,3C,2B(3C,3A,2C:3C,3A,3C,2B).
Row 6: 3B(3C,1A,3C,5B:3B), ☆3C, 1A, 3C, 5B, rep from ☆ to last 10(7:10) sts,
3C,1A,3C,3B(3C,1A,3C:3C,1A,3C,3B).
Row 7: 1A(1B,5C,3B,1A:1A), ☆3B, 5C, 3B, 1A, rep from ☆ to last 0(9:0) sts, work 0(3B,5C,1B:0).
Row 8: 2A(2B,3C,3B,3A:2A), ☆3B, 3C, 3B, 3A, rep from ☆ to last 11(8:11) sts,
3B,3C,3B,2A(3B,3C,2B:3B,3C,3B,2A).
Row 9: 3A(3B,1C,3B,5A:3A), ☆3B, 1C, 3B, 5A, rep from ☆ to last 10(7:10) sts,
3B,1C,3B,3A(3B,1C,3B:3B,1C,3B,3A).
Row 10: 4A(1A,5B,7A:4A), ☆5B, 7A, rep from ☆ to last 9(6:9) sts, 5B, 4(1:4)A.
Row 11: 1C(2A,3B,4A,1C:1C), ☆4A, 3B, 4A, 1C, rep from ☆ to last 0(9:0) sts, work 0(4A,3B,2A:0).
Row 12: 2C(3A,1B,4A,3C:2C), ☆4A, 1B, 4A, 3C, rep from ☆ to last 11(8:11) sts,
4A,1B,4A,2C(4A,1B,4A:4A,1B,4A,2C).
Row 13: As 3rd.
Row 14: 4C(1C,5A,7C:4C), ☆5A, 7C, rep from ☆ to last 9(6:9) sts, 5A, 4(1:4)C.
Row 15: 5C(2C,3A,9C:5C), ☆3A, 9C, rep from ☆ to last 8(5:8) sts, 3A, 5(2:5)C.
Row 16: 1B(3C,1A,5C,1B:1B), ☆5C, 1A, 5C, 1B, rep from ☆ to last 0(9:0) sts, 0(5C,1A,3C:0).
Row 17: 2B(8C,3B:2B), ☆9C, 3B, rep from ☆ to last 11(8:11) sts, 9C,2B(8C:9C,2B).
Row 18: 3B(7C,5B:3B), ☆7C, 5B, rep from ☆ to last 10(7:10) sts, 7C,3B(7C:7C,3B).
Rows 19–22: As 7th – 10th.
Row 23: 5A,3B(2A,3B:5A,3B), ☆9A, 3B, rep from ☆ to last 5(2:5) sts, 5(2:5)C.
Row 24: 6A,1B(3A,1B:6A,1B), ☆11A, 1B, rep from ☆ to last 6(3:6) sts, 6(3:6)A.
Work 2 rows in C.
Break off A and C and cont with B only.
Change to smaller needles.
Inc row: K6(2:6), ☆inc in next st, K6(6:5), rep from ☆ to last 7(3:7) sts, inc in next st, K to end: 110(118:126) sts.
Work 12 rows in K2, P2 rib, beg first row with P2 and 2nd row with K2.
Cast off loosely in rib.

FRONT

Work as given for back to ☆☆.
Change to larger needles.
Beg with a K row cont in st st until front measures 3 rows less than back to armhole shaping, thus ending with a K row.
Divide for neck

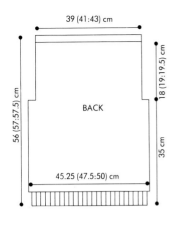

39 (41:43) cm

56 (57:57.5) cm

18 (19:19.5) cm

35 cm

BACK

45.25 (47.5:50) cm

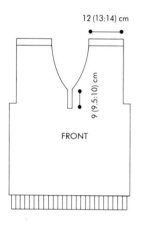

12 (13:14) cm

9 (9.5:10) cm

FRONT

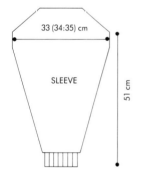

33 (34:35) cm

51 cm

SLEEVE

Next row: P54(57:60) sts, leave these sts on a spare needle, cast off 5 sts, P to end.

Cont working on last set of 54(57:60) sts first for left front.

Work 2 rows straight.

Shape armhole

Cast off 8 sts at beg of next row: 46(49:52) sts.

Work 17(19:21) rows straight.

Shape neck

Dec 1 st at neck edge on next and at same edge on 3 foll alternate rows: 42(45:48) sts.

P 1 row. ✰✰✰

Cont working in colour patt as given for back as follows:

Row 1: 1C(9A,1C:1C), ✰11A, 1C, rep from ✰ to last 5(11:11) sts, 3(9:9)A, K2 tog A.

Row 2: 3(9:9)A, ✰3C, 9A, rep from ✰ to last 2(11:2) sts, 2C(3C,8A:2C).

Row 3: 3(0:3)C, ✰7A, 5C, rep from ✰ to last 2(8:8) sts, 0(6:6)A, K2 tog A.

Row 4: 3(1:1)C, 0(5:5)A, 0(3:3)C, ✰1B, 3C, 5A, 3C, rep from ✰ to last 1(10:1) sts, 1B(1B,3C,5A,1C:1B).

✰✰✰✰ These 4 rows set colour patt. Cont in patt as given for back as set, dec 1 st at neck edge on next and at same edge on foll 9 alternate rows: 30(33:36) sts.

Work 1 row in patt.

With C work 2 rows in st st. Break off C and A. Cont with B only.

Change to smaller needles.

Inc row: K6(4:3), ✰inc in next st, K5, rep from ✰ to last 6(5:3) sts, inc in next st, K to end: 34(38:42) sts.

Beg first row with K2, work 13 rows in K2, P2 rib.

Cast off loosely in rib.

With RS of work facing, rejoin yarn to rem sts at neck edge for right front.

Work as given for first side to ✰✰✰.

Cont in colour patt as follows:

Row 1: K2 tog A, 3(9:9)A, ✰1C, 11A, rep from ✰ to last 1(10:1) sts, 1C(1C,9A:1C).

Row 2: 2(0:2)C, 9(8:9)A, ✰3C, 9A, rep from ✰ to last 6(12:12) sts, 3C, 3(9:9)A.

Row 3: K2 tog A, 0(6:6)A, ✰5C, 7A, rep from ✰ to last 3(0:3) sts, 3(0:3) C.

Row 4: 1(0:1)B, 3(1:3)C, ✰5A, 3C, 1B, 3C, rep from ✰ to last 0(6:6) sts, 0(5A,1C:5A,1C).

Cont in patt as set, working from ✰✰✰✰ to end, but working 14 rows in K2, P2 rib instead of 13.

SLEEVES

Using smaller needles and B, cast on 52(52:56) sts.

Work 25 rows in K2, P2 rib.

Inc row: Rib 5(5:8), ✰inc in next st, rib 7(5:7), rep from ✰ to last 6(5:8) sts, inc in next st, rib to end: 58(60:62) sts.

Break off B. Join in A.
Change to larger needles.
Beg with a K row, cont in st st, inc 1 st at each end of 7th and every foll 8th row until there are 84(86:88) sts.
Work 29 rows straight.

Shape top

Cast off 4 sts at beg of next 16 rows: 20(22:24) sts.
Cast off rem sts.

COLLAR

Using smaller needles and B, cast on 114(118:122) sts.
Beg first row with K2, work 28 rows in K2, P2 rib.
Cast off loosely in rib.

LEFT FRONT BORDER AND REVERS

Using smaller needles and B, cast on 50 sts.
☆☆☆☆☆ **Rows 1 and 2 (turning rows):** P2, K2, turn, sl 1, rib to end.
Rows 3 and 4: ☆P2, K2, rep from ☆ once, turn, sl 1, rib to end.
Rows 5 and 6: ☆P2, K2, rep from ☆ twice, turn, sl 1, rib to end.
Cont in this way working 4 more sts before turn, for a further 10 rows. ☆☆☆☆☆
Work 10 rows in K2, P2 rib across all sts.
Cast off loosely in rib.

RIGHT FRONT BORDER AND REVERS

Using smaller needles and B, cast on 50 sts.
Row 1: P2, ☆K2, P2, rep from ☆ to end.
Work in K2, P2 rib as given for left front border from ☆☆☆☆☆ to ☆☆☆☆☆ reading K for P and P for K.
Work 3 rows straight across all sts.

Make buttonholes

Row 1: Rib 3, cast off 3, rib 7, cast off 3, rib to end.
Row 2: Rib to end, casting on 2 sts over those cast off in previous row.
Work 4 more rows in rib. Cast off loosely in rib.

ARMHOLE BORDERS

Join shoulder seams, leaving centre 42 sts at back free.
Using smaller needles, B and with RS facing, rejoin yarn at underarm. Pick up and K 114(118:122) sts evenly around armhole edge.
Work 11 rows in K2, P2 rib as given for collar.
Cast off loosely in rib.
Work 2nd armhole to match.

TO MAKE UP

Press or block as appropriate for yarn used, avoiding ribbed sections.
Set in sleeves, catching down row ends of armhole borders to cast-off groups at underarms.
Join side and sleeve seams.
Sew down shaped edges of front borders and revers to correct fronts. Place left front border behind right front border, and sew down row ends to cast-off group at front neck.
Sew cast-off edge of collar around remainder of neck, then join row ends of collar and revers for 2.5cm/1".
With RS of work facing and using 3.50mm crochet hook, rejoin B and work 1 row dc evenly around rem edge of collar and revers.
Sew on buttons to correspond with buttonholes. Using 2 strands of yarn tog, embroider 'V' sts on front, using B and C as shown.

Layette in Lacy Stitch

For the dedicated knitter – a complete layette for a new baby – including shawl, matinée jacket, dress, angel top and vest.

MEASUREMENTS

To fit newborn to 6-months-old baby

Shawl
124cm/49″ square, including edging

Matinée Jacket and Angel Top
Length from back neck 24cm/9½″
Sleeve seam 11.5cm/4½″

Dress
Length from back neck 27cm/10½″
Sleeve seam 2cm/¾″

Christening robe
Length from back neck 65.5cm/26″
Sleeve seam 13cm/5″

Vest
Actual measurement 41cm/16″
Length from back neck 26cm/10¼″
Side seam 16.5cm/6½″

Bonnet
All round face edge 29cm/11½″

Leggings
Actual measurement at widest part 56.5cm/22¼″
Depth at front 18cm/7″
Inside leg seam 24cm/9½″

Mitts
Length 12cm/4¾″

Bootees
Length 10cm/4″

MATERIALS

Shawl
240g/9oz of a washable 2-ply baby yarn
A pair each of 3¾mm and 4mm knitting needles

Matinée jacket, Dress and Angel Top
60g/3oz of a washable 2-ply baby yarn for each garment
A pair each of 2¾mm and 3¼mm knitting needles
4 small buttons for jacket
3 small buttons for dress and angel top

Christening Robe
180g/7oz of a washable 2-ply baby yarn
A pair each of 3mm and 3¼mm knitting needles
5 small buttons
75cm/30″ of narrow ribbon
2 metres/2yd of 2cm/1¾″ wide ribbon

Vest
40g/2 oz of a washable 2-ply baby yarn
A pair of 3¼mm knitting needles

1 metre/1 yd narrow ribbon

Leggings
60g/3oz of a washable 2-ply baby yarn
A pair each of 2¾mm and 3¼mm knitting needles
Waist length of shirring elastic

Bonnet
20g/1oz of a washable 2-ply baby yarn
A pair of 2¾mm and 3¼mm knitting needles
2 metres/2yd of a 2cm/¾″ wide ribbon

Bootees and Mitts
20g/1oz of a washable 2-ply baby yarn
1 metre/1 yd of narrow ribbon

Note: Alter needle size if necessary to obtain correct tension for each garment.

TENSION

26 sts and 34 rows to 10cm/4″ measured over patt worked on 4mm needles
34 sts and 44 rows to 10cm/4″ measured over patt worked on 3¼mm needles
35 sts and 42 rows to 10cm/4″ measured over st st worked on 3¼mm needles

SHAWL

CENTRE

Using larger, needles cast on 281 sts.
Row 1: K1, *yf, skpo, K2 tog, yf, K1, rep from * to end.
Row 2 and every alternate row: P to end.
Row 3: K2, *yf, skpo, K3, K2 tog, yf, K3, rep from * ending last rep with K2.
Row 5: K3, *yf, skpo, K1, K2 tog, yf, K5, rep from * ending last rep with K3.
Row 7: K4, *yf, sl 1, K2 tog, psso, yf, K7, rep from * ending last rep with K4.
Row 9, 11 and 13: K1, *skpo, K2, yf, K1, yf, K2, K2 tog, K1, rep from * to end.
Row 14: As 2nd row.
These 14 rows form patt.
Rep 14 patt rows 25 more times.
Cast off.

EDGING

Using smaller needles cast on 18 sts.
Foundation row: K6, P7, K5.
Cont in patt as follows:
Row 1: Sl 1, K2, yf, K2 tog, K2, K2 tog, yf, K5, yf, K2 tog, [yf, K1] twice.
Row 2: K6, yf, K2 tog, P7, K2, yf, K2 tog, K1.
Row 3: Sl 1, K2, yf, K2 tog, K1, [K2 tog, yf] twice, K4, yf, K2 tog, [yf, K1] twice, K2.
Row 4: K8, yf, K2 tog, P7, K2, yf, K2 tog, K1.

Remember to check your tension.

Row 5: Sl 1, K2, yf, K2 tog, [K2 tog, yf] 3 times, K3, yf, K2 tog, [yf, K1] twice, K4.
Row 6: K10, yf, K2 tog, P7, K2, yf, K2 tog, K1.
Row 7: Sl 1, K2, yf, K2 tog, K1, [K2 tog, yf] twice, K4, yf, K2 tog, [yf, K1] twice, K6.
Row 8: Cast off 8 sts kw, K3, yf, K2 tog, P7, K2, yf, K2 tog, K1.
These 8 rows form edging patt.
Cont in patt until edging fits all round outer edges of centre, allowing for gathering at corners.
Cast off.

TO MAKE UP
Block, but do not press.
Join cast-on and cast-off edges of edging. Sew straight row ends to outer edges of centre, gathering edging at corners to keep Shawl flat.

MATINÉE JACKET
MAIN PART
(worked in one piece to armholes)
Using smaller needles, cast on 253 sts.
Work 7 rows in g st.
Change to larger needles.
Cont in patt as follows:
Row 1: K6, work as given for first patt row of shawl centre to last 6 sts, K6.
Row 2: K6, work as given for 2nd patt row of shawl centre to last 6 sts, K6.
Cont working as given for shawl centre, keeping 6 sts at each end in g st for front borders, until 4 complete patts and first 6 rows of 5th patt have been completed.
Divide sts for back and fronts
New row: K6, patt 58 sts and leave these 64 sts on a spare needle for right front, cast off 4 sts for underarm, patt 116 sts and leave these 117 sts on a spare needle for back, cast off 4 sts for underarm, patt to end.
Work on last set of 64 sts for left front as follows:
Keeping patt correct and 6 sts in g st for front border, dec 1 st at armhole edge on next 7 rows: 57 sts.
Break off yarn and leave these sts on a holder for yoke.
With WS of work facing, rejoin yarn to inner edge of 117 sts on holder for back.
Dec 1 st at each end of next 7 rows: 103 sts.
Break off yarn and leave these sts on a holder for yoke.
With WS of work facing, rejoin yarn to inner edge of 64 sts on spare needle for right front.
Work as given for left front.

SLEEVES
Using smaller needles cast on 33 sts.
Work 3 rows in g st.
Inc row: K2, *inc in next st, rep from * to last 3 sts, K3: 61 sts.

Change to larger needles.
Cont working in patt as given for shawl centre until 3 complete patts and 6th row of 4th patt have been completed, dec 1 st at end of last row: 60 sts.
Shape top
Rows 1 and 2: Keeping patt correct, cast off 3 sts, patt to end.
Row 3: Work 3 tog, patt to last 3 sts, work 3 tog: 50 sts.
Rep 3rd row twice more: 42 sts.
Dec 1 st at each end of next 2 rows: 38 sts.
Patt 1 row.
Break off yarn and leave sts on a holder for yoke.

YOKE
With WS of work facing, sl all sts onto a larger needle as follows:
left front, first sleeve, back, 2nd sleeve and right front: 293 sts.
Rejoin yarn and cont as follows:
Next row: K1, K2 tog, yrn (first buttonhole), K3, [K2 tog] 24 times, K3 across right front; K2 tog, K34, K2 tog across first sleeve; K3, [K2 tog] 49 times, K2 across back; K2 tog, K34, K2 tog across 2nd sleeve; K3, [K2 tog] 24 times, K6 across left front: 192 sts.
✩✩ Work 11 rows in g st.
Shape yoke
First dec row: K1, K2 tog, yrn (buttonhole), K3, ✩K2 tog, K1, rep from ✩ to last 6 sts, K6: 132 sts.
Work 11 rows in g st.
Next row: Rep first dec row: 92 sts.
Work 11 rows in g st.
2nd dec row: K7, ✩K2 tog, K1, rep from ✩ to last 7 sts, K7: 66 sts. ✩✩
First and 2nd turning rows: K to last 18 sts (first row), sl 1, K to last 18 sts (2nd row), turn.
3rd and 4th turning rows: Sl 1, K to last 24 sts, (3rd row), turn, sl 1, K to last 24 sts (4th row), turn.
Next row: Sl 1, K across all sts to end of row.
✩✩✩ Change to smaller needles.
Work 4 rows in g st, making a buttonhole as before at beg of 3rd row.
Cast off loosely. ✩✩✩

TO MAKE UP
Block, but do not press.
Join sleeve seams. Join tiny underarm seams.
Sew on buttons to correspond with buttonholes.

DRESS
MAIN PART
(worked in one place to armholes)
Using smaller needles cast on 241 sts.
Work 7 rows in g st.

Change to larger needles.

Work 76 rows in patt as given for shawl centre.

Divide sts for back and fronts

Patt 62 sts and leave these sts on a spare needle for left back, cast off 3 sts for underarm, patt across 110 sts and leave these 111 sts on spare needle for front, cast off 3 sts for underarm, patt to end.

Work on last set of 62 sts for right back as follows:

Keeping patt correct, dec 1 st at armhole edge on next 7 rows: 55 sts.

Break off yarn and leave these sts on a holder for yoke.

With WS of work facing, rejoin yarn to inner edge of 111 sts on spare needle for front.

Dec 1 st at each end of next 7 rows: 97 sts.

Break off yarn and leave these sts on holder for yoke.

With WS of work facing, rejoin yarn to inner edge of rem 62 sts on spare needle for left back, and complete to match right back.

SLEEVES

Using smaller needles cast on 41 sts.

Work 3 rows in g st.

Inc row: [K1, inc in next st] 20 times, K1: 61 sts.

Change to larger needles.

Work 6 rows in patt as given for shawl centre, dec 1 st at end of last row: 60 sts.

Shape top

Work as given for sleeve top of matinée jacket.

YOKE

With WS of work facing, sl all sts onto a larger needle as follows:

right back, first sleeve, front, 2nd sleeve, left back: 283 sts.

Rejoin yarn and cont as follows:

Next row: K7, [K2 tog] 24 times across left back; K2 tog, K34, K2 tog across first sleeve; K6, [K2 tog] 43 times, K5 across front; K2 tog, K34, K2 tog, across 2nd sleeve; [K2 tog] 26 times, K3 across right back, turn and cast on 6 sts for underflap: 192 sts.

Work as given for jacket yoke from ✿✿ to ✿✿.

✿✿✿✿ **First and 2nd turning rows:** K18 (first row), turn, sl 1, K to end (2nd row).

3rd and 4th turning rows: K11 (3rd row), turn, sl 1, K to end (4th row). ✿✿✿✿

Next row: K across all sts to end of row.

Rep from ✿✿✿✿ to ✿✿✿✿ once more.

Complete as given for matinée jacket, working from ✿✿✿ to ✿✿✿.

TO MAKE UP

Block, but do not press.

Join sleeve seams. Join tiny underarm seams.

Join back seam as far as yoke, then catch base of

underflap to WS.

Sew on buttons to correspond with buttonholes.

ANGEL TOP
MAIN PART

Work as given for main part of dress, but working 62 rows in patt instead of 76 before dividing sts for front and backs.

SLEEVES

Work as given for sleeves of matinée jacket, leaving 38 sts on a spare needle.

YOKE

Work as given for yoke of dress.

TO MAKE UP

As given for dress.

CHRISTENING ROBE
MAIN PART
(worked in one piece to armholes)

Using larger needles cast on 411 sts.

Work 5 rows in g st.

Work 223 rows in patt as given for shawl centre, ending with a 13th patt row and inc 1 st at end of last row: 412 sts.

Change to smaller needles.

Dec for waist as follows:

Next row: (WS): Cast on 6 sts for button under-flap, K these 6 sts, ✿K2 tog, K3 tog, pass K2 tog over K3 tog (4 sts dec) ✿, [K3 tog] 132 times, rep from ✿ to ✿ once more, K6 for buttonhole border: 146 sts.

Work 2 rows in g st.

Buttonhole and eyelet row: K3, yf, K2 tog (buttonhole), K2, ✿K2 tog, yf, rep from ✿ to last 7 sts, K7: 146 sts.

Work 3 rows in g st.

Cont working yoke patt as follows:

Row 1: K6, P2, ✿K2, yf, K2 tog, P2, rep from ✿ to last 6 sts, K6.

Row 2: K8, ✿P2, yrn, P2 tog, k2, rep from ✿ to last 6 sts, K6.

These 2 rows form yoke patt, Keeping 6 sts at each end in g st for buttonhole and button borders, rep 2 patt rows 4 more times.

Make buttonholes

Next row: K3, yf, K2 tog, K1, P2, ✿K2, yf, K2 tog, P2, rep from ✿ to last 6 sts, K6.

Divide sts for front and backs (WS)

Keeping patt correct, K6, patt 28 sts and leave these 34 sts on a spare needle for right back, cast off 8 sts for underarm, patt 61 sts and leave these 62 sts on a spare needle for front, cast off 8 sts for underarm, patt to end.

Cont on last set of 34 sts for left back as follows:
Keeping patt correct, dec 1 st at armhole edge on next row and 6 foll alternate rows, working button hole on last row: 27 sts.
Work 18 rows in patt, working a buttonhole on 14th row.

Shape shoulder

Keeping patt correct, cast off 4 sts at beg of next and 2 foll alternate rows: 15 sts.
Leave rem sts on a holder for neckband.
With RS facing, rejoin yarn to inner edge of 62 sts on spare needle for front and cont as follows:
Keeping patt correct, dec 1 st at each end of next and 6 foll alternate rows: 48 sts.
Work 4 rows in patt.

Divide sts for neck

Next row: Patt 18 sts and leave these sts on a spare needle for right front shoulder, patt next 12 sts and leave them on a holder for neckband, patt to end.
Cont on last set of 18 sts for left front shoulder as follows:

Shape neck

Dec 1 st at neck edge on next and 5 foll alternate rows: 12 sts.
Patt 1 row.

Shape shoulder

Cast off 4 sts at beg of next and foll alternate row: 4 sts.
Work 1 row. Cast off rem sts.
With RS of work facing, rejoin yarn to inner edge of 18 sts on spare needle for right front shoulder, and complete as given for left front shoulder, working 2 rows instead of 1 before shaping shoulder.
With RS of work facing rejoin yarn to inner edge of 34 sts on spare needle for right back and work as given for left back, omitting buttonholes, but working 17 rows instead of 18 before shaping shoulder and working 1 more row before leaving sts on holder for neckband.

SLEEVES

Using smaller needles, cast on 30 sts.
Work 8 rows in g st.
Inc row: K1, *inc in next st, K1, rep from * to last st, K1: 44 sts.
Cont working in patt as follows:
Row 1 (RS): P2, *K2, yf, K2 tog, P2, rep from * to end.
Row 2: K2, *P2, yrn, P2 tog, K2, rep from * to end.
These 2 rows form patt.
Work 40 more rows in patt.

Shape top

Keeping patt correct, cast off 4 sts at beg of next 2 rows. Dec 1 st at each end of next and 6 foll alternate rows: 22 sts.
Work 1 row. Cast off 2 sts at beg of next 6 rows: 10 sts.

Cast off rem sts.

NECKBAND

Join shoulder seams.
With RS facing and using smaller needles, K across 15 sts of left back neck, pick up and K 12 sts down left front neck, K across 12 sts on holder at centre front, pick up and K 12 sts up right front neck and K across 15 sts of right back neck: 66 sts.
Work 7 rows in g st, working a buttonhole on 4th row as before. Cast off.

FRILL

Using larger needles cast on 6 sts.
K 1 row.
Cont in patt as follows:
Row 1: K2, yf, K2 tog, yf, K2.
Row 2: K2, [yf, K1] twice, yf, K2 tog, K1.
Row 3: K2, yf, K2 tog, yf, K3, yf, K2.
Row 4: K2, yf, K5, yf, K1, yf, K2 tog, K1.
Row 5: K2, yf, K2 tog, yf, skpo, K3, K2 tog, yf, K2.
Row 6: K3, yf, skpo, K1, K2 tog, yf, K2, yf, K2 tog, K1.
Row 7: K2, yf, K2 tog, K2, yf, sl 1, K2 tog, psso, yf, K4.
Row 8: Cast off 7 sts, K2, yf, K2 tog, K1.
These 8 rows form patt.
Cont in patt until frill fits all round lower edge of skirt, casting off after 8th patt row.

TO MAKE UP

Block, but do not press.
Join sleeve seams. Set in sleeves. Close back seam as far as waist, then catch base of underflap to WS.
Sew on buttons to correspond with buttonholes.
Thread narrow ribbon through eyelet holes at waist and catch ends tog. Make a bow with wider ribbon, leaving ends to hang. Sew to centre-front at waist.
Join cast-on and cast-off edges of frill and sew to WS of lower edge, sewing straight edge of frill to last row of g st edging on skirt, leaving g st free.

VEST

Using needles as stated cast on 72 sts.
Work 5 rows in g st.
Beg with a K row work 58 rows in st st.

Shape sleeves

Inc 1 st at each end of next and 3 foll alternate rows.
P 1 row.
Cast on 10 sts at beg of next 2 rows: 100 sts.
Next row: K to end.
Next row: K4, P to last 4 sts, K4.
Rep last 2 rows 14 more times, then first row again.

Back neck border

Row 1: K4, P33, K26, P33, K4.
Row 2: K to end.

Rep last 2 rows twice more.

Divide for fronts

Next row: K4, P33, K4 and leave these 41 sts on a spare needle for left front, cast off 18 sts, K3 sts, P33, K4 and work on these last 41 sts for right front as follows:

Row 1: K to last 6 sts, inc 1, K5.

Row 2: K4, P to last 4 sts, K4.

Keeping 4 sts at each end in g st, work 10 rows in st st.

Shape front edge

Row 1: K to last 6 sts, inc 1, K5.

Row 2: K4, P to last 4 sts, K4.

Rep these 2 rows 12 times: 55 sts.

✿✿ **Shape sleeves**

Cast off 10 sts at beg of next row. Dec 1 st at same edge on each of 4 foll RS rows *at the same time*, cont inc 1 st at front edge as before on every RS row until 8 more inc rows have been worked: 49 sts.

Keeping 4 sts in g st at front edge, work 52 more rows in st st.

Work 5 rows in g st. Cast off.

With RS of work facing, rejoin yarn to inner edge of 41 sts on spare needle for left front and cont as follows:

Row 1: K4, inc 1, K to end.

Row 2: K4, P to last 4 sts, K4.

Keeping 4 sts at each end in g st, work 10 rows in st st.

Shape front edge

Row 1: K4, inc 1, K to end.

Row 2: K4, P to last 4 sts, K4.

Rep last 2 rows 11 more times, then first row again: 55 sts.

Work as given for right front from ✿✿ to end.

TO MAKE UP

Block, but do not press.

Join side and sleeve seams.

Sew 2 lengths of narrow ribbon to straight front edge of right front. Fold right front over left front, then sew 2 lengths of ribbon to left front to correspond.

LEGGINGS
RIGHT LEG

Using smaller needles, cast on 88 sts.

Work 12 rows in K1, P1 rib, inc 1 st at end of last row: 89 sts.

Change to larger needles.

Beg with a K row cont in st st. Work 2 rows straight.

Shape back

Rows 1 and 2: Work 11 sts, turn, sl 1, work to end.

Rows 3 and 4: Work 18 sts, turn, sl 1, work to end.

Rep 3rd and 4th rows 4 more times, working 7 sts more on each successive rep of 3rd row.

Cont in st st across all sts, inc 1 st at beg (back edge) of 3rd and at same edge on every foll 6th row until there are 99 sts.

Work 7 rows straight. (Mark each end of last row with a contrasting thread for crotch.)

Shape leg

Dec 1 st at each end of next and every foll 3rd row until 47 sts rem.

Work 2 rows straight. ✿✿

Shape instep

Next row: K40, turn and leave rem 7 sts on a safety-pin, P18, turn and leave rem 22 sts on a holder.

Work 16 rows straight in st st on these 18 sts.

Break off yarn.

With RS facing, rejoin yarn to rem sts and pick up and K 16 sts from one side of instep, K across 18 instep sts, pick up and K 16 sts from other side of instep and finally K 7 sts from safety-pin.

Next row: K to end, K22 sts from holder: 79 sts.

✿✿✿ K 12 rows.

Shape foot

Row 1: K5, K3 tog, K4, K3 tog, K25, K3 tog, K13, K3 tog, K20.

K 1 row.

Row 3: K4, K3 tog, K2, K3 tog, K23, K3 tog, K11, K3 tog, K19.

K 1 row.

Row 5: K3, [K3 tog] twice, K21, K3 tog, K9, K3 tog, K18: 55 sts.

K 1 row. Cast off rem sts.

LEFT LEG

Work as given for right leg to ✿✿ working 1 row instead of 2 before shaping instep.

Shape instep

Next row: K25, turn and leave rem 22 sts on a holder, P18, turn and leave rem 7 sts on a safety-pin.

Work 16 rows straight on these 18 sts. Break off yarn.

With RS facing, rejoin yarn to rem sts, pick up and K 16 sts from one side of instep, K across 18 instep sts, pick up and K 16 sts from other side of instep and finally K across 22 sts from holder.

Next row K to end, K 7 sts from safety-pin: 79 sts.

Work as given for right leg from ✿✿✿ working 13 rows instead of 12 before shaping foot.

TO MAKE UP

Block or press as appropriate for yarn used.

Join back and front seams as far as markers.

Join leg seams.

Beg at centre of toe end, join underfoot seam.

Run 5 rows of shirring elastic through WS of waist ribbing.

BONNET

Using larger needles, cast on 91 sts.
Work 5 rows in g st.
Work 14 rows in patt as given for shawl centre.
Work 9 rows in K1, P1 rib, beg first row with K1 and 2nd row with P1.
Beg with a K row (to reverse work) work 40 rows in st st.
Work 4 rows in g st.

Shape crown
Row 1: [K7, K2 tog] 10 times, K1: 81 sts.
Row 2: K to end.
Rep last 2 rows 7 more times, working 1 st less before dec on each successive rep: 11 sts.
Break off yarn leaving a long end. Run end through rem sts, draw up and fasten off. Join row ends across crown shaping only.

TO MAKE UP

Fold back patt rows to form a brim, then sew in place at each end.

Edging
Using smaller needles, rejoin yarn and pick up and K 80 sts along row ends of bonnet, working through double thickness at brim.
Work 6 rows in K1, P1 rib. Cast off in rib.
Cut ribbon into 2 pieces. Form 1 end of each into a rosette and sew rosette to each side of face edge.

BOOTEES

Using specified needles, cast on 41 sts.
Work 5 rows in g st.
Work 14 rows in patt as given for shawl centre.
Beg with a K row work 4 rows in st st, dec 1 st at end of last row: 40 sts.
Eyelet row: ☆K2, yf, K2 tog, rep from ☆ to end.
Next row: P to end. ☆☆
Next row K6, [K2 tog, K11] twice, K2 tog, K6: 37 sts.
Next row: P to end.

Divide for instep
Next row: K24, turn and leave rem 13 sts on a safety-pin, P11 and leave rem 13 sts on a safety-pin.
Work 16 rows in st st on these 11 sts. Break off yarn.

With RS facing, rejoin yarn and pick up and K 12 sts along one side of instep, K across 11 instep sts, pick up and K 12 sts from other side of instep and finally K 13 sts from safety-pin.
Next row: K to end, K 13 sts from other safety-pin: 61 sts.
Work 12 rows in g st.

Shape foot
Row 1: K2 tog, K23, K2 tog, K7, K2 tog, K23, K2 tog: 57 sts.
K 1 row.
Row 3: K2 tog, K22, K2 tog, K5, K2 tog, K22, K2 tog: 53 sts.
K 1 row.
Row 5: K2 tog, K21, K2 tog, K3, K2 tog, K21, K2 tog: 49 sts.
K 1 row.
Row 7: K2 tog, K20, K2 tog, K1, K2 tog, K20, K2 tog: 45 sts.
K 1 row. Cast off rem sts.
Make 2nd bootee in same way.

TO MAKE UP

Fold cast-off edge in half and join underfoot and back seam.
Thread ribbon through eyelets.

MITTS

Work as given for bootees to ☆☆.
Work 22 rows in st st.

Shape top
Row 1: [K2, K2 tog] 10 times: 30 sts.
Row 2: P to end.
Row 3: [K1, K2 tog] 10 times: 20 sts.
Row 4: P to end.
Row 5: [K2 tog] 10 times: 10 sts.
Break off yarn. Run end through rem sts, draw up and fasten off.
Make 2nd mitt in same way.

TO MAKE UP

Join seam. Thread ribbon through eyelet holes.

MATINEE JACKET

sleeve

1 FRONT OR BACK

2 BACK OR FRONT

3 FRONT OR BACK

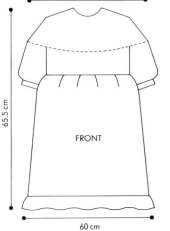

DRESS

FRONT

BACK

VEST

CHRISTENING ROBE

FRONT

BACK OPENING

SLEEVE

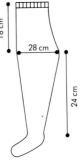

LEGGINGS

Christening Robe

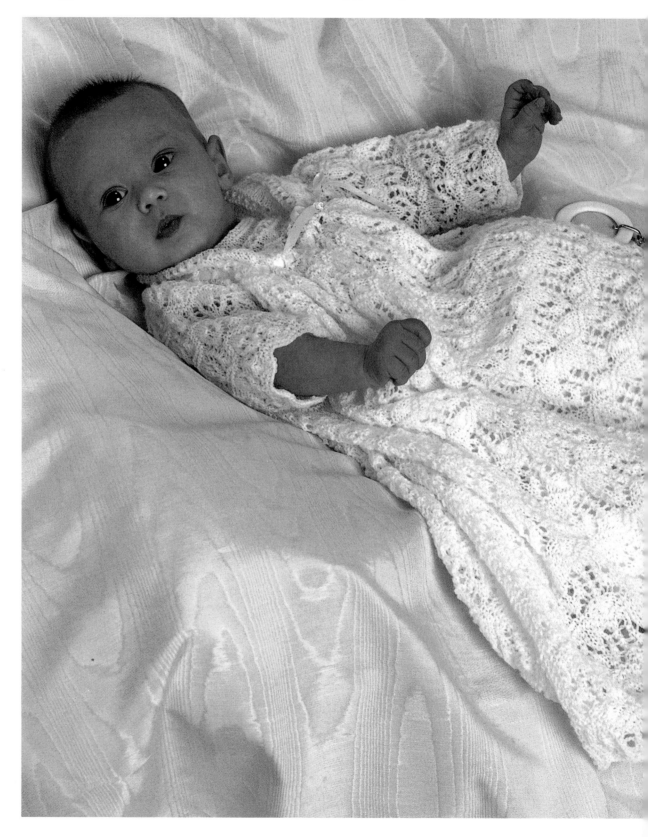

An exquisite design in delicate 2-ply yarn, for that special occasion.

MEASUREMENTS

To fit chest 46(48:51)cm/18(19:20)"
Actual measurements 122(130:138)cm/48(51:54½)"
Length from shoulders 56(59:64)cm/22(23¼:25¼)"
Sleeve seam 14(15:17)cm/5½(6:6¾)"
Instructions are given for smallest size first, with larger sizes in ( ).

MATERIALS

120(120:160)g/5(5:6)oz of a 2-ply baby yarn
A pair each of 2¾mm, 3¼mm and 3¾mm knitting needles (or sizes to obtain correct tension)
3 buttons
1.3 metres/1½ yards baby ribbon

TENSION

1 patt repeat (10 sts) measures 4cm/1½" worked on larger needles.
10 rows to 5cm/2" measured over patt worked on larger needles.

Remember to check your tension.

INSTRUCTIONS

BACK AND FRONT (alike)

Using largest needles cast on 153(163:173) sts.
Row 1: Sl 1, K to end.
Rows 2–5: As row 1.
Row 6: Sl 1, P1, ☆yrn, P3, P3 tog, P3, yrn, P1, rep from ☆ to last st, K1.
Row 7: Sl 1, K2, ☆yf, K2, sl 1, K2 tog, psso, K2, yf, K3, rep from ☆ to end.
Row 8: Sl 1, P3, ☆yrn, P1, P3 tog, P1, yrn, P5, rep from ☆ to last 9 sts, yrn, P1, P3 tog, P1, yrn, P3, K1.
Row 9: Sl 1, K4, ☆yf, sl 1, K2 tog, psso, yf, K7, rep from ☆ to last 8 sts, yf, sl 1, K2 tog, psso, yf, K5.
Row 10: Sl 1, P2, ☆K2, P3, rep from ☆ to last 5 sts, K2, P2, K1.
Row 11: Sl 1, K1, ☆yf, skpo, P1, yon, sl 1, K2 tog, psso, yrn, P1, K2 tog, yf, K1, rep from ☆ to last st, K1.
Row 12: Sl 1, P3, ☆K1, P3, K1, P5, rep from ☆ to last 9 sts, K1, P3, K1, P3, K1.
Row 13: Sl 1, K2, ☆yf, skpo, yf, sl 1, K2 tog, psso, yf, K2 tog, yf, K3, rep from ☆ to end.
Row 14: Sl 1, P2, ☆K1, P5, K1, P3, rep from ☆ to last 10 sts, K1, P5, K1, P2, K1.
Row 15: Sl 1, K2, ☆P1, K1, yf, sl 1, K2 tog, psso, yf, K1, P1, K3, rep from ☆ to end.
Row 16: Sl 1, P2, ☆K1, P5, K1, P3, rep from ☆ to last 10 sts, K1, P5, K1, P2, K1.
These 16 rows form the patt.
Cont in patt until work measures 25(27:30)cm/9¾ (10½:11¾)" from beg, ending with a wrong-side row.

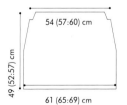

54 (57:60) cm

49 (52:57) cm

61 (65:69) cm

22 (22:26) cm

19 (20:22) cm

Change to medium-sized needles.
Cont in patt until work measures 44(47:52)cm/
17¼(18½:20½)" from beg, ending with a wrong-side
row.

Shape armholes
Cast off 8 sts at beg of next 2 rows.
Keeping patt correct, dec 1 st at each end of next and
every foll alternate row until 127(137:147) sts remain.
Break off yarn and leave these sts on a spare needle.

SLEEVES
Using medium-sized needles cast on 63(63:73) sts.
Work in patt as given for back and front until sleeve
measures 14(15:17)cm/5½(6:6¾)" from beg, ending
with a wrong-side row.

Shape top
Cast off 8 sts at beg of next 2 rows.
Keeping patt correct, dec 1 st at each end of next and
every foll alternate row until 37(37:47) sts remain.
Break off yarn and leave these sts on a spare needle.

YOKE
1st and 2nd sizes only
With right side facing slip the first 66(71) sts of back
onto a holder, join yarn to next st, and using
medium-sized needles cast on 5 sts. K across these 5
sts, then work across rem 61(66) sts of back as follows:
[K2 tog] 8(12) times, [K3 tog] 15(14) times, now work
across 37 sts from top of first sleeve as follows: K1, [K2
tog, K2] 9 times, work across 127(137) sts of front as
follows: [K3 tog] 13(12) times, [K2 tog] 23(31) times,
[K3 tog] 14(13) times, work across 37 sts of second
sleeve as follows: [K2, K2 tog] 9 times, K1, then work
across 66(71) sts from holder on back as follows: [K3
tog] 15(14)times, [K2 tog] 8(12) times, K5: 162(174) sts.
3rd size only
With right side facing slip the first 76 sts of back onto a
holder, join yarn to next st, and using medium-sized
needles cast on 5 sts, K across these 5 sts then work
across remaining 71 sts of back as follows: [K2 tog] 16
times, [K3 tog] 13 times, now work across 47 sts from
top of first sleeve as follows: [K2 tog] 5 times, [K1, K2
tog] 9 times, [K2 tog] 5 times, work across 147 sts of
front as follows: [K3 tog] 11 times, [K2 tog] 39 times,
[K3 tog] 12 times, work across 47 sts of second sleeve
as follows: [K2 tog] 5 times, [K2 tog, K1] 9 times, [K2
tog] 5 times, then work across 76 sts from holder on
back as follows: [K3 tog] 13 times, [K2 tog] 16 times, K5:
186 sts.
All sizes
Row 1: Sl 1, K to end.
Row 2: As row 1.
Row 3: Sl 1, K4, ✷yrn, P2 tog, rep from ✷ to last 5 sts, K5.

Rows 4–6: As row 1.
Row 7: Sl 1, K4, P to last 5 sts, K5.
Row 8: Sl 1, K4, [K1, K2 tog] 7(8:9) times, K31, [K2 tog,
K1] 16(18:20) times, K31, [K2 tog, K1] 7(8:9) times, K5:
132(140:148) sts.
Row 9: Sl 1, K4, P to last 5 sts, K5.
Row 10: Sl 1, K to last 3 sts, yf, K2 tog, K1.
Rows 11 and 12: Rep row 1 twice.
Row 13: As row 3.
Rows 14–16: Rep row 1 three times.
Row 17: As row 7.
Row 18: Sl 1, K4, [K2 tog, K2] 12(13:14) times, [K2 tog,
K3] 4 times, [K2 tog, K2] 13(14:15) times, K2 tog, K5:
102(108:114) sts.
Row 19: Sl 1, K4, P to last 5 sts, K5.
Row 20: Sl 1, K to last 3 sts, yf, K2 tog, K1.
Rows 21 and 22: Rep row 1 twice.
Row 23: As row 3.
Rows 24–26: Rep row 1 three times.
Row 27: As row 7.
Row 28: Sl 1, K4, [K2 tog, K3] 18(19:20) times, K2 tog,
K5(6:7): 83(88:93) sts.
Row 29: Sl 1, K4, P to last 5 sts, K5.
Change to smallest needles.
Next row: Sl 1, K to last 3 sts, yf, K2 tog, K1.
Next row: Sl 1, K to end.
Rep the last row 3 more times.
Cast off.

TO MAKE UP
Press or block as appropriate for yarn used. Join
semi-raglan seams up to yoke. Join side and sleeve
seams. Sew on buttons. Thread ribbon through first
cyelet hole row on yoke, keeping ends at the front. Tie
into a bow at front.

Big Top

A smart bomber jacket-style cardigan in a brilliantly coloured abstract design knitted in warm double knitting yarn.

MEASUREMENTS

To fit chest 56(61:64)cm/22(24:25)″
Actual measurements 64(68:72)cm/25¼(26¾:28¼)″
Length from shoulders 32(35:38)cm/12½(13¾:15)″
Sleeve seam 26(28:32)cm/10¼(11:12½)″
Instructions are given for smallest size first, with larger sizes in ( ).

MATERIALS

100(100:150)g/4(4:6)oz of a double knitting yarn in main colour A
100g/4oz of same in each of contrasting colours B and C
50g/2oz of same in each of contrasting colours D and E
A pair each of 3¼mm and 4mm knitting needles (or sizes to obtain correct tension)
6 buttons

Remember to check your tension.

TENSION

24 sts and 28 rows to 10cm/4″ measured over st st worked on larger needles.

INSTRUCTIONS

BACK

Using smaller needles and A, cast on 72(76:80) sts.
Work 4cm/1½″ in K1, P1 rib, ending with a RS row.
Inc row: P11(10:10), ✶inc in next st, P9(10:11), rep from ✶ to last 11(11:10) sts, inc in next st, P to end: 78(82:86) sts.
Change to larger needles.
Reading odd-numbered (K) rows from right to left and even-numbered (P) rows from left to right, work in patt from chart for back, working armhole and shoulder shaping as indicated.

RIGHT FRONT

Using smaller needles and A, cast on 36(38:40) sts.
Work 4cm/1½″ in K1, P1, rib, ending with a right-side row.
Inc row: P8, [inc in next st, P9] twice, inc in next st, P7(9:11): 39(41:43) sts.
Change to larger needles.
Work in patt from chart for right front, working armhole and neck shaping as indicated.

LEFT FRONT

Work as given for right front, following chart for left front.

SLEEVES

Using smaller needles and A, cast on 42(48:48) sts.
Work 6cm/2½″ in K1, P1, rib, ending with a right-side row.
Inc row: P6, ✶inc in next st, P5(4:4), rep from ✶ to last 6(7:7) sts, inc in next st, P5(6:6): 48(56:56) sts.
Change to larger needles.
Work in patt from chart for sleeve, working increases as indicated.

BUTTONHOLE BORDER

With RS facing, using smaller needles and A, pick up and K74(84:94) sts up right front to beg of neck shaping.
Work 3 rows K1, P1 rib.
Buttonhole row (RS): Rib 4, ✶yrn, P2 tog, rib 10(12:14), rep from ✶ to last 8 sts, yrn, P2 tog, rib to end.
Rib 3 more rows.
Cast off in rib.

BUTTON BORDER

Work as given for buttonhole border, picking up sts down left front edge and omitting buttonholes.

NECKBAND

Join shoulder seams.
With RS facing, using smaller needles and A, pick up and K6 sts across buttonhole border, 19 sts up right side of front neck, 28 sts across back neck, 19 sts down left side of front neck, then 6 sts across button border: 78 sts.
Work 3cm/1¼″ in K1, P1 rib.
Cast off in rib.

TO MAKE UP

Press or block as appropriate for yarn used. Sew in sleeves, then join side and sleeve seams. Sew on buttons.

designed by Annabel Fox [ES]

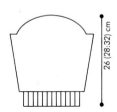

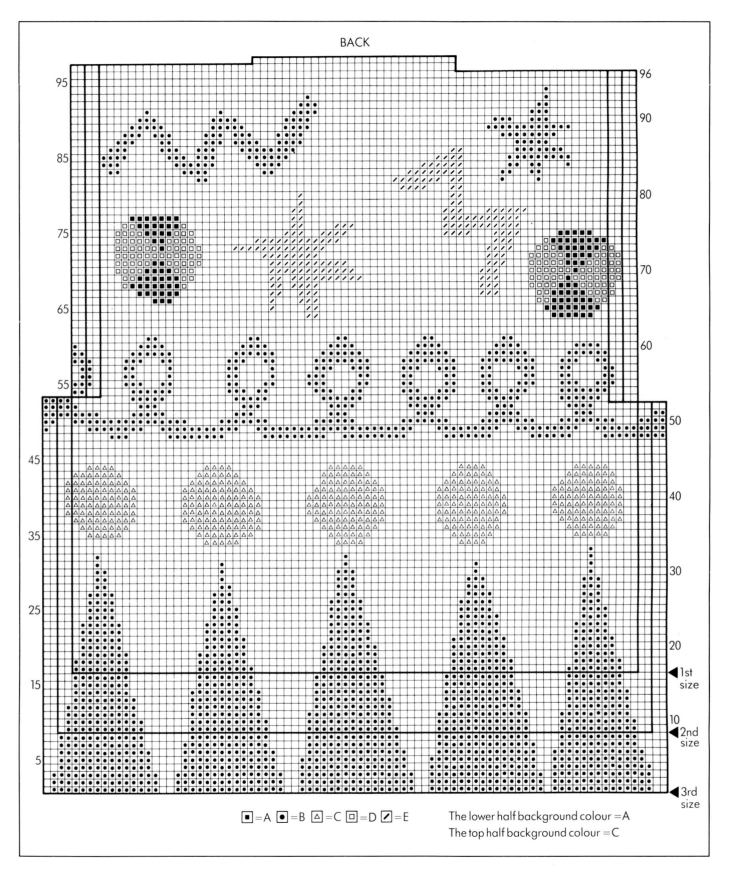

BACK

■ = A   ● = B   △ = C   ▣ = D   ╱ = E

The lower half background colour = A
The top half background colour = C

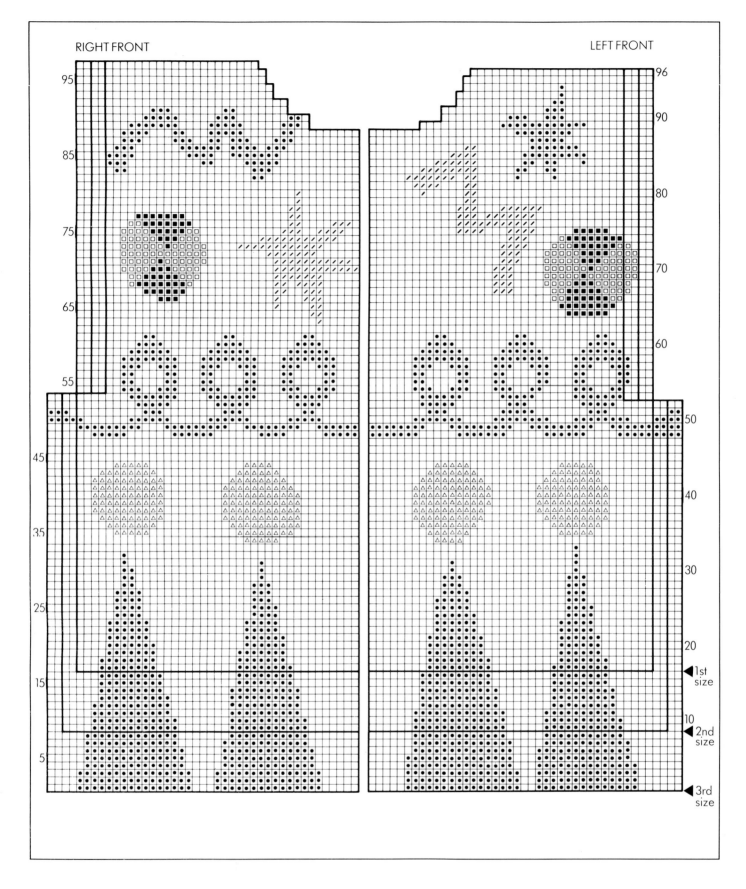

RIGHT FRONT

LEFT FRONT

SLEEVE

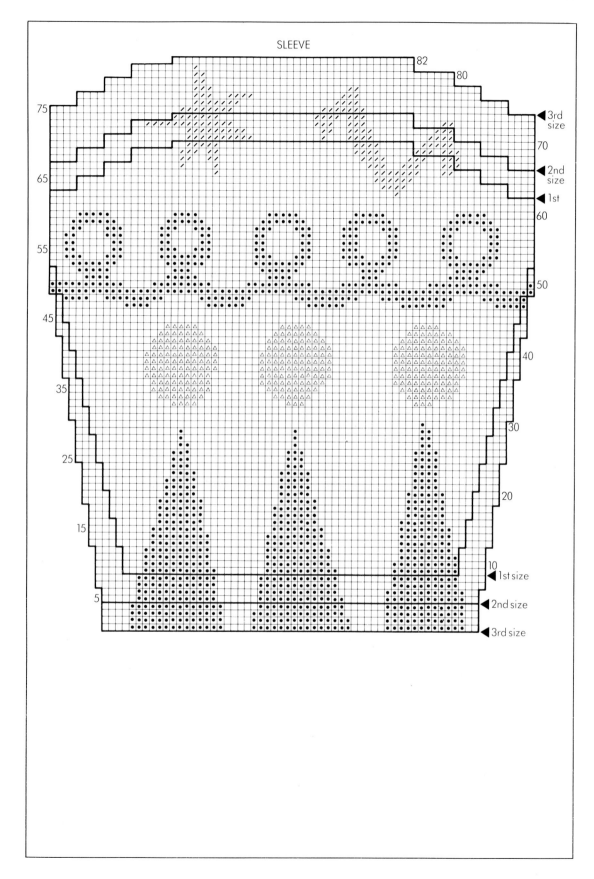

Basketweave

A round-neck pullover with shoulder fastening. The interesting woven effect is created by interweaving moss, stocking and reverse stocking stitch.

MEASUREMENTS

To fit chest 46–51(51–56)cm/18–20(20–22)″
Actual measurements 52(64)cm/20½(25)″
Length from shoulders 28(31)cm/11(12¼)″
Sleeve seam 21(23)cm/8¼(9)″
Instructions are given for smallest size first, with larger size in ( ).

MATERIALS

150(200)g/6(7)oz of a 4-ply yarn
A pair each of 2¼mm and 3mm knitting needles (or sizes to obtain correct tension)
4 buttons

Remember to check your tension.

TENSION

36 sts and 48 rows to 10cm/4″ measured over patt worked on larger needles.

INSTRUCTIONS

BACK

Using smaller needles cast on 94(114) sts.
Row 1: K2, ✫P2, K2, rep from ✫ to end.
Row 2: K1, P1, ✫K2, P2, rep from ✫ to last 4 sts, K2, P1, K1.
Rep these 2 rows for 4cm/1½″, ending with rib row 1.
Inc row: Rib 16(24), ✫inc in next st, rib 15, rep from ✫ to last 14(26) sts, inc in next st, rib to end: 99(119) sts.
Change to larger needles.
Cont in patt as foll:
Row 1: K2, ✫[K1, P1] twice, K6, rep from ✫ to last 7 sts, [K1, P1] twice, K3.
Row 2: K1, P1, ✫[K1, P1] twice, K1, P5, rep from ✫ to last 7 sts, [K1, P1] twice, K1, P1, K1.
Rows 3–8: Rep rows 1 and 2 three times.
Row 9: K2, P15(5), ✫K5, P15, rep from ✫ to last 22(12) sts, K5, P15(5), K2.
Row 10: K1, P1, K15(5), ✫P5, K15, rep from ✫ to last 22(12) sts, P5, K15(5), P1, K1.
Rows 11–14: Rep rows 9 and 10 twice.
Rows 15–22: Rep rows 1 and 2 four times.
Row 23: K2, P5(15), ✫K5, P15, rep from ✫ to last 12(22) sts, K5, P5(15), K2.
Row 24: K1, P1, K5(15), ✫P5, K15, rep from ✫ to last 12(22) sts, P5, K5(15), P1, K1.
Rows 25–28: Rep rows 23 and 24 twice.
These 28 rows form the patt.
Cont in patt until back measures approximately

26(29)cm/10¼(11½)″ from beg, ending with row 18(4).
Shape neck
Next row: Patt across 35(41) sts, turn and leave rem sts on a spare needle.
Keeping patt correct, dec 1 st at neck edge on every row until 27(33) sts remain.
Cast off.
Return to sts on spare needle.
With right side facing, sl first 29(37) sts onto a holder, rejoin yarn to next st and using smaller needles, work in moss st to end of row.
Cont in moss st, dec 1 st at neck edge on every row until 27(33) sts rem.
Cast off.

FRONT

Work as given for back until 22 rows less than back to shoulders have been worked, ending with row 6(20).
Shape neck
Next row: Patt across 39(45) sts, turn and leave rem sts on a spare needle.
Keeping patt correct, dec 1 st at neck edge on every row until 27(33) sts remain.
Work straight until front measures same as back to shoulders.
Change to smaller needles and work buttonhole border as follows:
Work 4 rows moss st.
Next row (buttonhole row): Moss st 7(9), ✫yrn, sl 1, K1, psso, moss st 6(8), rep from ✫ once more, yrn, sl 1, K1, psso, moss st 2.
Work 3 rows moss st.
Cast off.
Return to sts on spare needle.
With right side facing, slip first 21(29) sts onto a holder, rejoin yarn and patt to end.
Keeping patt correct, dec 1 st at neck edge on every row until 27(33) sts remain.
Work straight until front measures same as back to right shoulder, ending with a wrong-side row.
Cast off.

SLEEVES

Using smaller needles cast on 46(54) sts.
Work 4cm/1½″ in rib as given for back, ending with rib row 1.
Inc row: Rib 4(2), ✫inc in next st, rib 2(11), rep from ✫ to last 5(3) sts, inc in next st, rib 4(2): 59 sts.
Change to larger needles.
Now working in patt as given for first size of back, inc

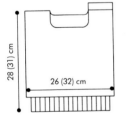

and work into patt 1 st within the 2 st border at each end of 5th and every following 4th row until there are 79(89) sts.

Work straight until sleeve measures approximately 21(23)cm/8¼(9)″ from beg, ending with row 28(8). Cast off.

NECKBAND

With right side facing and using smaller needles, pick up and K26 sts down left side of front neck, K across 21(29) sts on front neck holder, pick up and K18 sts up right side of front neck and 8 sts down right side of back neck, K across 29(37) sts on back neck holder, then pick up and K8 sts up left side of back neck:

110(126) sts. Now P 1 row.

Work 5 rows in rib as given for back.

Buttonhole row: Rib to last 5 sts, P2 tog, yrn, rib to end.

Work 5 more rows in rib.

Cast off.

TO MAKE UP

Block the work gently if necessary.

Overlap buttonhole border on left shoulder and catch together at armhole edge.

Sew in sleeves, then join side and sleeve seams.

Sew on buttons.

Barnacle Bill

A traditional Guernsey design – in miniature!

MEASUREMENTS

To fit chest 51(56)cm/20(22)"
Actual measurements 61(66)cm/24(26)"
Length from shoulders 31(33.5)cm/12(13)"
Sleeve seam 23(25.5)cm/9(10)"
Instructions are given for smallest size first, with figures for larger sizes in ( ).

MATERIALS

250(300)g/9(11)oz of Guernsey 5 ply
A pair of 2¼mm knitting needles
A set of four 2¼mm double-pointed needles (or sizes to obtain correct tension)

Remember to check your tension.

TENSION

32 sts and 44 rows to 10cm/4" measured over st st

SPECIAL TECHNIQUE

Guernsey grafting Hold the wrong sides of work together, with the points of the needles holding the sts both facing the same way. Using a spare needle sl 1 st from each needle in turn onto the third needle until all sts for grafting are on one needle; cast off as follows: (K2 tog) twice, pass the first st on RH needle over the second to cast it off, K the next 2 sts tog, then pass the first st on RH needle over the second again to cast it off; cont in this way until all the sts are cast off.

INSTRUCTIONS

BACK

Using pair of needles cast on 90(102) sts.
Work 16 rows g st. Cont in rib as follows:
Row 1: K1, P1, K2, ☆P2, K2, rep from ☆ to last 2 sts, P1, K1.
Row 2: ☆K2, P2, rep from ☆ to last 2 sts, K2.
Rep these 2 rows twice more, then rib row 1 again.
Next row: (RS) K15(21), ☆inc in next st, K9(14), rep from ☆ to last 15(21) sts, inc in next st, K to end: 97(107) sts.
Next row: K1, P to last st, K1.
Always working K1 at each end of every P row, cont in st st until work measures 18(20.5)cm/7(8)" from beg, ending with a P row. Place a marker at each end of last row to denote beg of armhole. Cont as follows:
Row 1: K6, P6, K to last 12 sts, P6, K6.
Row 2: K1, P to last st, K1.
Rep these 2 rows until work measures 30.5(33)cm/12(13)" from beg, ending with row 2.
Cut off yarn and leave sts on a spare needle.

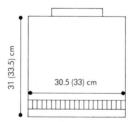

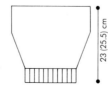

FRONT

Work as given for back.

NECK GUSSETS

Holding wrong sides of back and front tog, sl the first 22(27) sts from each needle onto spare needles for first shoulder seam, and join tog using the Guernsey grafting technique; do not fasten off but leave the final st on a spare needle for the neck gusset.
Sl 53 neck sts at centre of each piece onto spare needles, with points facing the grafted shoulder seam.
Using the needle with 1 st from shoulder grafting, K1 from the front needle holding 53 sts: 2 sts on RH needle, turn.
Next row: Sl the first st, P1, then P1 from second set of 53 sts: 3 sts on RH needle, turn.
Next row: Sl 1, then K2, K1 from first set of sts: 4 sts, turn. Cont in this way, working across 1 more st each time until there are 11 sts on the needle.
Break yarn and leave these sts on a holder.
Graft the 2nd set of 22(27) shoulder sts and work neck gusset in same way as first.

NECKBAND

Using the set of four needles, work 7 rounds in K2, P2 rib over 108 sts on holders at neck. Cast off purlwise.

SLEEVES

Using pair of needles cast on 54 sts.
Row 1: ☆K2, P2, rep from ☆ to last 2 sts, K2.
Row 2: K1, P1, K2, ☆P2, K2, rep from ☆ to last 2 sts, P1, K1.
Rep these 2 rows for 5(6.5)cm/2(2½)", ending with rib row 2.
Work in st st, inc 1 st each end of next and every foll 4th row until there are 82 sts.
Work straight until sleeve measures 21.5(24)cm/8½(9½)" from beg, ending with a P row.
Work 7 rows in rib as given for cuff. Cast off knitwise.

UNDERARM GUSSETS

Using pair of needles cast on 1 st.
Working in st st, inc 1 st at beg of every row until there are 13 sts, then dec 1 st at beg of every row until 1 st remains. Fasten off.

TO MAKE UP

Press or block as appropriate for yarn used.
Sew in sleeves between markers, then sew in underarm gussets. Leaving lower edges open below ribbing, join side and sleeve seams.

Nellie the Elephant

Baby's cardigan with marching elephants around the bottom and matching bootees.

MEASUREMENTS

Cardigan

To fit chest 41–46cm/16–18″
Actual measurements 51cm/20″
Length from shoulders 25cm/10″
Sleeve seam 13cm/5¼″
Instructions are given for smaller size first, with figures for larger size in ( ).

Bootees

To fit 0–6 months

MATERIALS

Cardigan

100g/4oz of a 3-ply yarn in main colour A
50g/2oz of same in contrasting colour B
A pair each of 2¼mm, 3mm and 3¼mm knitting needles (or sizes to obtain correct tension)
6 buttons

Bootees

1 ball of same in main colour A
2 buttons

Remember to check your tension.

TENSION

32 sts and 36 rows to 10cm/4″ measured over st st worked on medium-sized needles.

INSTRUCTIONS

CARDIGAN

BACK AND FRONT

(worked in one piece to armholes)
Using smallest needles and A, cast on 177 sts.
Row 1: K2, ✭P1, K1, rep from ✭ to last st, K1.
Row 2: K1, ✭P1, K1, rep from ✭ to end.
Rep these 2 rows twice more.
Next row (Buttonhole row): K2, P1, yrn, P2 tog, rib to end.
Beg with rib row 2, work 3 more rows in rib.
Next row: Rib 7 and slip these sts onto a safety-pin, change to medium-sized needles and K to last 7 sts, turn and leave rem sts on a safety-pin: 163 sts.
Beg with a P row, work 3 rows st st.
Change to largest needles.
Work elephant motifs from chart as follows:
Row 1: K3A, [3B, 5A, 3B, 3A, 2B, 4A] 8 times.
Row 2: P3A, [3B, 3A, 3B, 5A, 3B, 3A] 8 times.
Cont in patt from chart until row 16 has been completed. Change to medium-sized needles.

Cont in st st until work measures 15cm/6″ from beg, ending with a P row.

Divide for back and fronts

Next row: K40 and slip these sts onto a holder for right front, K the next 83 sts, turn and leave rem 40 sts on a holder for left front.
Working on sts for back, cast off 5 sts at beg of next 2 rows.
Work 1 row.
Next row: K2, K2 tog tbl, K to last 4 sts, K2 tog, K2.
Next row: Purl.
Rep the last 2 rows until 61 sts rem.
Work straight until back measures 25cm/10″ from beg, ending with a P row.

Shape shoulders

Cast off 19 sts at beg of next 2 rows.
Break off yarn and leave rem 23 sts on a holder.
Return to sts on holder for right front.
With WS facing, join on A, cast off 5 sts, then P to end: 35 sts.
✭✭ Dec 1 st of armhole edge as given for back on next and every foll alternate row until 29 sts rem.
Work straight until front measures 20cm/8″ from beg, ending at front edge.
Next row: Work across first 4 sts then slip these sts onto a safety-pin, work to end.
Work 1 row.
Dec 1 st at neck edge on next and every foll alternate row until 19 sts rem.
Work straight until front measures same as back to shoulders, ending with a P row.
Cast off. ✭✭
Return to sts on holder for left front.
With RS facing, join on A, cast off 5 sts, then K to end: 35 sts.
Work 1 row.
Now complete as given for right front from ✭✭ to ✭✭.

SLEEVES

Using smallest needles and A, cast on 43 sts.
Work 10 rows rib as given for back and fronts.
Change to medium-sized needles.
Inc row: K1, ✭inc into next st, K1, rep from ✭ to end: 64 sts.
Working in st st, inc 1 st at each end of 11th and every foll 10th row until there are 70 sts.
Work straight until sleeve measures 13cm/5¼″ from beg, ending with a P row.

Shape top

Cast off 5 sts at beg of next 2 rows.
Working shaping as given for back, dec 1 st each end of

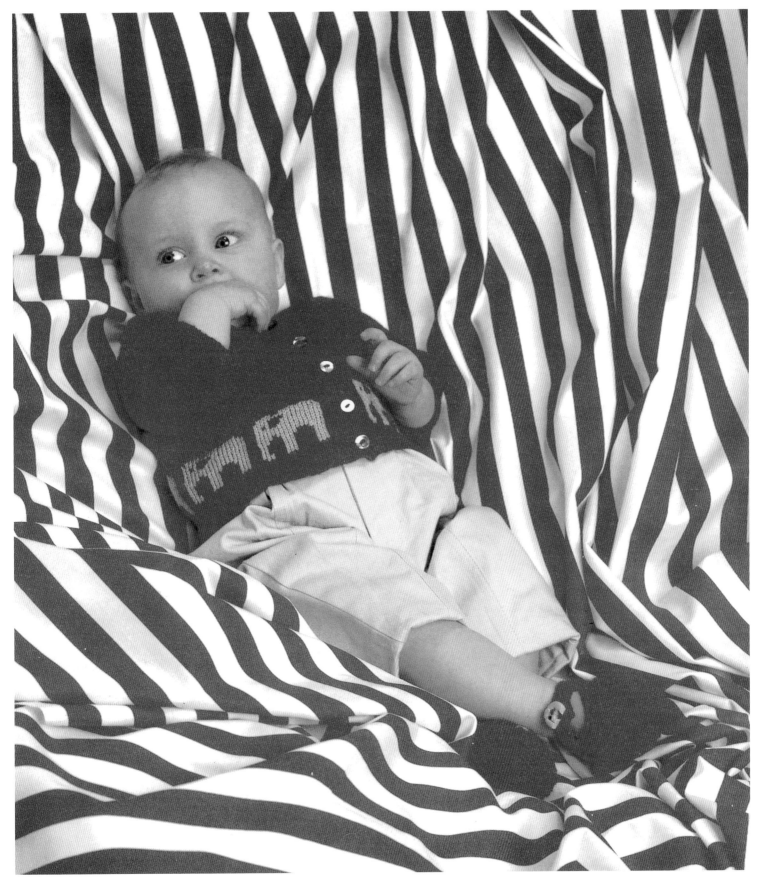

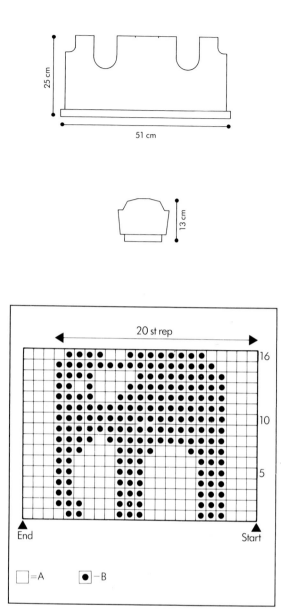

20 st rep

□ = A   ● = B

End

Start

next and every foll alternate row until 48 sts rem, ending with a P row.
Cast off 6 sts at beg of next 4 rows: 24 sts.
Cast off.

BUTTON BORDER

With RS facing, slip the 7 sts on holder at lower edge of left front onto a smallest-size needle, join on A, inc into first st, [K1, P1] twice, K2: 8 sts.
Next row: [K1, P1] 4 times.
Cont in rib until border, when slightly stretched, fits up front to beg of neck shaping. Break off yarn and leave sts on holder. Sew on the border and mark the position for 5 buttons, the first one to match first buttonhole, the top one 4cm/1¼", from top of border and the others spaced evenly in between.

BUTTONHOLE BORDER

With WS facing, slip the 7 sts on holder at lower edge of right front onto a smallest-size needle, join on A, inc into first st, [P1, K1] 3 times.
Next row: K2, [P1, K1] 3 times.
Complete as given for button border, working buttonholes to correspond with markers as follows:
Buttonhole row (RS): K2, P1, yrn, P2 tog, K1, P1, K1.

NECKBAND

Sew on buttonhole border and join shoulder seams.
With RS facing, using smallest needles and A, rib across 7 sts of buttonhole border, K the last st of buttonhole border tog with first of 4 sts on safety-pin at right front neck, K the next 3 sts, pick up and K16 sts up right front neck, K across 23 sts from back neck holder, pick up and K16 sts down left front neck, K3 sts from safety-pin at left front and K the last st on safety-pin tog with first st from button border, then rib 7:77 sts.
Next row (WS): K1, *P1, K1, rep from * to end.
Buttonhole row: K2, P1, yrn, P2 tog, rib to end.
Work 11 more rows rib, making a second buttonhole on the eighth row. Cast off in rib.

TO MAKE UP

Press or block as appropriate for yarn used.
Fold neckband in half to WS and slipstitch in place. Join sleeve seams, then sew in sleeves.

BOOTEES

Using largest needles and 2 strands of yarn tog throughout, cast on 31 sts.
K 1 row.
Shape sole as follows:
Row 1 (RS): Inc in first st, K14, inc in next st, K14, inc in last st.
Row 2 and every alternate row: K to end.

Row 3: Inc in first st, K15, inc in next st, K16, inc in last st.

Row 5: Inc in first st, K17, inc in next st, K17, inc in last st.

Row 7: Inc in first st, K18, inc in next st, K19, inc in last st.

Row 9: Inc in first st, K20, inc in next st, K20, inc in last st.

Row 11: Inc in first st, K21, inc in next st, K22, inc in last st: 49 sts.

Row 12: K to end.

Work in patt as follows:

Row 1: (RS): K1, ☆yf, sl 1 pw, yon, K1, rep from ☆ to end.

Row 2: K1, K2 tog, ☆yf, sl 1 pw, yon, K2 tog, rep from ☆ to last st, K1.

Row 3: K1, ☆yf, sl 1 pw, yon, K2 tog, rep from ☆ to last 2 sts, yf, sl 1 pw, yon, K1.

Rep rows 2 and 3 five more times, then work row 2 again.

Next row (RS): K2, ☆K2 tog, K1, rep from ☆ to last 4 sts, K2 tog, K2.

Next row: K20, [K2 tog] twice, K1, [K2 tog] twice, K20.

Next row: K18, [K2 tog] twice, K1, [K2 tog] twice, K18.

Next row: K16, [K2 tog] twice, K1, [K2 tog] twice, K16.

Next row: K14, [K2 tog] twice, K1, [K2 tog] twice, K14: 33 sts.

Next row: K10, cast off 13 sts, K to end.

Work on first set of 10 sts for button strap.

Next row: K to end.

Next row: Cast on 8 sts, K to end: 18 sts. K 3 rows. (For bootee, work buttonhole on first of these rows.) Cast off.

With RS facing, join yarn to rem 10 sts, cast on 8 sts, then K to end: 18 sts.

K 1 row.

Next row (Buttonhole row): K3, yrn, skpo, K to end. (For 2nd bootee, K this row.)

K 2 rows.

Cast off.

Make 2nd bootee in same way, reversing buttonhole on strap as indicated.

TO MAKE UP

Join sole and centre back seam.
Sew on buttons.

Freddy Frog

A cotton top with a handsome frog motif.

MEASUREMENTS

To fit chest 46(51:56)cm/18(20:22)"
Actual measurements 53(59:64)cm/21(23:25)"
Length from shoulders 28(30.5:33)cm/11(12:13)"
Sleeve seam 6(8:10)cm/2½(3:4)"
Instructions are given for smallest size first, with figures for larger sizes in ( ).

MATERIALS

150(200:200)g/6(8:8)oz of a double knitting weight cotton yarn in main colour A
50(100:100)g/2(4:4)oz of same in contrasting colour B
A pair each of 3¼mm and 4mm knitting needles (or sizes to obtain correct tension)
2 buttons

Remember to check your tension.

TENSION

22 sts and 28 rows to 10cm/4" measured over st st

INSTRUCTIONS

BACK

✿✿ Using smaller needles and B, cast on 55(61:67) sts.
Row 1: K2, ✿P1, K1, rep from ✿ to last st, K1.
Row 2: K1, ✿P1, K1, rep from ✿ to end.
Rep these 2 rows 4 more times.
Change to larger needles.
Break off B. Join on A.
Inc row: K10(14:16), ✿inc in next st, K10, rep from ✿ to last 12(14:18) sts, inc in next st, K to end: 59(65:71) sts. ✿✿
Beg with a P row, work in st st until back measures 15(16.5:19)cm/6(6½:7½)" from beg, ending with a P row.
Shape raglans
Cast off 3(3:4) sts at beg of next 2 rows: 53(59:63) sts.
Work 2 rows st st.
Next row: K1, K2 tog tbl, K to last 3 sts, K2 tog, K1.
Next row: Purl.
Rep these 2 rows until 21(23:27) sts rem, ending with a P row.
Break off yarn and leave rem sts on a holder.

SLEEVES

Using smaller needles and B, cast on 41(45:47) sts.
Work 6 rows in rib as given for back.
Change to larger needles.
Break off B. Join on A.
Inc row: K8(9:10), ✿inc in next st, K7(8:9), rep from ✿ to last 9(9:10) sts, inc in next st, K to end: 45(49:51) sts.

Beg with a P row, work in st st until sleeve measures 6(8:10)cm/2½(3¼:4)" from beg, ending with a P row.
Shape raglan
Cast off 3(3:4) sts at beg of next 2 rows: 39(43:43) sts.
Work 2 rows st st.
Next row: K1, K2 tog tbl, K to last 3 sts, K2 tog, K1.
Next row: Purl.
Rep these 2 rows until 7 sts rem, ending with a P row.
Break off yarn.
Leave sts on a holder.

FRONT

Work as given for back from ✿✿ to ✿✿.
Beg with a P row, work 3 rows st st.
Now work frog motif from chart as follows:
Row 1: K26(29:32)A, 1B, 5A, 1B, 26(29:32)A.
Row 2: P24(27:30)A, 3B, 5A, 3B, 24(27:30)A.
Cont in patt from chart until row 30 has been completed.
Cont in A only until front measures same as back to beg of raglan shaping, ending with a P row.
Shape raglans
Work raglan shaping as given for back until 49(55:59) sts rem, ending with a P row.
Divide for neck
Next row: K1, K2 tog tbl, K19(22:24), turn and leave rem sts on a spare needle.
Next row: Join on B and cast on 5 sts for button band, over these 5 sts work [K1, P1] twice, K1, change to A and P to end.
✿✿✿ Always twisting A and B tog when changing colour to avoid making a hole, keep 5 st border worked in moss st and B as set and *at the same time* cont raglan shaping as before in A until 17(20:22) sts rem, ending with a WS row. ✿✿✿
Shape neck
Next row: K1, K2 tog tbl, K4(6:6), K2 tog, K1, turn and leave rem sts on a safety-pin.
Next row: P1, P2 tog, P to end.
Next row: K1, K2 tog tbl, K to last 3 sts, K2 tog, K1.
Next row: P1, P2 tog, P to end: 4(5:5) sts.
Now cont to dec at raglan edge only as before until 2 sts rem.
Cast off.
Return to sts on spare needle.
With RS facing, join B to first st and K5, join on A then K to last 3 sts, K2 tog, K1.
Cont to dec at raglan edge on every alternate row as before and working 5 st border in moss st and B, work as given for first side of neck from ✿✿✿ to ✿✿✿, working buttonhole on the 7th row as follows:

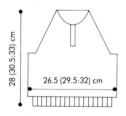

Buttonhole row: (RS) K1, P1, yrn, sl 1, K1, psso, K1, change to A and K to last 3 sts, K2 tog, K1.

Shape neck
Do not cut off B. Sl first 7(8:10) sts onto a safety-pin, using A only K1, K2 tog tbl, K to last 3 sts, K2 tog, K1. Dec 1 st at neck edge on next 2 rows and *at the same time* cont to dec at raglan edge as before until 2 sts rem.
Cast off.

COLLAR
With RS facing and using smaller needles and yarn from right front border at neck edge, work across sts on safety-pin as follows: K1, P1, yrn, sl 1, K1, psso, K3(4:6), pick up and K9(11:11) sts up right side of front neck, K across 7 sts from top of right sleeve, 21(23:27) sts across back neck and 7 sts across top of left sleeve, pick up and K9(11:11) sts down left side of front neck, K the first 3(4:6) sts from safety-pin, then [P1, K1] twice: 67(75:83) sts.
Work 2 rows in moss st. Cont in moss st, cast off 2 sts at beg of next 2 rows.
Work a further 16 rows moss st.
Cast off.

TO MAKE UP
Press or block as appropriate for yarn used.
Join raglan seams, then join side and sleeve seams.
Catch button border in place at base of buttonhole border. Sew on buttons.

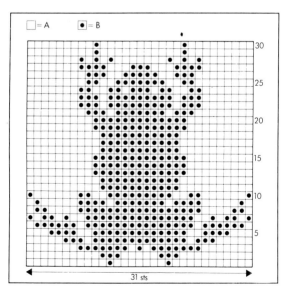

Mucky Pup!

Teddy bear bibs for baby and bear.

MATERIALS

Child's bib or teddy's bib
50g/2oz of a 3-ply weight cotton yarn in main colour A
Small amount of yarn for teddy motif in contrasting colour B
Oddment of black for embroidered features
A pair of 3¾mm double-pointed knitting needles for child's bib
A pair of 2¾mm double-pointed knitting needles for Teddy's bib (or sizes to obtain correct tension)

TENSION

24 sts and 36 rows to 10cm/4" measured over moss st worked on larger needles using yarn double
30 sts and 48 rows to 10cm/4" measured over moss st worked on smaller needles using yarn single

NOTE

Instructions given are for teddy's bib, the instructions for the child's bib are given in ( ). The teddy's bib is worked using the yarn single throughout, and the child's bib is worked using the yarn double.

INSTRUCTIONS

Using smaller(larger) needles and 1(2) strands of A, cast on 23 sts.
Row 1: K twice into first st, [P1, K1] to last 2 sts, P twice into next st, K1: 25 sts.
Row 2: K twice into first st, [K1, P1] to last 2 sts, P twice into next st, K1: 27 sts.
Rep these 2 rows 3 more times: 39 sts.
Work 16 rows straight in moss st.
Now work from chart below as follows:
Row 1: Moss st 7, K25, moss st 7.
Row 2: Moss st 7, P25, moss st 7.
Row 3: Moss st 7A, K4A, 5B, 7A, 5B, 4A, moss st 7A.
Row 4: Moss st 7A, P3A, 7B, 5A, 7B, 3A, moss st 7A.
Working 7 sts in moss st at each end of the rows, cont in patt from chart until row 25 has been completed.
Using A only, work 6 rows st st.
Work 10 rows moss st across all sts, so ending with a RS row.
Shape neck
Next row: Moss st 14, cast off 11 sts, moss st to end.
Working on first 14 sts only, dec 1 st at neck edge on next 5 rows: 9 sts.
Work 5 rows moss st.

Shape shoulder
Next row: Cast off 5 sts, K to end.
Next row: P to end: 4 sts.
Now cont in tubular knitting as follows:
K1 row.
☆ Slide the sts to the other end of the needle, then bringing the yarn across the back of the work and pulling it fairly tightly, K the 4 sts again. ☆
Rep from ☆ to ☆ until tubular piece of knitting measures approximately 23(25.5)cm/9(10)". Cast off.
Return to rem sts.
With RS facing, join yarn to rem sts and complete to match first side of neck, reversing all shaping and working 1 extra row before shaping shoulder.

TO MAKE UP

Press or block as appropriate for yarn used.
Darn in all ends neatly, gathering tops of ties to close.

Remember to check your tension.

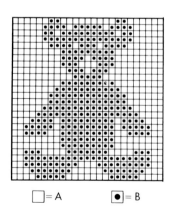

☐ = A   ⦿ = B

Beach Belle

This fetching sundress (with or without anchors) is made from two identical pieces – back and front – which are joined at the sides. The skirt and the top are continuous. You simply reduce the number of stitches by half at the waistband.

MEASUREMENTS

To fit chest 46(51:56)cm/18(20:22)"
Actual measurements 51(56:61)cm/20(22:24)"
Length from shoulders 40.5(43:46)cm/16(17:18)"
Instructions are given for smallest size first, with figures for larger sizes in ( ).

MATERIALS

150(200:200)g/6(8:8)oz of a 3-ply-weight cotton yarn in main colour A
50g/2oz of same in contrasting colour B (if motifs required)
A pair each of 2¼mm and 2¾mm knitting needles
Two short double-pointed 2¼mm knitting needles for tubular knitting (or sizes to obtain correct tension)

Remember to check your tension.

TENSION

32 sts and 44 rows to 10cm/4" measured over st st worked on larger needles

SPECIAL TECHNIQUE

Tubular knitting Using double-pointed needles and working over 5 sts, K 1 row.
Do not turn work but sl the 5 sts to the other end of the needle, bring the yarn across the back of the work and pulling yarn tightly K the row again from right to left.
Cont in this way, always keeping the RS of the fabric facing and always working from right to left across the work, thus creating a tubular piece of knitting.

INSTRUCTIONS

BACK AND FRONT (alike)

Using smaller needles and A, cast on 171(183:195) sts.
Beg with a K row, work 8 rows st st.
Next row: K1, *yf, K2 tog, rep from * to end.
Change to larger needles.
Beg with a P row, work 9 rows st st.
With wrong sides together, fold work along eyelet hole row and make hem as follows:
Next row: K1, pick up first loop from cast-on edge and K tog with next st on LH needle, *pick up next loop from cast-on edge and K tog with next st on LH needle, rep from * to end.
Work 3 rows st st.

Now working from chart, place motifs (if required) as follows:
Row 1: K6A, *3B, 9A, rep from * to last 9 sts, 3B, 6A.
Row 2: P5A, *1B, 1A, 1B, 1A, 1B, 7A, rep from * to last 10 sts, 1B, 1A, 1B, 1A, 1B, 5A.
Cont in this way working from chart until row 12 has been completed.
Break off B.
Using A only, cont in st st until skirt measures 14(15:18)cm/5½(6:7)" (or length desired) from beg, ending with a WS row.
Dec row: K1, *K2 tog, rep from * to end: 86(92:98) sts.
Next row: K to end.
Beg with a P row, work in rev st st until bodice measures 15(16.5:16.5)cm/5¾(6½:6½)" from dec row, ending with a K row.
☆☆ Shape armholes
Cast off 4 sts at beg of next 2 rows: 78(84:90) sts.
Dec 1 st at each end of every row to 60(66:72) sts, then at each end of every foll alternate row until 52(58:64) sts rem, ending with a K row.
Work 2 rows straight.
Shape neck
Next row (RS): P21(24:26), cast off next 10(10:12) sts, P to end.
Working on first set of sts only, dec 1 st at neck edge on next and every foll alternate row until 5 sts rem.
Work 1 row, then changing to double pointed needles, work 18(20:20)cm/7(8:8)" of tubular knitting.
Break off yarn and thread through sts, draw up tight and fasten off securely.
Return to rem sts.
With WS facing, join yarn to first st and complete to match first side of neck.

TO MAKE UP

Press or block as appropriate for yarn used.
Join side seams.
Allowing neck and armhole edges to roll, tie straps into a bow to fit. ☆☆

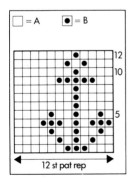

= A   ● = B

12

10

5

12 st pat rep

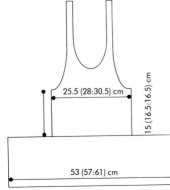

25.5 (28:30.5) cm

15 (16.5:16.5) cm

53 (57:61) cm

Fair Isle Accessories

These colourful accessories consist of a pair of mittens, a pull-on hat and tube socks, which are socks worked in the round without a heel. All of them are decorated with stripes, contrast ribbing and a Fair Isle pattern worked from a simple chart.

MEASUREMENTS

To fit age 3(4:5) years
Width at top of sock 16(17:17)cm/6½(7:7)"
Around head for cap: 44cm/17½"
Around hand for mittens: 14cm/5½"
Instructions are given for the smallest size first with figures for larger sizes in ( ).

MATERIALS

Socks
50g/2oz of a machine-washable double knitting yarn in main colour A
25g/1oz in each of 3 contrasting colours B, C and D

Mittens
25g/1oz in each of 4 colours A, B, C and D

Cap
50g/2oz in main colour A 25g/1oz in each of 3 contrasting colours B, C and D

Whole set
75g/3oz in main colour A
50g/2oz in contrasting colour B
25g/1oz in each of 2 contrasting colours C and D
1 pair each of 3¼mm and 4mm knitting needles (or size to obtain correct tension)
1 set each of 4 double-pointed 3¼mm and 4mm knitting needles (for socks) (or size to obtain correct tension)

TENSION

22 sts and 28 rows to 10cm/4" measured over st st worked on larger needles

INSTRUCTIONS

CAP

Using smaller needles and B, cast on 98 sts. Work 2cm/¾" in K1, P1 rib.
Change to larger needles and C. Work 6 rows in st st beg with a K row. Cont in st st, work 2 rows in A, then 2 rows in D.
Cont in Fair Isle patt from chart as follows:
Row 1: K1A, ✳1A, 3B, 2A, rep from ✳ to last st, K1A.
Row 2: P1A, ✳2A, 3B, 1A, rep from ✳ to last st, P1A.
These 2 rows set the patt. Cont working 3rd–9th rows from chart reading K rows from right to left and P rows

from left to right, and working edge sts in A as set.
Cont in st st, work 1 row in A, then 2 rows in D. Now with A only, work straight until cap measures 12cm/5".
Shape crown
Row 1: [K4, K2 tog] 8 times, [K3, K2 tog] 10 times: 80 sts.
Row 2 and every alternate row: Purl.
Row 3: [K2 tog, K2] to end of row: 60 sts.
Row 5: [K2 tog, K1] to end of row: 40 sts.
Row 7: [K2 tog] to end: 20 sts.
Row 9: [K2 tog] to end: 10 sts.
Break yarn and thread through rem sts. Draw up yarn and fasten off securely.

SOCKS (both alike)

Using set of four double-pointed smaller needles and B, cast on 36(40:40) sts.
Divide sts between three needles using fourth needle to work in rounds. Work in K2, P2 rib, working 6 rows in B, 2 rows in A, 2 rows in C, 2 rows in D. Now work 4 rows in B inc 2 sts evenly across last row on 2nd and 3rd sizes only: 36(42:42) sts.
Change to larger needles and C. Work 6 rows in st st (K every round).
Cont in st st work 2 rounds in A, then 2 rounds in D. Now work Fair Isle patt from chart as follows:
Round 1: ✳K1A, 3B, 2A; rep from ✳ to end of round.
Round 2: As first round.
These 2 rounds set the patt. Cont working 3rd–9th rounds from chart reading every row on chart from right to left. Cont in st st work 1 round in A, then 2 rounds in D. With A only work straight until sock measures 25cm/10". Change to B.
Shape toe as follows:
2nd and 3rd sizes only
Next round: [K5, K2 tog] 6 times: 36 sts.
Next round: Knit.
All Sizes
Round 1: [K4, K2 tog] 6 times: 30 sts.
Round 2 and every alternate round: Knit.
Round 3: [K3, K2 tog] 6 times: 24 sts.
Round 5: [K2, K2 tog] 6 times: 18 sts.
Round 7: [K1, K2 tog] 6 times: 12 sts.
Round 9: [K2 tog] 6 times: 6 sts.
Break off yarn and thread through rem sts. Draw up and fasten off securely.

RIGHT-HAND MITTEN

Using smaller needles and B, cast on 30 sts. Work in K1, P1 rib for 5cm/2".
Change to larger needles and A.

Remember to check your tension.

Cont in st st work 2 rows.

Shape thumb gusset

Row 1: K15, inc into next st, K1, inc into next st, K12.

Rows 2–4: Work in st st.

Row 5: K15, inc into next st, K3, inc into next st, K12.

Cont in this way, inc 1 st on each side of gusset on every 4th row until there are 38 sts on needle.

Next row: Purl.

Next row: K27, turn and cast on 2 sts.

Next row: P12, turn and cast on 2 sts.

Cont on these 14 sts for 2.5cm/1″ ending with a P row.

Next row: [K2 tog] to end: 7 sts. Break off yarn and thread through rem sts. Draw up and fasten off securely.

Join thumb seam.

With RH needle pick up and K4 sts from base of thumb, K to end of row: 32 sts.

Next row: Purl.

Cont in st st work 2 rows in D.

Now work 1st–9th rows in Fair Isle patt from chart as given for cap.

Cont in st st, work 1 row in A, then 2 rows in D.

Change to A.

Shape top

Row 1: K1, K2 tog, K11, K2 tog, K1, K2 tog, K10, K2 tog, K1.

Row 2 and every alternate row: Purl.

Row 3: K1, K2 tog, K9, K2 tog, K1, K2 tog, K8, K2 tog, K1.

Row 5: K1, K2 tog, K7, K2 tog, K1, K2 tog, K6, K2 tog, K1.

Row 6: Purl.

Cast off.

LEFT-HAND MITTEN

Work as given for right-hand mitten reversing shaping for thumb gusset as follows:

Row 1: K12, inc into next st, K1, inc into next st, K15.

Rows 2–4: Work in st st.

Cont in this way inc 1 st on each side of gusset on every 4th row until there are 38 sts.

Next row: Purl.

Next row: K21, turn and cast on 2 sts.

Next row: P12, turn and cast on 2 sts: 14 sts.

Complete as given for right-hand mitten.

TO MAKE UP

Press or block all pieces as appropriate for yarn used. Join back seam on cap and mitten seams invisibly. Thread shirring elastic through sock tops if required.

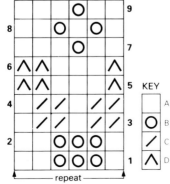

Pretty Maids in a Row

Pretty as a picture, this colourful cardigan will make any little girl smile with delight.

MEASUREMENTS

To fit chest 56(61:66)cm/22(24:26)"
Actual measurements 57.5(63:68.5)cm/22½(24¾:27)"
Length from shoulders 32.5(35.5:40.5)cm/12¾(14:16)"
Sleeve seam 23(25.5:28)cm/9(10:11)"
Instructions are given for smallest size first, with figures for larger sizes in ( ).

MATERIALS

100(150:150)g/4(6:6)oz of a machine-washable 4-ply yarn in main colour, A
50g/2oz in each of contrasting colours B and C
A pair each of 2¾mm and 3¼mm knitting needles (or sizes to obtain correct tension)
6 buttons

Remember to check your tension.

TENSION

29 sts and 38 rows to 10cm/4" measured over st st worked on larger needles

INSTRUCTIONS

BACK AND FRONTS (worked in 1 piece to armholes)
Using smaller needles and B, cast on 161(177:193) sts
Row 1: K1, *P1, K1, rep from * to end.
Row 2: P1, *K1, P1, rep from * to end.
Work 16 more rows in rib as set.
☆☆ Change to larger needles.
Beg with a K row cont working in st st throughout.
Cont working border patt, joining and breaking off colours as required, in colours as follows:
☆☆ **Rows 1 and 2:** With A, to end.
Row 3: 1C, *3A, 1C, rep from * to end.
Row 4: 2C, 1A, *3C, 1A, rep from * to last 2 sts, 2C.
Row 5: With C, to end.
Row 6: With A, to end.
Row 7: 1A, *2B, 3A, 2B, 1A, rep from * to end.
Row 8: 1A, *1B, 5A, 1B, 1A, rep from * to end.
Row 9: 4B, *1A, 7B, rep from * ending last rep with 4B.
Row 10: 3B, *3A, 5B, rep from * ending last rep with 3B.
Row 11: 2B, *5A, 3B, rep from * ending last rep with 2B.
Row 12: 1C, *3A, 1C, rep from * to end.
Row 13: 2C, *1A, 1C, 1A, 1C, 1A, 3C, rep from * ending last rep with 2C.
Row 14: As 10th, using C instead of B.
Row 15: As 11th, using C instead of B.
Row 16: 1C, *7A, 1C, rep from * to end.

Row 17: 1A, *2C, 3A, 2C, 1A, rep from * to end.
Rows 18 and 19: 2C, *5A, 3C, rep from * ending last rep with 2C.
Break off B and C and cont with A only ☆☆.
Cont in st st until work measures 21(23.5:26)cm/8¼(9¼:10¼)" from beg, ending with a K row.
Divide for back and fronts
Next row: P40(44:48) sts, leave these sts on a spare needle for left front, P81(89:97) and leave these sts on a spare needle for back, P to end.
Cont working on last set of sts for right front.
Shape raglan and front edge
Row 1: K2 tog, K to last 4 sts, K2 tog, K2.
Row 2: P2, P2 tog, P to end.
Row 3: K to end.
Row 4: As 2nd row.
Row 5: As first row.
Row 6: P to end.
Row 7: K to last 4 sts, K2 tog, K2.
☆☆☆ Rep last 6 rows 6(6:7) more times, then 0(2nd – 6th: 2nd – 4th) rows once more: 3(3:4) sts. ☆☆☆
First size only
Next row: P1, P2 tog.
2nd and 3rd sizes only
Next row: K2 tog, K to end.
Next row: P to end.
All sizes
K rem 2(2:3) sts tog and fasten off.

BACK
With RS of work facing, rejoin yarn to inner edge of 81(89:97) sts on spare needle.
Shape raglans
Row 1: K2, skpo, K to last 4 sts, K2 tog, K2.
Row 2: P2, P2 tog, P to last 4 sts, P2 tog, P2.
Row 3: K to end.
Row 4: As 2nd.
Row 5: As first.
Row 6: P to end.
Rep last 6 rows 6(7:8) more times.
First size only Rep first and 2nd rows once more.
2nd size only
Rep first and 6th rows once more.
All sizes
Cast off rem 21(23:25) sts.

LEFT FRONT
With RS of work facing, rejoin yarn to inner edge of rem 40(44:48) sts.
Shape raglan and front edge
Row 1: K2, skpo, K to last 2 sts, K2 tog.

Row 2: P to last 4 sts, P2 tog tbl, P2.
Row 3: K to end.
Row 4: As 2nd row.
Row 5: As first row.
Row 6: P to end.
Row 7: K2, skpo, K to end.
Work as given for right front from ✩✩✩ to ✩✩✩.
First size only
Next row: P2 tog tbl, P1.
2nd and 3rd sizes only
Next row: K to last 2 sts, skpo.
Next row: P to end.
All sizes
Complete as given for right front.

SLEEVES
Using smaller needles and B, cast on 35(37:39) sts.
Work 17 rows in rib as given for back.
Inc row: Rib 4(1:2), inc in next st, ✩rib 1(2:1), inc in next st, rep from ✩ to last 4(2:2) sts, rib to end: 49(49:57) sts.
Cont working in patt as given for back and fronts from ✩✩ to ✩✩ and taking extra sts into patt when working border patt, inc 1 st at each end of 9th and every foll 8th (6th:8th) row until there are 63(71:75) sts.
Cont without shaping until sleeve measures 23(25.5:28)cm/9(10:11)″ from beg, ending with a WS row.
Shape top
Work 6 raglan shaping rows as given for back until 7(7:11) sts rem, then rep first – 3rd rows again for 3rd

size only: 7(7:7) sts.
First and 2nd sizes only
Next row: K2, K3 tog, K2.
Next row: P1, P3 tog, P1.
3rd size only
Next row: P2, P3 tog, P2.
Next row: K1, K3 tog, K1.
Next row: P3.
All sizes
K3 tog and fasten off.

FRONT BAND
Join raglan seams.
Using smaller needles and B, cast on 8 sts.
Work 2 rows in K1, P1 rib.
Make buttonholes
Row 1: Rib 3, cast off 2, rib to end.
Row 2: Rib to end, casting on 2 sts over those cast off in previous row.
Rib 12(14:16) rows. Rep last 14(16:18) rows 4 more times, then 2 buttonhole rows once more.
Cont in rib, omitting buttonholes, until band fits up right front, around neck and down left front, when slightly stretched.

TO MAKE UP
Press or block as appropriate for yarn used.
Join sleeve seams. Sew front band into position, placing last buttonhole level with first front dec.
Sew on buttons to correspond with buttonholes.

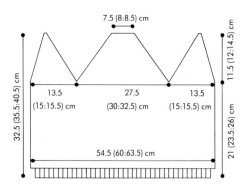

BACK AND FRONTS WORKED IN ONE PIECE TO ARMHOLES

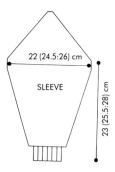

Three-Piece Sweet

A warm jacket, hat and mitts in chunky tweed yarn will keep a little girl cosy in cold weather. Although in these days of equality, a young boy would look just as good wearing them.

MEASUREMENTS

Jacket

To fit chest 56(61:66)cm/22(24:26)"
Actual measurements 60.5(66.5:72.5)cm/
23¾(26¼:28½)", fastened
Length from shoulders 32.5(34.5:36.5)cm/
12¾(13½:14¼)"
Sleeve seam 18.5(20.5:23)cm/7¼(8:9)" with cuff turned
back

Hat

To fit average head

Mitts

Length 15.5cm/6"
Jacket instructions are given for smallest size first with
figures for larger sizes in ( ).

MATERIALS

400(450:500)g/16(18:20)oz of a chunky knitting yarn
for the set
A pair each of 5½mm and 6mm knitting needles (or
sizes to obtain correct tension)

Remember to check your tension.

TENSION

13 sts and 19 rows to 10cm/4" measured over st st
worked on larger needles

INSTRUCTIONS

JACKET

(worked in one piece to neck shaping)
BACK
Using smaller needles cast on 40(44:48) sts.
Row 1: K3, ✸P2, K2, rep from ✸ to last 5 sts, P2, K3.
Row 2: P3, ✸K2, P2, rep from ✸ to last 5 sts, K2, P3.
Rep last 2 rows 3 more times.
Change to larger needles.
Beg with a K row cont working in st st throughout.
Work 36(38:40) rows straight.
Shape sleeves
Next row: Cast on 24(27:30) sts for first sleeve, K to
end, turn and cast on 24(27:30) sts for 2nd sleeve:
88(98:108) sts.
Work 13(15:17) rows straight.
Divide sts for neck
Next row: K37(42:47), turn and leave rem sts on a
spare needle.

RIGHT FRONT

Cont on first set of sts as follows:
Work 15 rows straight.
Next row: K to end, turn and cast on 4 sts for neck:
41(46:51) sts.
Work 5 rows straight.
Next row: Cast off 24(27:30) sts to complete sleeve, K

to end: 17(19:21) sts.
Work 35(37:39) rows straight.
Change to larger needles.
Cont working in rib for lower edge as follows:
Row 1: P2(0:2), ✸K2, P2, rep from ✸ to last 3 sts, K3.
Row 2: P3, ✸K2, P2, rep from ✸ to last 2(0:2) sts,
K2(0:2).
Rep last 2 rows 3 more times. Cast off in rib.
With RS of work facing, return to rem sts. Rejoin yarn
and cast off next 14 sts for centre back neck, K to end:
37(42:47) sts.

LEFT FRONT

Cont on last set of sts as follows:
Work 15 rows straight.
Next row: Cast on 4 sts for neck, K to end.
Work 4 rows straight.
Next row: Cast off 24(27:30) sts to complete 2nd
sleeve, P to end: 17(19:21) sts.
Work 36(38:40) rows straight.
Change to smaller needles.
Cont working in rib for lower edge as follows:
Row 1: K3, ✸P2, K2, rep from ✸ to last 2(0:2) sts,
P2(0:2).
Row 2: K2(0:2) sts, ✸P2, K2, rep from ✸ to last 3 sts, P3.
Rep last 2 rows 3 more times. Cast off in rib.

CUFFS

With RS of work facing and using smaller needles, pick
up and K 26(30:34) sts around lower edge of sleeve.
Row 1: K2, ✸P2, K2, rep from ✸ to end.
Row 2: P2, ✸K2, P2, rep from ✸ to end.
Rep last 2 rows twice more then first row again. Cast
off in rib.
Work 2nd cuff in same way.

COLLAR

Using smaller needles, cast on 60(64:68) sts.
Work 13 rows in rib as given for back. Cast off loosely
in rib.

BUTTON BAND

Using smaller needles, cast on 32(36:40) sts.
Work 6 rows in rib as given for back.
Cast off in rib.

BUTTONHOLE BAND

Using smaller needles, cast on 32(36:40) sts.
Work 2 rows in rib as given for back.
Make buttonholes
Row 1: Rib 1(2:2), ✸cast off 2, rib 7(8:9), rep from ✸
twice more, cast off 2, rib to end.
Row 2: Work in rib, casting on 2 sts over those cast off
in previous row.

Rib 2 more rows. Cast off in rib.

TO MAKE UP
Press or block as appropriate for yarn used.
Join side seams. Sew on cuffs. Join sleeve seams.
Sew front bands in place. Sew on collar, beg and ending in centre of front bands. Turn back cuffs.
Sew on buttons to correspond with buttonholes.

HAT
Using smaller needles, cast on 60 sts.
Work 31 rows in K2, P2 rib.
Change to larger needles.
K 1 row.

Shape crown
Row 1: P3, [P2 tog, P4] 4 times, P2 tog, P2, [P2 tog, P4] 4 times, P2 tog, P3: 50 sts.
Work 4 rows straight in st st.
Row 6: K2, [K2 tog, K3] 4 times, K2 tog, K2, [K2 tog, K3] 4 times, K2 tog, K2: 40 sts.
Row 7: P1, [P2 tog, P2] 9 times, P2 tog, P1: 30 sts.
Row 8: [K2 tog] 15 times.
Break off yarn, leaving a long end. Thread end through rem sts, draw up and fasten off securely.

TO MAKE UP
Press or block as for jacket.
Join seam, reversing seam for brim. Turn brim to RS.

MITTS
LEFT MITT
Using smaller needles cast on 21 sts.
Row 1: K3, *P2, K2, rep from * to last 2 sts, P2.
Row 2: K2, *P2, K2, rep from * to last 3 sts, P3.
Rep last 2 rows 5 more times.
Change to larger needles.
K 1 row. ☆☆

Shape thumb
Row 1: P7, inc in next st, P2, inc in next st, P to end.
Row 2: K to end.
Row 3: P8, inc in next st, P2, inc in next st, P to end.
Row 4 and every alternate row: K to end.
Row 5: P9, inc in next st, P2, inc in next st, P to end.
Row 7: P10, inc in next st, P2, inc in next st, P to end: 29 sts.

Divide sts for thumb
Break off yarn, sl first 8 sts onto a safety-pin, rejoin yarn to next st, K9, turn and work on these sts only for thumb. Leave rem 12 sts on a spare needle.
☆☆☆ **Thumb**
Work 5 rows in st st.
Next row: *K2, K2 tog, rep from * once more, K1.
Break off yarn, leaving a long end. Thread this end through rem 7 sts, draw up tightly and fasten off.

Join thumb seam. ☆☆☆
With RS of work facing, rejoin yarn to 8 sts on safety-pin, K these 8 sts, pick up and K 2 sts from base of thumb, K across 12 sts on spare needle: 22 sts.
☆☆☆☆ Work 4 rows in st st.

Shape top
Row 1: P2, P2 tog, P3, P2 tog, P4, P2 tog, P3, P2 tog, P2: 18 sts.
Row 2: K to end.
Row 3: [P2, P2 tog] 4 times, P2: 14 sts.
Row 4: K to end.
Row 5: P1, P2 tog, P1, P2 tog, P2, P2 tog, P1, P2 tog, P1: 10 sts.
Row 6: [K2 tog] 5 times.
Break off yarn, leaving a long end. Thread this end through rem sts, draw up and fasten off.

RIGHT MITT
Work as given for left mitt to ☆☆.

Shape thumb
Row 1: P10, inc in next st, P2, inc in next st, P to end.
Row 2 and every alternate row: K to end.
Row 3: P11, inc in next st, P2, inc in next st, P to end.
Row 5: P12, inc in next st, P2, inc in next st, P to end.
Row 7: P13, inc in next st, P2, inc in next st, P to end: 29 sts.

Divide sts for thumb
Break off yarn, sl first 12 sts onto a spare needle, rejoin yarn to next st, K9, turn and leave rem sts on a safety-pin.
Work as given for left mitt from ☆☆☆ to ☆☆☆.
With RS of work facing, rejoin yarn to 12 sts on spare needle, K these sts, pick up and K 2 sts from base of thumb, then K across 8 sts on safety-pin: 22 sts.
Work as given for left mitt from ☆☆☆☆ to end.

TO MAKE UP
Press or block as for jacket. Join seam.

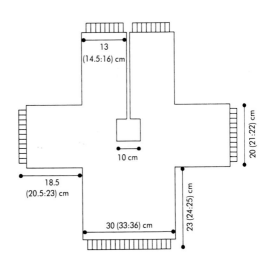

Sweater and Dungarees

Mix and match sweater and dungarees are pretty and practical for a busy and active toddler.

MEASUREMENTS

Sweater

To fit chest 51(56:61)cm/20(22:24)"
Actual measurements 53(58:63)cm/20¾(22¾:24¾)"
Length from shoulders 29(33.5:36.5)cm/
11½(13¼:14¼)"
Sleeve seam 23(26.5:30)cm/9(10¼:11¾)"

Dungarees

Length from waist to ankle 43.5(51:58.5)cm/17(20:23)", including ribbing

Instructions are given for smallest size first with figures for larger sizes in ( ).

MATERIALS

Sweater

100(150:150)g/4(6:6)oz of a double knitting yarn in main colour A
50(50:100)g/2(2:4)oz in contrasting colour B
1 press stud

Dungarees

150(200:200)g/6(8:8)oz of same yarn in main colour A
50(50:50)g/2(2:2)oz in contrasting colour B
8 buttons
A pair each of 3¼mm and 3¾mm knitting needles for both garments (or sizes to obtain correct tension)

TENSION

24 sts and 35 rows to 10cm/4" measured over patt worked on larger needles
24 sts and 32 rows to 10cm/4" measured over st st worked on larger needles

Remember to check your tension.

INSTRUCTIONS

SWEATER

BACK

Using smaller needles and A, cast on 64(70:76) sts.
Work 12 rows in K1, P1 rib.
Change to larger needles.
Cont working in patt as foll:
Rows 1–4: Using A and beg with a K row, work 4 rows in st st.
Rows 5 and 6: Using B, K to end.
These 6 rows form patt and are rep throughout.
Cont straight until back measures 19(22.5:24)cm/
7½(8¾:9½)" from beg, ending with a WS row. ✩✩
Shape raglan armholes
Cast off 3 sts at beg of next 2 rows. Dec 1 st at each end of next and every foll alternate row until 24(26:28) sts rem.
Work 1 row. Leave rem sts on a spare needle.

FRONT

Work as given for back to ✩✩.
Shape raglan armholes
Cast off 3 sts at beg of next 2 rows. Dec 1 st at each end of next and foll alternate rows until 40(42:44) sts rem, ending with a dec row.
Divide for neck
Next row: Patt 12 sts and leave these sts on a holder for first half of neck, patt 16(18:20) sts and leave these sts on a holder for centre front neck, patt to end.
Cont working on last set of sts as follows:
Dec 1 st at each end of next row and foll 2 alternate rows, then at armhole edge only on foll 4 alternate rows: 2 sts.
Work 1 row. K2 tog.
Fasten off.
With RS of work facing, rejoin yarn to rem 12 sts on holder. Complete as given for first side, reversing shaping.

SLEEVES

Using smaller needles and A, cast on 30(32:36) sts.
Work 19 rows in K1, P1 rib.
Inc row: Rib 4(2:4), ✩inc 1 st in next st, rib 2, rep from ✩ to last 2(0:2) sts, rib 2(0:2): 38(42:46) sts.
Change to larger needles.
Cont working in patt as given for back, inc 1 st at each end of 7th and every foll 6th row until there are 50(54:58) sts.
Work straight until sleeve measures 23(26.5:30)cm/
9(10¼:11¾)" from beg, ending with a WS row.
Shape raglans
Work as given for armhole shaping on back until 10 sts rem.
Work 1 row. Leave rem sts on a holder.

NECKBAND

Join right sleeve to back and front, then left sleeve to front only.
With RS of work facing and using smaller needles, rejoin A and K across 10 sts of left sleeve, pick up and K15 sts down left front neck, K across centre front sts, pick up and K15 sts up right front neck, K across 10 sts of right sleeve and K across 24(26:28) sts of back neck, cast on 4 sts for placket: 94(98:102) sts.
Work 6 rows in K1, P1 rib.
Cast off in rib.

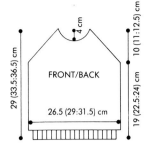

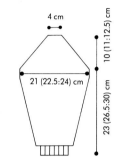

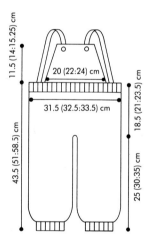

TO MAKE UP

Press or block as appropriate for yarn used.
Join rem raglan seam, leaving ribbing at neck free. Join side and sleeve seams. Close neck ribbing with a press stud.

DUNGAREES

FRONT – RIGHT LEG

Using smaller needles and A, cast on 16(18:18) sts.
Work 11 rows in K1, P1 rib, inc 1 st at end of last row for 3rd size only: 16(18:19) sts.
Inc row: Inc into each st to end: 32(36:38) sts.
Change to larger needles.
Beg with a K row cont in st st, until leg measures 25(30:35)cm/9 ¾(11¾:13¾)″ from beg, ending with a WS row. Leave sts on a spare needle.

LEFT LEG

Work as given for right leg.
Cont as follows:
Joining row: K across 32(36:38) sts of left leg, cast on 10 sts, K across 32(36:38) sts of right leg: 74(82:86) sts.
Next row: P to end.
Shape crotch
Row 1: K31(35:37) sts, skpo, K8, K2 tog, K to end.
Row 2 and every alternate row: P to end.
Row 3: K31(35:37), skpo, K6, K2 tog, K to end.
Row 5: K31(35:37), skpo, K4, K2 tog, K to end.
Row 7: K31(35:37), skpo, K2, K2 tog, K to end.
Row 9: K31(35:37), skpo, K2 tog, K to end: 64(72:76) sts.
Cont in st st and work 41(49:57) rows without shaping.
✧✧✧
Waist ribbing
Change to smaller needles.
Work 2 rows in K1, P1 rib.
Make buttonholes
Row 1: Rib 3, [yrn] twice, K2 tog, rib to last 5 sts, P2 tog, [yrn] twice, rib to end.
Row 2: Rib to end, dropping extra loops off needle.
Work 2 rows in rib.
Rep 2 buttonhole rows once more.
Next row: Cast off 8 sts, rib to end.
Next row: Cast off 9 sts, rib to end: 47(55:59) sts.
Bib
Change to larger needles.
Row 1: K1, P1, K1, P2 tog, K to last 5 sts, P2 tog, K1, P1, K1.
Row 2: P1, K1, P1, K1, P to last 4 sts, K1, P1, K1, P1.
Row 3: Rib 4, K to last 4 sts, rib 4.
Row 4: Rib 4, P to last 4 sts, rib 4.
Rep last 4 rows 6(8:9) more times: 33(37:39) sts.
Rep 3rd and 4th rows once more, then first and 2nd rows again: 31(35:37) sts.

Next row: K1, *P1, K1, rep from * to end.
Next row: P1, *K1, P1, rep from * to end.
Buttonhole row: K1, K2 tog, [yrn] twice, P1, K1, K2 tog, [yrn] twice, P2 tog, K1.
Work 2 more rows in rib, dropping extra loops on first of these rows.
Cast off in rib.

BACK

Work as given for front, to ✧✧✧ but working 40(48:56) rows instead of 41(49:57) rows before waist ribbing.
Shape back
Rows 1 and 2: P to last 8 sts, turn, K to last 8 sts, turn.
Rows 3 and 4: P to last 16 sts, turn, K to last 16 sts, turn.
Rows 5 and 6: P to last 24 sts, turn, K to last 24 sts, turn.
Next row: P across all sts, turn and cast on 4 sts for placket: 68(76:80) sts.
Next row: ✧K1, P1, rep from ✧ to end, turn and cast on 4 sts for placket: 72(80:84) sts.
Next row: ✧K1, P1, rep from ✧ to end.
Work 7 more rows in rib.
Cast off in rib.

STRAPS (make 2)

Using smaller needles and A, cast on 9 sts.
Beg odd numbered rows with K1, and even numbered rows with P1, cont in K1, P1 rib until strap measures 26(29:33)cm/10¼(11½:13)″.
Cast off in rib.

POCKETS (make 2)

Using larger needles and A, cast on 20 sts.
Work 24 rows in patt as given for back of sweater.
Change to smaller needles.
Working in A only, K 1 row, then work 2 rows in K1, P1 rib.
Cast off in rib.

TO MAKE UP

Press or block as for sweater.
Join side seams and inside leg seams. Sew one end of each strap to inside of back waist ribbing, placing straps 6(7:8)cm/2¼(2¾:3)″ apart.
Sew 2 buttons on each strap and 2 buttons on both plackets of waist ribbing, to correspond with buttonholes.
Sew one pocket on right front and one on left back.

Nautical Set

A jaunty beret and a stylish cardigan, shown here in red, white and French navy.

MEASUREMENTS

To fit chest 56(61:66:71)cm/22(24:26:28)"
Actual measurements 58.5(63.5:68.5:73.5)cm/23(25:27:29)"
Length from shoulders 36.5(39:41.5:44)cm/14¼(15¼:16¼:17¾)"
Sleeve seam 25(27.5:30:32.5)cm/9¾(10¾:11¾:12¾)"
Instructions are given for smallest size first with figures for larger sizes in ( ).

MATERIALS

Cardigan
120(120:160:160)g/5(5:6:6)oz of a machine-washable double crepe or a double knitting yarn in main colour A 40(40:40:40)g/2(2:2:2)oz in each of contrasting colours B and C; 6 buttons

Beret
40g/2oz of same yarn in main colour A

Small quantity of B or C
A pair each of 3¾mm and 4mm knitting needles (or sizes to obtain correct tension) for each garment
4.00mm crochet hook

Remember to check your tension.

TENSION

24 sts and 31 rows to 10 cm/4" measured over st st worked on larger needles

NOTE

Where the figure '0' is given this means that there are no sts to be worked on this section for your size

INSTRUCTIONS

CARDIGAN

BACK

Using smaller needles and A, cast on 72(78:84:90) sts.
Work 16 rows in K1, P1 rib.
✷✷ Change to larger needles.
Beg with a K row, cont working in st st, joining in colours as required and using separate balls of yarn for each boat, in patt as follows:
Rows 1–6: Work each row in B. ✷✷
Row 7: ✷3B, 3A, rep from ✷ to end.
Row 8: ✷4A, 2B, rep from ✷ to end.
Rows 9 and 10: ✷3A, 3B, rep from ✷ to end.
Row 11: ✷2B, 4A, rep from ✷ to end.
Rows 12–14: Work each row in A.
Row 15: 13(16:19:22)A, ✷5B, 16A, rep from ✷ ending last rep with 12(15:18:21)A.
Row 16: 10(13:16:19)A, ✷8B, 13A, rep from ✷ ending last rep with 12(15:18:21)A.
Row 17: 11(14:17:20)A, ✷11B, 10A, rep from ✷ ending last rep with 8(11:14:17)A.
Row 18: 8(11:14:17)A, ✷3B, 3A, 1B, 14A, rep from ✷ ending last rep with 15(18:21:24)A.
Row 19: 15(18:21:24)A, ✷1B, 20A, rep from ✷ ending last rep with 14(17:20:23)A.
Row 20: 5(8:11:14)A, ✷9C, 1B, 1A, 7C, 3A, rep from ✷ ending last rep with 7(10:13:16)A.
Row 21: 8(11:14:17)A, ✷6C, 1A, 1B, 8C, 5A, rep from ✷ ending last rep with 6(9:12:15)A.
Row 22: 7(10:13:16)A, ✷7C, 1B, 1A, 5C, 7A, rep from ✷ ending last rep with 9(12:15:18)A.
Row 23: 10(13:16:19)A, ✷4C, 1A, 1B, 6C, 9A, rep from ✷ ending last rep with 8(11:14:17)A.
Row 24: 9(12:15:18)A, ✷5C, 1B, 1A, 3C, 11A, rep from ✷ ending last rep with 11(14:17:20)A.
Row 25: 12(15:18:21)A, ✷2C, 1A, 1B, 4C, 13A, rep from ✷ ending last rep with 10(13:16:19)A.
Row 26: 11(14:17:20)A, ✷3C, 1B, 1A, 1C, 15A, rep from ✷ ending last rep with 13(16:19:22)A.

Row 27: 15(18:21:24)A, ✷1B, 2C, 18A, rep from ✷ ending last rep with 12(15:18:21)A.
Row 28: 13(16:19:22)A, ✷1C, 1B, 19A, rep from ✷ ending last rep with 15(18:21:24)A.
Row 29: 15(18:21:24)A, ✷1B, 20A, rep from ✷ ending last rep with 14(17:20:23)A.
Rows 30–34: Work each row in A.
These 34 rows form patt.
Rep 34 patt rows once more, marking each end of 22nd(28th:34th) row to indicate end of side seams for first, 2nd and 3rd sizes.
Cont with A only work a further 22(30:38:46) rows, marking each end of 6th row to indicate end of side seams for 4th size only.

Shape shoulders

Cast off 11(12:13:14) sts at beg of next 4 rows:
28(30:32:34) sts.
Break off yarn and leave rem sts on a spare needle.

LEFT FRONT

Using smaller needles and A, cast on 38(42:44:48) sts.
Beg with P1, work 15 rows in K1, P1 rib.
Next row: Rib 7 and leave these sts on a holder for button band, rib to end inc 1 st at end of row for first and 3rd sizes only: 32(35:38:41) sts.
Work first 6 patt rows as given for back from ✷✷ to ✷✷.
Row 7: 2A(2B:3A:2A:2B:3A), ✷3B, 3A, rep from ✷
Row 8: 0(3:0:3)A, 2B, ✷4A, 2B, rep from ✷ to end.
Row 9: ✷3A, 3B, rep from ✷ to last 2(5:2:5) sts, 2A(3A:2B:2A:3A:2B).
Row 10: 2B(2A:3B:2B:2A:3B), ✷3A, 3B, rep from ✷
Row 11: ✷2B, 4A, rep from ✷ to last 2(5:2:5) sts, 2B, 0(3:0:3)A.
Rows 12–14: With A to end.
Row 15: 16(19:22:25)A, 5B, 11A.
Row 16: 9A, 8B, 15(18:21:24)A.
Row 17: 14(17:20:23)A, 11B, 7A.
Row 18: 7A, 3B, 3A, 1B, 18(21:24:27)A.
Row 19: 18(21:24:27)A, 1B, 13A.
Row 20: 4A, 9C, 1B, 1A, 7C, 10(13:16:19)A.
✷✷✷ These 20 rows set position for patt.
Keeping patt correct as set, cont as given for back and work a further 36(42:48:54) rows, marking end of last row to indicate end of side seam.
Patt a further 15(17:17:19) rows.

Shape neck

Next row: Patt 10(11:12:13) sts and leave these sts on a holder for first side of neck, patt to end.
Cont straight until front measures same as back to shoulder, ending at side edge.

Shape shoulder

Cast off 11(12:13:14) sts at beg of next row:
11(12:13:14) sts. Work 1 row.
Cast off rem sts.

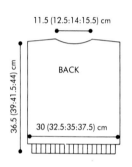

11.5 (12.5:14:15.5) cm

BACK

36.5 (39:41.5:44) cm

30 (32.5:35:37.5) cm

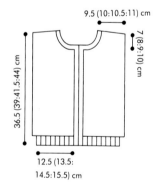

9.5 (10:10.5:11) cm

7 (8:9:10) cm

36.5 (39:41.5:44) cm

12.5 (13.5:14.5:15.5) cm

22 (23.5:24:25.5) cm

SLEEVE

25 (27.5:30:32.5) cm

RIGHT FRONT

Using smaller needles and A, cast on 38(42:44:48) sts.
Work 15 rows in K1, P1 rib.

Inc row: Inc 1(0:1:0) st in first st, rib to last 7 sts, turn
and leave these sts on a holder for buttonhole band:
32(35:38:41) sts.

Work first 6 patt rows as given for back from ✿✿ to ✿✿.

Row 7: 2A(2B,3A:2A:2B,3A), ✿3B, 3A, rep from ✿
Row 8: ✿4A, 2B, rep from ✿ to last 2(5:2:5) sts,
2A(4A,1B:2A:4A,1B).
Row 9: 2B(2A,3B:2B:2A,3B), ✿3A, 3B, rep from ✿
Row 10: ✿3A, 3B, rep from ✿ to last 2 (5:2:5) sts,
2A(3A,2B:2A:3A,2B).
Row 11: 2A(1B,4A:2A:1B,4A), ✿2B, 4A, rep from ✿
Rows 12–14: With A to end.
Row 15: 10A, 5B, 17(20:23:26)A.
Row 16: 15(18:21:24)A, 8B, 9A.
Row 17: 8A, 11B, 13(16:19:22)A.
Row 18: 13(16:19:22)A, 3B, 3A, 1B, 12A.
Row 19: 12A, 1B, 19(22:25:28)A.
Row 20: 10(13:16:19)A, 9C, 1B, 1A, 7C, 4A.

These 20 rows set patt for right front.

Work as for left front from ✿✿✿ to end, marking *beg of
row* to indicate side seam and working 1 more row
before shaping neck.

SLEEVES

Using smaller needles and A, cast on 38(40:42:44) sts.
Work 16 rows in K1, P1 rib.
Change to larger needles.
Beg with a K row cont in st st, inc 1 st at each end of 5th
and every foll 8th row until there are 52(56:58:62) sts.
Work 3(3:11:11) rows straight.
Break off A. Join in B. Work 6 more rows straight.
Cast off.

BUTTON BAND

Using smaller needles, A, and with RS facing, rib across
7 sts from holder on left front.
Work 67(77:87:97) rows in rib. Break off yarn and
leave sts on a safety-pin.

BUTTONHOLE BAND

Using smaller needles, A, and with WS facing, rib across
7 sts from holder on right front.

Make buttonholes

Row 1: Rib 2, cast off 2, rib to end.
Row 2: Rib to end, casting on 2 sts over those cast off.
previous row.
Rib 12(14:16:18) rows.
Rep last 14(16:18:20) rows 3 more times, then 2
buttonhole rows again.
Work 10(12:14:16) more rows in rib.
Do not break off yarn.

NECKBAND

Join shoulder seams.

With RS facing, rib across buttonhole band sts, K across
10(11:12:13) sts from holder on right front, pick up and
K 15(15:17:17) sts from right front neck shaping, K
across back neck sts dec 1 st, pick up and K
15(15:17:17) sts from left front neck shaping, K across
10(11:12:13) sts from holder on left front, then rib
across button band sts: 91(95:103:107) sts.

Row 1: ✿P1, K1, ✿ rep from ✿ to ✿ 7(8:8:9) times, P1
and mark this st for corner, K1, rep from ✿ to ✿
28(28:32:32) times, P1 and mark this st for corner,
✿✿K1, P1, rep from ✿✿ 7(8:8:9) times.
Row 2: Work in rib to within 2 sts of marked st, P2 tog,
K marked st, P2 tog, rep from ✿ once more, rib to end.
Row 3: Work in rib to within 2 sts of marked st, K2 tog,
P marked st, K2 tog, rep from ✿ once more, rib to end.
Rep 2nd and 3rd rows once more, then 2nd row again,
at the same time, make a buttonhole at right front edge
as before on first and 2nd of these rows.
Cast off in rib.

TO MAKE UP

Press or block as appropriate for yarn used.
Set in sleeves above markers, matching centre of sleeve
tops to shoulder seams. Sew front bands in place. Sew
on buttons to correspond with buttonholes.

BERET

Using smaller needles and A, cast on 92 sts.
Cont in K1, P1 rib working 2 rows A, 2 rows B and 2
rows A.
Change to larger needles. Cont with A in st st as follows:
Row 1: K1, ✿K8, incs 1 st in next st, rep from ✿ 9 more
times, K1: 102 sts.
Rows 2–4: P 1 row, K 1 row, P 1 row.
Row 5: K1, ✿K9, inc in next st, rep from ✿ 9 more
times, K1: 112 sts.
Rep 2nd–5th rows 3 more times, working 1 extra st
between incs on each rep of 5th row: 142 sts. P 1 row.
Join in B. Using B, work 8 rows straight.
Break off B and cont with A only.

Shape crown

Row 1: K1, ✿K12, K2 tog, rep from ✿ to last st, K1: 132
sts.
Row 2: P to end.
Row 3: K1, ✿K11, K2 tog, rep from ✿ to last st, K1: 122
sts.
Rep 2nd and 3rd rows 10 more times, working 1 st less
between decs on each rep of 3rd row: 22 sts.
P 1 row.
Next row: ✿K2 tog, rep from ✿ to end: 11 sts.
Break yarn, leaving an end. Run end through rem sts and
fasten off. Join seam. Sew a pompom to top.

Fancy Rib Sweater

A classic sweater for all the family, knitted in fancy rib; make it with a polo neck or crew neck.

MEASUREMENTS

To fit bust/chest 61(66:71:76:81:86:91:97:102:107)cm/ 24(26:28:30:32:34:36:38:40:42)"

Actual measurements 66(71:76:81:86:91:96:101:106: 111)cm/26(28:30:32:34:36:37¾:39¾:41¾:43¾)"

Length from shoulders 37.5(41.5:45:49:54:55:56.5:59: 60:61.5)cm/14¾(16¼:17¾:19¼:21¼:21½:22¼: 23¼:23½:24¼)"

Sleeve seam 22(26:30.5:35:41:41:41:44.5:44.5:44.5)cm/ 8¾(10¼:12:13¾:16:16:16:17½:17½:17½)"

Instructions are given for smallest size first, with figures for larger sizes in ( ).

MATERIALS

Crew-neck version

200(200:250:300:350:400:450:450:500:500)g/ 8(8:10:12:14:16:18:18:20:20)oz of a double knitting yarn

Polo-neck version

250(250:300:350:400:450:500:500:550:550)g/ 10(10:12:14:16:18:20:20:22:22)oz of a double knitting yarn

A pair each of 3¼mm and 4mm knitting needles (or sizes to obtain correct tension)

Remember to check your tension.

TENSION

24 sts and 32 rows to 10cm/4" measured over patt with ribs slightly stretched, worked on larger needles

INSTRUCTIONS

BACK

Using smaller needles cast on 78(84:90:96:102:108:114:120:126:132) sts.

Work 12 rows in K1, P1 rib, inc 1 st at end of last row: 79(85:91:97:103:109:115:121:127:133) sts.

Change to larger needles.

Cont working in patt as follows:

Row 1 (RS): K1, *P1, K1, rep from * to end.

Row 2: P2, K3, *P3, K3, rep from * to last 2 sts, P2.

These 2 rows form patt and are rep throughout.

Cont in patt until back measures 21.5(24:26.5:29:32.5:32.5:32.5:34:34:34)cm/ 8½(9½:10½:11½:12¾: 12¾:12¾:13½:13½:13½)" from beg, ending with a WS row.

Shape raglan armholes

Rows 1 and 2: Cast off 1 st, patt to end.

Row 3: K3, skpo, patt to last 4 sts, K2 tog, K2.

Row 4: K1, P2, patt to last 3 sts, P2, K1. **☆☆**

Rep last 2 rows until 29(31:33:35:37:39:41:43:45:47) sts rem.

Next row: K2, sl 1, K2 tog, psso, patt to last 5 sts, K3 tog, K2.

Next row: K1, P2, patt to last 3 sts, P2, K1: 25(27:29:31:33:35:37:39:41:43) sts.

Break off yarn and leave rem sts on a spare needle.

FRONT

Work as given for back to **☆☆**. Rep 3rd and 4th shaping rows until 41(43:47:49:53:55:59:61:65:67) sts rem, then 3rd row once more: 39(41:45:47:51:53:57:59:63:65) sts.

Divide for neck

Next row Patt 13(14:16:16:18:18:20:21:23:24) sts and leave these sts on a spare needle for right front, patt across next 13(13:13:15:15:17:17:17:17:17) sts and leave them on a holder for centre front neck, patt to end.

Work on last set of 13(14:16:16:18:18:20:21:23:24) sts for left front.

Dec 1 st at armhole edge as before on next and every foll alternate row 5(5:6:6:7:7:8:8:9:9) times in all, *at the same time* dec 1 st at neck edge on next 4(5:6:6:7:7:8:9:10:11) rows, then foll alternate row: 3 sts.

Work 1 row. K3 tog and fasten off.

With WS of work facing, rejoin yarn to rem sts at neck edge and complete to match first side, reversing shaping.

SLEEVES

Using smaller needles cast on 42(42:42:48:48:48:54:54:54:60) sts.

Work 16(16:16:16:20:20:20:24:24:24) rows in K1, P1 rib, inc 1 st at end of last row: 43(43:43:49:49:49:55:55:55:61) sts.

Change to larger needles.

Work 4 rows in patt as given for back. Keeping patt correct and taking extra sts into patt when possible, inc 1 st at each end of next and every foll 10th(8th:8th:12th:10th:8th:8th:8th:6th:6th) row until there are 51(55:59:63:69:73:77:81:85:89) sts.

Cont without shaping until sleeve measures 22(26:30.5:35:41:41:41:44.5:44.5:44.5)cm/ 8¾(10¼:12:13 ¾:16:16:16:17½:17½:17½)" from beg, ending with a WS row.

Shape raglans

Rows 1 and 2: Cast off 1 st, patt to end.

Row 3: K3, patt to last 3 sts, K3.

Row 4: K1, P2, patt to last 3 sts, P2, K1.

Row 5: K2, skpo, patt to last 4 sts, K2 tog, K2.
Row 6: As row 4.
Rep 3rd–6th rows 2(2:2:2:2:2:2:3:3:3) more times,
then rep 5th and 6th rows only until 7(7:7:7:7:7:7:9:9:9)
sts rem, ending with a 6th row.
First, 2nd, 3rd and 4th sizes only
Next row: K2, sl 1, K2 tog, psso, K2.
Next row: K1, P3, K1.
Break off yarn and leave rem 5(5:5:5:7:7:7:9:9:9) sts on
a holder.

NECKBAND
Join right raglan seam and left sleeve to front only. With
RS facing and using smaller needles, rejoin yarn to left
sleeve.
K across sts at top of left sleeve, pick up and K
11(12:13:14:15:16:17:18:19:20) sts down left side of
neck, K across 13(13:13:15:15:17:17:17:17:17) sts at
centre front neck, pick up and K
11(12:13:14:15:16:17:18:19:20) sts up right side of
neck, K across sts at top of right sleeve, then K across
25(27:29:31:33:35:37:39:41:43) sts at back neck:

70(74:78:84:92:98:102:110:114:118) sts.
Crew neck
☆ Work 5(5:5:5:7:7:7:9:9:9) rows in K1, P1 rib. ☆
Foldline: P to end.
Rep from ☆ to ☆ once more.
Cast off loosely in rib.
Polo collar
Work 10(10:10:10:14:14:14:18:18:18) rows in K1, P1
rib.
Change to larger needles.
Work a further 13(13:13:13:17:17:17:23:23:23) rows in
rib.
Cast off loosely in rib.

TO MAKE UP
Do not press.
Join rem raglan seam, then cont across neckband
ribbing with a flat seam. Join side and sleeve seams.
Fold crew neck in half to WS along foldline, and catch in
place.
Fold polo collar to RS.

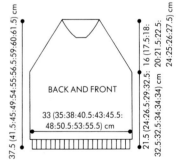

BACK AND FRONT

37.5 (41.5:45:49:54:55:56:59:60:61.5) cm

16 (17.5:18: 20:21.5:22.5: 24:25:26:27.5) cm

33 (35:38:40.5:43:45.5: 48:50.5:53:55.5) cm

21.5 (24:26.5:29:32.5: 32.5:32.5:34:34:34) cm

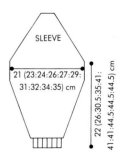

SLEEVE

21 (23:24:26:27:29: 31:32:34:35) cm

22 (26:30.5:35:41: 41:41:44.5:44.5:44.5) cm

191

Ski Sweater

Unisex ski sweater with a contrasting decorative pattern in traditional Scandinavian style.

MEASUREMENTS

To fit bust/chest 81(86:91:97:102:107)cm/
32(34:36:38:40:42)"
Actual measurements 85.5(90:97:101:105.5:112)cm/
33¾(35½:38:39¾:41½:44)"
Length from shoulders 64(64.5:65.5:70.5:71.5:72.5)cm/
25¼(25½:25¾:27¾:28¼:28½)"
Sleeve seam 43.5(43.5:43.5:49.5:49.5:49.5)cm/
17¼(17¼:17¼:19½:19½:19½)"
Instructions are given for smallest size first with figures
for larger sizes in ( ).

MATERIALS

360(360:400:440:480:520)g/15(15:16:17:19:21)oz of a
chunky knitting yarn in main colour A
160(200:200:200:200:200)g/7(8:8:8:8:8)oz in
contrasting colour B
A pair each of 3¾mm, 4½mm and 5mm knitting
needles (or sizes to obtain correct tension)
A 60cm/24" 4mm and an 80cm/30" 4½mm circular
knitting needle (or sizes to obtain correct tension)
A set of 4 3¾mm double-pointed knitting needles (or
size to obtain correct tension)

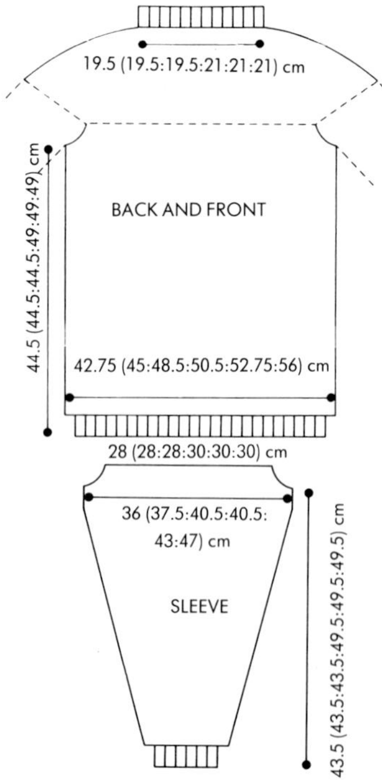

TENSION

18 sts and 23 rows to 10cm/4" measured over st st
worked on largest needles

INSTRUCTIONS

BACK AND FRONT (alike)

Using smallest needles and B, cast on
77(81:87:91:95:101) sts.
Row 1: K1, ✩P1, K1, rep from ✩ to end.
Row 2: P1, ✩K1, P1, rep from ✩ to end.
Work 12(12:12:14:14:14) more rows in rib as set.
Change to largest needles.
Join in A. Beg with a K row cont working in st st
throughout in colour patt as follows:
Rows 1–3: 5(4:4:0.5:5)B, ✩1A, 5B, rep from ✩ to last
6(5:5:1:6:6) sts, 1A, 5(4:4:0:5:5)B.
Row 4: 1A,3B(3B:3B:2A,3B:1A,3B:1A,3B), ✩3A, 3B,
rep from ✩ to last 1(6:6:2:1:1) sts,
1A(3A,3B:3A,3B:2A:1A:1A).
Row 5: 2(1:1:0:2:2)A, ✩1B, 2A, rep from ✩ to last
0(2:2:1:0:0) sts, 0(1:1:1:0:0)B, 0(1:1:0:0:0)A.
Row 6: As 4th row, but working A for B and B for A.
Rows 7–9: 2(1:1:3:2:2)B, ✩1A, 5B, rep from ✩ to last
3(2:2:4:3:3) sts, 1A,2B(1A,1B:1A, 1B:1A, 1B:1A,3B:1A,2B).

Rows 10–15: Work as 6th row back to first row.
Row 16: As 4th.
Row 17: As 7th.
Row 18: As first.
Row 19: As 10th.
Row 20: As 18th.
Row 21: Work in A only to end.
Row 22: As 17th.
These 22 rows complete border patt.
Change to medium-sized needles.
Cont in A only in st st until work measures
44.5(44.5:44.5:49:49:49)cm/
17½(17½:17½:19¼:19¼:19¼)" from beg, ending
with a WS row.

Shape armholes

Cast off 3(4:6:3:4:6) sts at beg of next 2 rows.
Dec 1 st at each end of next and every foll alternate
row until 63(63:63:71:71:71) sts rem.
P 1 row. Leave sts on a spare needle.

SLEEVES

Using smallest needles and B, cast on
43(43:43:49:49:49) sts. Work 14(14:14:16:16:16) rows
in rib as given for back.
Change to largest needles.
Join in A. Work 8 rows in patt as given for back, foll
figures for 4th size only for all sizes.
Keeping patt correct to match back and taking extra sts
into patt, inc 1 st at each end of next and foll 8th row:
47(47:47:53:53:53) sts.
Patt 5 rows straight.
Change to medium-sized needles.
Cont with A only. Patt 2 rows straight.
Inc 1 st at each end of next and every foll
6th(5th:4th:6th:5th:4th) row until there are
65(69:75:75:79:85) sts.
Work straight until sleeve measures
43.5(43.5:43.5:49.5:49.5:49.5/
17¼(17¼:17¼:19½:19½:19½)" from beg, ending
with a WS row.

Shape top

Work as given for armhole shaping on back until
51(51:51:55:55:55) sts rem.
Break off yarn and leave sts on a spare needle.

YOKE

Using larger circular needle and with RS facing, rejoin
yarn and work across sts of one sleeve, front, 2nd
sleeve and then back as follows:
Next round: K2(2:2:10:10:10), ✩K2 tog,
K11(11:11:8:8:8), rep from ✩ to last 5(5:5:12:12:12) sts,

Remember to check your tension.

19.5 (19.5:19.5:21:21:21) cm

44.5 (44.5:44.5:49:49:49) cm

BACK AND FRONT

42.75 (45:48.5:50.5:52.75:56) cm

28 (28:28:30:30:30) cm

36 (37.5:40.5:40.5:43:47) cm

SLEEVE

43.5 (43.5:43.5:49.5:49.5:49.5) cm

K2 tog, K3(3:3:10:10:10): 210(210:210:228:228:228) sts.
Cont working in rounds (every row K), marking first st with a contrasting thread to indicate beg of rounds, in yoke patt as follows:

Round 1: ✫1B, 5A, rep from ✫ to end.
Round 2: Work in A to end.
Round 3: 3A, ✫1B, 5A, rep from ✫ to last 3 sts, 1B, 2A.
Round 4: 2A, ✫3B, 3A, rep from ✫ to last 4 sts, 3B, 1A.
Round 5: As round 3.
Round 6: As round 1.
Round 7: 2B, ✫3A, 3B, rep from ✫ to last 4 sts, 3A, 1B.
Round 8: 3B, ✫1A, 5B, rep from ✫ to last 3 sts, 1A, 2B.
Rounds 9 and 10: As round 8.
Round 11: As round 7.
Round 12: ✫1B, 2A, rep from ✫ to end.
Change to smaller circular needle.
Round 13: As round 4.
Round 14: ✫1A, 5B, rep from ✫ to end.
Round 15: ✫1A, 2B, K2 tog B, 1B, rep from ✫ to end: 175(175:175:190:190:190) sts.
Round 16: ✫1A, 4B, rep from ✫ to end.
Round 17: 2A, ✫2B, 3A, rep from ✫ to last 3 sts, 2B, 1A.
Round 18: ✫1B, 1A, K2 tog B, 1A, rep from ✫ to end: 140(140:140:152:152:152) sts.
Round 19: ✫1B, 3A, rep from ✫ to end.
Round 20: 2B, ✫1A, 3B, rep from ✫ to last 2 sts, 1A, 1B.

Rounds 21 and 22: As round 20.
Break off A and cont with B only.
Shape yoke top
Round 1: ✫K5(5:5:6:6:6), skpo, rep from ✫ to end: 120(120:120:133:133:133) sts.
K 3 rounds.
Round 5: ✫K4(4:4:5:5:5), skpo, rep from ✫ to end: 100(100:100:114:114:114) sts.
K 3 rounds.
Round 9: ✫K3(3:3:4:4:4), K2 tog, rep from ✫ to end: 80(80:80:95:95:95) sts.
K 3 rounds.
Round 13: ✫K6(6:6:3:3:3), skpo, rep from ✫ to end: 70(70:70:76:76:76) sts.
K 1 round.
Change to set of 4 double-pointed needles.
Work 7 rounds in K1, P1 rib.
P 1 round for fold-line.
Work 7 more rounds in rib. Cast off loosely in rib.

TO MAKE UP
Press or block as appropriate for yarn used.
Join underarm seams. Join side and sleeve seams.
Fold neckband in half to WS and catch in place.

Rice Stitch Cardigan

A comfortable, casual cardigan for the man about the house to wear at weekends.

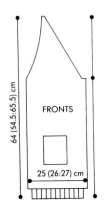

15 (15.5:16) cm

23.5 (24:25) cm

40.5 cm

BACK

50 (52.5:55) cm

Remember to check your tension.

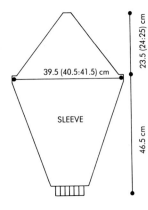

64 (54.5:65.5) cm

FRONTS

25 (26:27) cm

23.5 (24:25) cm

46.5 cm

39.5 (40.5:41.5) cm

SLEEVE

MEASUREMENTS

To fit chest 97(102:107)cm/38(40:42)"
Actual measurements 101(105:110.5)cm/
39¾(41¼:43½)"
Length from shoulders 64(64.5:65.5)cm/
25¼(25½:25¾)"
Sleeve seam 46.5cm/18¼"
Instructions are given for the smallest size first, with figures for larger sizes in ( ).

MATERIALS

600(600:650)g/24(24:26)oz of a double knitting yarn
A pair each of 3mm and 4mm knitting needles (or sizes to obtain correct tension)
5 buttons

TENSION

25 sts and 34 rows to 10cm/4" measured over patt worked on larger needles

INSTRUCTIONS

BACK

Using smaller needles cast on 125(131:137) sts.
Row 1: K1, *P1, K1, rep from * to end.
Row 2: P1, *K1, P1, rep from * to end.
Work 20 more rows in rib as set.
Change to larger needles.
Cont in patt as follows:
Row 1: K1, *P1, K1, rep from * to end.
Row 2: K to end.
These 2 rows form the patt. Cont in patt until work measures 40.5cm/16" from beg, ending with a WS row.

Shape raglan

Keeping patt correct cast off 5(6:7) sts at beg of next 2 rows: 115(119:123) sts.
Next row: K1, K2 tog tbl, patt to last 3 sts, K2 tog, K1.
Next row: P2, K to last 2 sts, P2.
Rep last 2 rows until 37(39:41) sts rem. Cast off in patt.

POCKET LININGS (make 2)

Using larger needles, cast on 35 sts. Work 34 rows in patt as given for back. Break off yarn and leave sts on a spare needle.

LEFT FRONT

Using smaller needles cast on 61(63:67) sts. Work 22 rows in rib as given for back.

Change to larger needles.
Cont working throughout in patt as given for back.
Work 34 rows. ✩✩

Place pocket

Next row: Patt 16(18:22) sts, leave rem 45 sts on a spare needle, patt across 35 sts of one pocket lining: 51(53:57) sts.
Work 12 rows in patt. Break off yarn and leave sts on a holder.
With RS of work facing, rejoin yarn to inner edge of 45 sts on spare needle, and cont working on these sts.
Cast off 4 sts at beg of next row, 7 sts at beg of 4 foll alternate rows and 3 sts at beg of foll alternate row: 10 sts.
Joining row: K10, K across 51(53:57) sts on holder: 61(63:67) sts.
✩✩✩ Cont working in patt until front measures same as back to beg of raglan shaping, ending at side edge. ✩✩✩

Shape raglan and front edge

Row 1: Cast off 5(6:7) sts, patt to end.
Row 2: K to last 2 sts, P2.
Row 3: K1, K2 tog tbl, patt to last 2 sts, K2 tog.
Row 4: As row 2.
Row 5: K1, K2 tog tbl, patt to end.
✩✩✩✩ Rep rows 2 to 5 14(14:16) more times, then rows 4 and 5 9(10:7) times: 2 sts. K2 tog. Fasten off.

RIGHT FRONT

Work as given for left front to ✩✩.

Place pocket

Next row: Patt 45 sts, turn and leave rem 16(18:22) sts on a spare needle.
Cast off 4 sts at beg of next row, 7 sts on foll 4 alternate rows and 3 sts at same edge on foll alternate row: 10 sts.
Work 1 row in patt. Leave these sts on a holder.
Using larger needles, rejoin yarn and patt across 35 sts of 2nd pocket lining, then with same needle, patt across 16(18:22) sts from spare needle: 51(53:57) sts.
Work 12 rows in patt.
Joining row: K to end, then K across 10 sts on holder: 61(63:67) sts.
Cont working in patt as given for left front from ✩✩✩ to ✩✩✩.

Shape raglan and front edge

Row 1: Cast off 5(6:7) sts, K to end.
Row 2: K2 tog, patt to last 3 sts, K2 tog, K1.
Row 3: P2, K to end.
Row 4: Patt to last 3 sts, K2 tog, K1.
Row 5: As row 3.
Complete as given for left front, from ✩✩✩✩ to end.

SLEEVES

Using smaller needles, cast on 49(53:57) sts. Work 22 rows in rib as given for back.

Change to larger needles.

Taking extra sts into patt as they occur, cont in patt as given for back, inc 1 st at each end of 5th and every foll 5th row until there are 97(101:105) sts.

Cont without shaping until sleeve measures 46.5cm/ 18¼″ from beg, ending with a WS row.

Shape raglan

Work as given for armhole shaping on back until 9 sts rem. Cast off in patt.

FRONT BORDER

Join raglan seams.

Using smaller needles cast on 9 sts.

Row 1: K2, ✫P1, K1, rep from ✫ to last st, K1.

Row 2: K1, ✫P1, K1, rep from ✫ to end.

Cont in rib as set. Rep last 2 rows once more.

Buttonhole row: Rib 3, cast off 3, rib to end.

Next row: Rib to end, casting on 3 sts over those cast off in previous row.

Work 30 more rows in rib.

Rep last 32 rows 3 more times, then 2 buttonhole rows once more.

Cont in rib until band fits up left front, across back neck and down right front when slightly stretched.

Cast off in rib.

POCKET TOPS (make 2)

With RS of work facing and using smaller needles, rejoin yarn, then pick up and K 33 sts across top of pocket. Beg with a 2nd row work 8 rows in rib as given for back. Cast off in rib.

TO MAKE UP

Press lightly or block as appropriate for yarn used. Join side and sleeve seams. Sew front border in place, placing top buttonhole level with first front dec. Sew on buttons to correspond with buttonholes. Sew row ends of pocket tops to RS and pocket linings to WS.

Traditional Guernsey

Easy to knit, a traditional Guernsey is designed to provide comfort and warmth for all outdoor types.

MEASUREMENTS

To fit chest 91(97:102:107:112)cm/36(38:40:42:44)" loosely

Actual measurements 102(105.5:112:115:121.5)cm/ 40(41½:44:45½:47¾)"

Length from shoulders 63(63:64:64:65.5)cm/ 24¾(24¾:25¼:25¼:25¾)"

Sleeve seam 48.5cm/19"

Instructions are given for the smallest size first with larger sizes in ( ).

MATERIALS

700(750:750:800:850)g/28(30:30:32:34)oz of a 5-ply Guernsey yarn

A pair each of 2¾mm and 3mm knitting needles (or sizes to obtain correct tension)

A set of 4 double-pointed 2¾mm knitting needles (or size to obtain correct tension)

TENSION

25 sts and 33 rows to 10cm/4" measured over st st worked on larger needles

INSTRUCTIONS

BACK AND FRONT (alike)

Using smaller needles cast on 120(124:130:134:140) sts. K 26 rows.

Inc row: K7(9:6:8:9) sts, inc in next st, ✫K14(14:12:12:10), inc in next st, rep from ✫ until 7(9:6:8:9) sts rem, K to end: 128(132:140:144:152) sts.

Cont working in rib as follows:

Row 1: K1, ✫P2, K2, rep from ✫ ending last rep with K1.

Row 2: P1, ✫K2, P2, rep from ✫ ending last rep with P1.

Rep last 2 rows twice more.

Change to larger needles.

Beg with a K row cont working in st st throughout, until work measures 40.5cm/16" from beg. Mark each end of last row with a contrasting thread to indicate end of side seams. Work 8 more rows in st st.

Next row: K4, P6, K to last 10 sts, P6, K4.

Next row: P to end.

Rep last 2 rows 33(33:35:35:37) more times.

Break off yarn and leave sts on a spare double-pointed needle.

Neckband and shoulders

With WS of shoulder sts of back and front tog and using larger needles, rejoin yarn to sleeve edge and working through back and front sts tog, cast off

31(33:36:38:41) sts (1 st left on needle).

Row 1: K1 from front needle, turn: 2 sts.

Row 2: Sl 1, P1, P1 from back needle, turn.

Row 3: Sl 1, K2, K1 from front needle, turn.

Row 4: Sl 1, P3, P1 from back needle, turn.

Cont in this way, working 1 extra st alternately on front and back needle at end of row, for 14 more rows: 19 sts. P46(46:48:48:50) sts from back needle. Break off yarn and leave these 65(65:67:67:69) sts on a spare needle.

Turn work, and work 2nd shoulder in the same way. A total of 130(130:134:134:138) sts.

Arrange these 130(130:134:134:138) sts evenly onto 3 double-pointed needles. Using 4th double-pointed needle, rejoin yarn and K 1 round dec 1 st in centre of each shoulder gusset: 128(128:132:132:136) sts.

Work 19 rounds in K2, P2 rib. Cast off in rib.

SLEEVES

Using smaller needles cast on 78(78:80:80:84) sts.

Work 36 rows in rib as given for back and front.

Change to larger needles.

Beg with a K row cont working in st st, inc 1 st at each end of 3rd and every foll 8th(8th:6th:6th:6th) row until there are 100(100:108:108:112) sts.

Work 23(23:25:25:25) rows in st st.

Shape gusset

Inc 1 st at each end of next and every foll alternate row until there are 112(112:120:120:124) sts. P 1 row.

Next row: K7, ✫P2, K2, rep from ✫ to last 9 sts, P2, K7.

Next row: P7, ✫K2, P2, rep from ✫ to last 9 sts, K2, P7.

Rep last 2 rows twice more. Cast off.

TO MAKE UP

Press or block as appropriate for yarn used.

Sew cast-off sts at top of sleeve to row ends, between markers on back and front. Join side and sleeve seams, leaving row ends of g st free at lower edges.

Remember to check your tension.

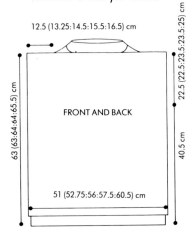

12.5 (13.25:14.5:15.5:16.5) cm

22.5 (22.5:23.5:23.5:25) cm

63 (63:64:64:65.5) cm

FRONT AND BACK

40.5 cm

51 (52.75:56:57.5:60.5) cm

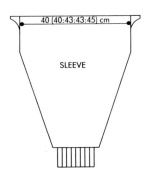

40 (40:43:43:45) cm

SLEEVE

Cricket Sweater

Knitted in white – of course – club colours can be incorporated in the contrasting bands of the trim.

MEASUREMENTS

To fit chest 82(88:92:97:100:105)cm/
32(34:36:38:40:42)"
Actual measurements 87(93:97:102:106:111)cm/
34(36½:38:40:42:44)"
Length from shoulders 63(63.5:64:66:67:67.5)cm/
24¾(25:25¼:26:26¼:26½)"
Sleeve seam 43.5cm/17"
Instructions are given for smallest size first, with figures
for larger sizes in ( ).

MATERIALS

450(500:550:600:650:700)g/18(20:22:24:26:28)oz of a
double knitting yarn in main colour A
50g/2oz in each of contrasting colours B and C
A pair each of 3¼mm and 4mm knitting needles (or
sizes to obtain correct tension)
A cable needle

TENSION

30 sts and 29 rows to 10cm/4" measured over patt
when slightly stretched, worked on larger needles

SPECIAL ABBREVIATION

C6B – cable 6 back as follows: sl next 3 sts onto cable
needle and hold at back of work, K3, then K3 from
cable needle.

INSTRUCTIONS

BACK

Using smaller needles and A, cast on
131(139:145:153:159:167) sts.
Row 1: Using A, K1, *P1, K1, rep from * to end.
Row 2: Using A, P1, *K1, P1, rep from * to end.
Rep 2 rib rows, working 10 more rows in A, 2 in B, 2 in
A, 2 in C and 12 in A.
Cont with A only.
Change to larger needles.
Cont working in patt as follows:
Row 1: P4(P8:P2,K6,P3:P0:P3:P7), *K1, P1, K1, P3, K6,
P3, rep from * to last 7(11:14:3:6:10) sts, K1, P1, K1,
then P4(P8:P3,K6,P2:P0:P3:P7).
Row 2: K4(K8:K2,P6,K3:P0:K3:K7), *P3, K3, P6, K3, rep
from * to last 7(11:14:3:6:10) sts, P3, then
K4(K8:K3,P6,K2:P0:K3:K7).
Rows 3–6: As rows 1 and 2.
Row 7: P4(P8:P2,C6B,P3:P0:P3:P7), *K1, P1, K1, P3,
C6B, P3, rep from * to last 7(11:14:3:6:10) sts, K1, P1,

K1, then P4(P8:P3,C6B,P2:P0:P3:P7).
Row 8: As row 2.
These 8 rows form patt and are rep throughout.
Cont in patt until back measures
40(40:40:41.5:41.5:41.5)cm/
15¾:(15¾:15¾:16¼:16¼:16¼:16¼)" from beg,
ending with a WS row. ✳✳

Shape armholes

Keeping patt correct, cast off 6(6:6:7:7:7) sts at beg of
next 2 rows. Dec 1 st at each end of next 5(5:7:7:7:9)
rows, then every foll alternate row until
101(107:111:117:121:127) sts rem.
Cont without shaping until armholes measure
23(23.5:24:24.5:25.5:26)cm/9(9¼:9½:9¾:10:10¼)"
from beg, ending with a WS row.

Shape shoulders

Cast off 7(7:7:8:8:8) sts at beg of next 6 rows, then
5(7:8:7:8:10) sts at beg of foll 2 rows:
49(51:53:55:57:59) sts.
Break off yarn and leave rem sts on a holder.

FRONT

Work as given for back to ✳✳, working 1 row less than
back to beg of armhole shaping.

Divide for neck

Next row: Patt 65(69:72:76:79:83) sts and leave these
sts on a spare needle for right front, cast off 1 st for
centre front neck, patt to end.
Work on last set of 65(69:72:76:79:83) sts first for left
front as follows:

Shape armhole and front edge

Row 1: Cast off 6(6:6:7:7:7) sts, patt to last 2 sts, dec 1
st.
Row 2: Patt to end.
✳✳✳ Dec 1 st at armhole edge on next 5(5:7:7:7:9)
rows and at same edge on foll 4(5:4:4:5:4) alternate
rows, at the same time dec 1 st at neck edge on first of
these rows and every foll alternate row:
42(44:46:49:49:50:53) sts.
Patt 1 row. Dec 1 st at neck edge only on next row and
foll 11(10:11:13:13:13) alternate rows, then every foll
4th row 4(5:5:4:4:5) times in all: 26(28:29:31:32:34) sts.
Work a few rows straight until front measures same as
back to shoulder, ending at side edge.

Shape shoulder

Cast off 7(7:7:8:8:8) sts at beg of next and foll 2
alternate rows: 5(7:8:7:8:10) sts.
Work 1 row. Cast off rem sts.
With RS of work facing, rejoin A to rem sts at neck
edge for right front and cont as follows:
Row 1: Dec 1 st, patt to end.

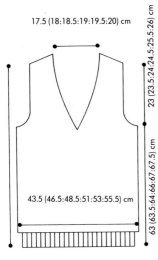

Remember to check your tension.

17.5 (18:18.5:19:19.5:20) cm

23 (23.5:24:24.5:25.5:26) cm

63 (63.5:64:66:67:67.5) cm

43.5 (46.5:48.5:51:53:55.5) cm

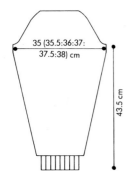

35 (35.5:36:37:37.5:38) cm

43.5 cm

Row 2: Cast off 6(6:6:7:7:7) sts, patt to end.
Complete to match first side, from ☆☆☆ to end.

SLEEVES

Using smaller needles and A, cast on
63(65:67:71:73:75) sts. Cont working in rib as given for
back as follows:
12 rows A, 2 rows B, 2 rows A, 2 rows C and 11 rows
A.

Inc row: Rib 3(4:5:2:3:4), inc in next st, ☆ rib
4(4:4:5:5:5), inc in next st, rep from ☆ to last 4(5:6:2:3:4)
sts, rib to end: 75(77:79:83:85:87) sts.
Change to larger needles.
Cont working in patt with A only, as follows:
Row 1: K3(K4:K5:P1,K6:P2,K6:P3,K6), P3, K1, P1, K1,
P3, ☆K6, P3, K1, P1, K1, P3, rep from ☆ to last
3(4:5:7:8:9) sts, K3(K4:K5:K6,P1:K6,P2:K6,P3).
Row 2: P3(P4:P5:K1,P6:K2,P6:K3,P6), K3, P3, K3, ☆P6,
K3, P3, K3, rep from ☆ to last 3(4:5:7:8:9) sts,
P3(P4:P5:P6,K1:P6,K2:P6,K3).
These 2 rows set the position of the patt.
Keeping patt correct, cont in patt as given for back,
working extra sts into patt where possible, inc 1 st at
each end of 5th and every foll 6th row until there are
105(107:109:113:115:117) sts.
Cont without shaping until sleeve measures 43.5cm/17″
from beg, ending with a WS row.
Shape top
Cast off 6(6:6:7:7:7) sts at beg of next 2 rows. Dec 1 st
at each end of next 7 rows, then every foll alternate
row until 59 sts rem.
Work 1 row. Dec 1 st at each end of next 12 rows: 35
sts. Cast off rem sts.

NECKBAND

Join right shoulder seam.
With RS facing, using smaller needles and A, pick up
and K55(57:59:61:63:65) sts down left side of neck, 2
sts from centre front, 55(57:59:61:63:65) sts up right
side of neck and 49(51:53:55:57:59) sts across back
neck:161(167:173:179:185:191) sts.
Row 1: P1, ☆K1, P1, ☆ rep from ☆ to ☆ to centre front
sts, P2 centre sts, P1, rep from ☆ to ☆ to end.
Row 2: Rib to within 2 sts of centre front sts, K2 tog, K2
centre front sts, K2 tog, rib to end.
Row 3: Rib to within 2 sts of centre front sts, P2 tog, P2
centre front sts, P2 tog, rib to end.
Cont to dec 1 st at each side of centre front sts as
before, cont in rib working 1 row A, 2 rows B, 2 rows
A, 2 rows C and 4 rows A.
Cast off in rib, dec as before.

TO MAKE UP

Do not press.
Join rem shoulder seam, then cont across neckband
with a flat seam.
Set in sleeves. Join side and sleeve seams.

Allsorts

These colourful giant sweets are quick to knit in chunky yarn and garter stitch. Filled with foam, they're also fun to play with.

MATERIALS

Black and orange cube
100g/4oz chunky yarn in black (A)
50g/2oz in orange (B)
Yellow and black cube
200g/8oz in yellow (C)
50g/2oz in black (A)
Black and white allsort
100g/4oz in black (A)
50g/2oz in white (D)
Black and white round allsort
100g/4oz in black (A)
50g/2oz in white (D)
Pink and black allsort
200g/8oz in pink (E)
50g/2oz in black (A)
Whole set
350g/14oz in black (A)
50g/2oz white (D)
200g/8oz in pink (E)
50g/2oz in orange (B)
200g/7oz in yellow (C)
1 pair 7mm needles
Solid foam or chippings for the stuffing

INSTRUCTIONS

BLACK AND ORANGE CUBE

SIDE PIECES (make 4)
With A, cast on 22 sts.
Work in g st stripes as follows:
Rows 1–8: A.
Rows 9–16: B.
Rep these 16 rows once more, then the first 8 rows again. Cast off.

END PIECES (make 2)
Using A, cast on 22 sts.
Work 40 rows in g st. Cast off.

TO MAKE UP
Do not press. Sew up cube leaving one seam open. Stuff and close rem seam.

YELLOW AND BLACK CUBE
SIDE PIECES (make 4)
With C, cast on 22 sts. Work 16 rows in g st. Cont in g st, work 8 rows in A, then 16 rows in C. Cast off.

END PIECES (make 2)
With C, cast on 22 sts. Work 40 rows in g st. Cast off.

TO MAKE UP
Complete as given for black and orange cube.

BLACK AND WHITE ALLSORT
SIDE PIECES (make 4)
With A, cast on 22 sts. Work 8 rows in g st. Cont in g st, work 8 rows in D, then 8 rows in A. Cast off.

END PIECES (make 4)
Work as given for black and orange cube.

TO MAKE UP
Complete as given for black and orange cube.

BLACK AND WHITE ROUND ALLSORT CHART 1
SIDE PIECE
With A, cast on 22 sts. Work 80 rows in g st. Cast off.

END PIECES (make 2)
With A, cast on 6 sts. Work in g st from chart I as follows: Work 2 rows straight. Cast on 2 sts at beg and end of next row. Work I row.
Next row: With A, inc I st into next st, K3, K2D, with A, K3, inc I st into last st.

Next row: K5A, 2D, 5A.
Cont working from chart I, inc I st at each end of foll 3rd row, then dec as shown until chart is complete. Cast off.

TO MAKE UP
Darn in loose ends. Join long seam of side piece to make tube. Sew one end piece in position. Stuff with foam chippings or rolled up sheet foam. Sew on rem end piece.

PINK AND BLACK ALLSORT CHART II
SIDE PIECE
With E, cast on 22 sts. Work 140 rows in g st. Cast off.

END PIECES (make 2)
With E, cast on 8 sts. Work in g st from chart II, inc at each end of 3rd, 5th, 7th, 9th, 13th and 17th rows and joining in A on 15th row as shown. Follow chart to complete shaping. Cast off.

TO MAKE UP
Complete as given for other cushion.

CHART 11

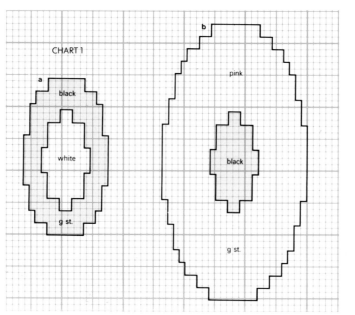

202

Pastoral Cushions

These unusual knitted cushions feature two picture panels: a sheep in a field and cherry trees. Soft colours enhance the natural effect.

MEASUREMENTS

Finished cushion measures 35.5cm/14" square
Knitted panel measures 23cm/9" square

MATERIALS

Sheep cushion
Oddments of 4-ply yarns in 11 colours and assorted textures (see key to chart I for details)
Cushion pad 35cm/14" square

Cherry tree cushion
Oddments of 4-ply yarns in 10 colours and assorted textures (see key to chart II for details)
Cushion pad 35cm/14" square
1 pair 3¼mm needles (or size to obtain correct tension)
40cm/½yd of 140cm/54" wide fine tweed fabric (for each cushion)
25cm/10" zip (for each cushion)

Remember to check your tension.

TENSION

26 sts and 36 rows to 10cm/4" measured over st st worked on 3¼mm needles

INSTRUCTIONS

SHEEP PANEL

Cast on 58 sts.
Using colours as indicated in key, follow chart I Beg with a K row work in st st, reading odd-numbered (K) rows from right to left and even-numbered (P) rows from left to right. When 81 rows of chart have been completed cast off.

CHERRY TREE PANEL

Cast on 58 sts.
Using colours as indicated in key, follow chart II, working in st st as given for Sheep panel. On K rows work from A to B twice, then from A to C. On P rows work from C to A, then from B to A twice. When 81 rows of chart have been completed cast off.

TO MAKE UP

Press or block if necessary as appropriate for yarn used. Darn in loose ends securely. Make up both covers alike. Pin out panel to 23cm/9" square. Textured yarns such as mohair can be raised by gentle brushing to give more depth and life to the landscape.
Cut fabric following layout. Sew borders together taking in 2cm/¾" seams to make a frame as shown. Press seams open. Position knitted panel in centre of frame and oversew joins on WS. Sew back of cushion to front taking in 2cm/¾" seams leaving 25cm/10" open on one side for zip. Insert zip.

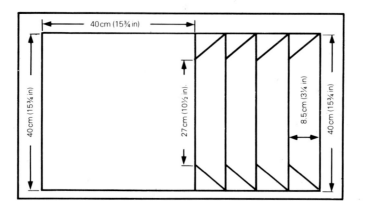

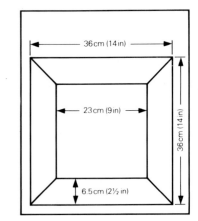

CHART I
1 grey
2 dark brown
3 lovat green
4 light green
5 bottle green
6 mixed wool, medium green
7 mid green
8 green mohair stripes
9 mixture, light green
10 white boucle
11 black

CHART II
1 grey
2 light brown boucle
3 pink for blossoms
4 light green
5 light brown
6 turquoise/pink for flowers
7 dark brown
8 green and yellow mixed
9 green/pink boucle mixture
10 green mohair

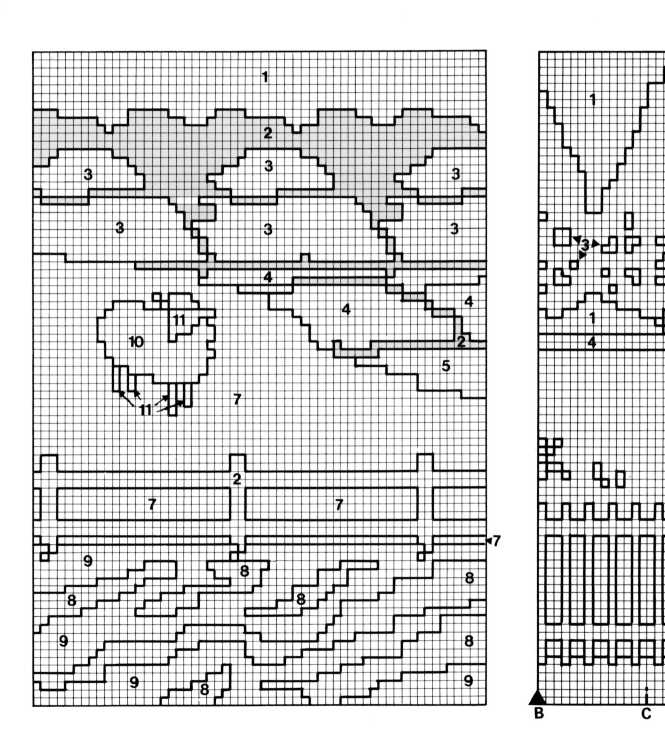

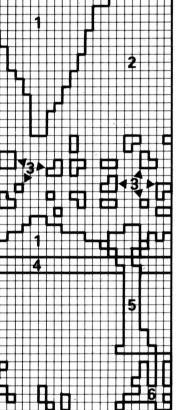

205

Christmas Stocking

A traditional Christmas stocking complete with fir trees and reindeer.

MATERIALS

150g/6oz of a double knitting yarn in main colour A
50g/2oz each of same in contrasting colours B and C
25g/1oz of a lightweight glitter yarn in contrasting colour D (used double)
A set of four 4mm and 4½mm double-pointed knitting needles (or sizes to obtain correct tension)

Remember to check your tension.

TENSION

24 sts and 30 rows to 10cm/4" measured over st st worked on smaller needles

INSTRUCTIONS

Using smaller needles and A, cast on 72 sts and arrange over 3 needles, so placing 24 sts on each needle.
K 36 rounds.
Next round: (Picot edge): ☆yf, skpo, rep from ☆ to end.
K a further 40 rounds.
Using the larger needles for the motif rows and the smaller needles for the plain rows, work in patt from chart, rep the 24 sts patt 3 times in each round, until row 59 completed. Change to smaller needles.
K 2 rounds.

Shape ankle
Next round: K1, skpo, K to last 3 sts, K2 tog, K1.
K 4 rounds.
Rep these last 5 rounds until 58 sts rem.

Shape heel
Break off A. Re-arrange sts as follows:
Sl last 15 sts of third needle and first 16 of first needle onto fourth needle. (There should now be 31 sts on this needle.)
Divide rem 27 sts onto rem 2 needles and leave.
Join on C and work backwards and forwards in rows on 31 sts of first needle only, as follows:
Row 1: K to end.
Row 2: P to end.
Dec 1 st at beg of next 22 rows: 9 sts.
Now inc 1 st at end of next 22 rows by picking up corresponding decreased loop of previous 22 rows: 31 sts. Break off C.
Join on A; working in rounds over all 58 sts, K 1 round re-arranging sts so that there are 20 sts on first needle and 19 on each of second and third and noting that round now begins at side edge of foot.
K 36 rounds. Break off A.
Join on C and K 6 rounds.
Shape toe

Round 1: [K1, skpo, K23, K2 tog, K1] twice.
Round 2: K to end.
Round 3: [K1, skpo, K21, K2 tog, K1] twice.
Round 4: K to end.
Cont to dec in this way on every alternate round until 22 sts rem. Cast off.

TO MAKE UP

Turn stocking inside out and join toe seam. Fold hem at top of stocking to WS and slipstitch into place. Either by crochet, plaiting or using the tubular knitting technique (see page 174), make a length of cord 20cm/8" long and stitch to back at top edge of stocking.

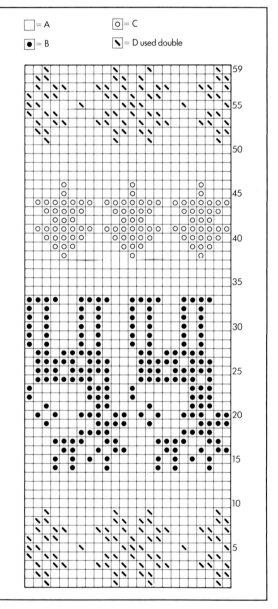

9 Design

Once you have become familiar with knitting patterns and the stages involved in knitting a garment, you may develop a yen to alter a pattern in some way – or even to create your own original design. You may, for example, find a yarn you like but then find that none of the designs for that yarn are quite to your taste. You may be looking for a cardigan pattern, but the only appealing designs are for pullovers. Perhaps you've found exactly the right pattern but its instructions do not include your size. Or perhaps the yarn recommended for the design is no longer available.

For designing you need both inspiration – such as magazine clippings and yarn samples – and information. A notebook and calculator are essential. For charting shapes, either ordinary graph paper or a tension grid is also required.

Your first steps in knitting design will probably consist of altering an existing pattern. Alterations to patterns vary considerably in difficulty; some are more work than designing a simple garment from scratch. Many, however, can be achieved by a person with only a moderate amount of experience. In the following pages you will find instructions for making a variety of pattern alterations, as well as the basic principles and steps involved in designing a complete garment.

MATERIALS FOR DESIGNING

Adapting and designing knitting patterns requires a few additional pieces of equipment besides those shown on page 13. These include a calculator, a notebook for writing down measurements and calculations, a sketch-book for planning original designs, and large sheets of graph paper and/or tension grids for charting some shapings. A tension grid is a kind of graph paper in which the lines correspond to the shape of knitting stitches. It is especially useful when designing colour patterns. Magazine clippings and other sources of inspiration can be kept in a file or large manilla envelope. Small tags are useful for labelling stitch samples.

SUBSTITUTING DIFFERENT YARNS

The simplest type of yarn substitution is to replace the recommended yarn with another of the same type – for example Brand B double knitting for Brand A. Even in this case, however, a little extra work is involved.

CALCULATING THE AMOUNT TO BUY

Different brands vary in the length per unit of weight, so you may need to buy more – or fewer – balls. If the length is given on the ball bands, you can calculate the amount yourself. If it is not, you must ask for assistance from the salesperson, who will have this information in the yarn catalogues supplied by the spinners.

Let us assume that both Brand A and Brand B come in 50g/1¾ oz balls, and that A contains an average 115 metres/126 yards in a ball, whereas B contains only 100 metres/109 yards. The number of balls of A specified is 9. Multiply 9 times 115/126, which gives 1,035 metres/1,134 yards. This is the total length of yarn required. Now divide this figure by the metres/yards in a ball of Brand B: 1,035 (m) ÷ 100 (m) = 10.35 (balls); 1,134 (yds) ÷ 109 (yds) = 10.4. (The small difference is caused by the rounding off that is done in most metric-imperial conversions.) To be on the safe side, you should buy 11 balls of Brand B.

CHECKING THE TENSION

You will need to check your tension in any case (see page 25), but if you are substituting a yarn for the one recommended, you may have slightly more trouble getting the tension right. Change to different needles as necessary until you get the tension specified by the pattern.

SUBSTITUTING A DIFFERENT TYPE OF YARN

Using a totally different kind of yarn can dramatically change the character of a garment. By substituting a soft kid mohair for a double knitting, for example, you could turn a casual-looking pullover into a dressy one.

To ensure a successful substitution you must first make sure that your chosen yarn will knit to the same tension as the original. Buy one ball, and work a tension swatch in the specified stitch pattern. Change the needle size if necessary. If you can achieve the correct tension, it may be safe to substitute the new yarn, and you can proceed to calculate the required amount as described above.

A WORD OF WARNING

If getting the correct tension entails a drastic adjustment of needle size, you may end up with an unsatisfactory – even though technically correct – tension. Any yarn has its own natural tension – a range of stitches and rows in which its texture and weight are displayed to best advantage. Some manufacturers will print this tension, along with the recommended needle size for achieving it, on the ball band. You can usually go up or down two sizes from this, but if you depart drastically from it and force the yarn to yield a radically different tension, you will get a fabric that is inappropriately flimsy or stiff. (An exception to this rule is deliberately to change the character of a solid stitch pattern, such as garter stitch, giving it an openwork texture. This is done by working it on unusually large needles.)

Your tension swatch will also reveal whether the texture of the substitute yarn is suitable for the stitch pattern. If the garment is worked mainly in stocking stitch, virtually any yarn can be used. If it is worked in a highly textured stitch pattern, you should be more critical. A fuzzy or multicoloured yarn, for example, may obscure the texture of the stitch.

CHANGING THE FABRIC

A somewhat more adventurous way of changing a pattern is to transform the character of the fabric, by adding a colour pattern (or substituting one for another) or by changing the stitch.

INTRODUCING A COLOUR PATTERN

It is a relatively easy matter to add a colour pattern to a plain stocking stitch garment. Horizontal stripes, or vertical stripes worked by the intarsia method (page 68), can easily be added to such a garment without any effect on the tension.

You will, however, need to make sure that a horizontal stripe pattern matches at the armhole. Work the back and front first. Before knitting the sleeves, measure down from the beginning of the armhole shaping, and see which colour you should begin with in order to ensure that you will be working the correct colour when you begin the sleeve head shaping.

Colour patterns worked by stranding/weaving (see pages 69–70) must be treated as a change of stitch pattern (see below), because they will almost certainly produce a change in the tension. The same applies to slipstitch colour patterns.

CHANGING THE STITCH PATTERN

A change of stitch pattern can be very simple – or very difficult. It all depends on what you wish to substitute for what.

The very simplest substitution would be reverse stocking stitch for stocking stitch; all you do is purl the knit rows and vice versa. This may not seem a very exciting or original idea, but the difference in texture may give quite a different character to the garment. You might also add a fat cable on one or

Working a sample will reveal the possibilities and limitations of a yarn. The Nut Pattern (mauve) works well in double knitting yarn but loses its definition in a fuzzy mohair blend. However, the mohair can be successfully used in some lace patterns, as the sample of Open Chevron Lace demonstrates. (For Nut Pattern see page 36; for Open Chevron Lace see page 40.)

both sides, to contrast with the reverse stocking stitch and provide an interesting design element. (Remember, though, that even one cable will draw the fabric in slightly, so make sure that the overall measurements are generous enough to allow for this.)

Substituting a textured stitch for a flat one, or one textured stitch for another, will almost certainly produce a change of tension; and if you were simply to cast on the specified number of stitches and work in the different pattern, the finished garment might be far too small or too large.

In some cases it may be possible to achieve the stated tension simply by adjusting the needle size. In many cases, however, you will need to do some calculations and adjust the number of stitches to cast on. If the garment involves only simple shaping, this can be relatively straightforward. But if the shaping is complex (raglan sleeves, for example), you are getting into deeper waters and would probably be better off designing the garment from scratch.

Another potential problem is the number of stitches in the pattern repeat. For your first attempt at substituting a stitch pattern, you would be wise to choose one with a repeat divisible by 2, or one with the same number in the repeat as the original stitch. Then, assuming you can get the same tension, the substitution should not present any problems.

Remember, though, to consider the mutual suitability of stitch pattern and yarn. If the yarn specified in the pattern is an Aran weight, for example, a lacy pattern would probably appear uncharacteristically coarse.

Finally, if you are replacing a flat stitch pattern with a highly textured one, you will need considerably more yarn. It is a good idea to calculate your yarn requirements using the method described on page 208.

STYLING ALTERATIONS

It is also possible to make certain alterations to the style of a pattern. Of course, these vary considerably in difficulty. Some adjustments are so complex that they should be attempted only by someone who has a measure of experience in designing original garments. Others are fairly simple. Among the latter are the following.

CREW NECK TO POLO NECK

This is among the easiest of all adjustments. You simply pick up the same number of stitches specified for the original neckband and work to the required depth for the collar.

To substitute a crew neck for a polo neck, reverse the method, working fewer rows. A crew neck is normally about 2.5cm/1″ deep. It can simply be cast off at this depth or worked to twice the depth, folded under and slipstitched to the wrong side.

PULLOVER TO CARDIGAN

This alteration is fairly easy if the pullover has a simple round neckline. Take, as an example, a pullover in which the tension is 30 stitches over 10cm/4″, or 3 sts per cm/7½ per inch respectively, and the number of stitches to cast on for front and back is 139. Work the back as instructed. For the front, the steps are as follows:

1 Divide the number of cast-on stitches by 2: 139 ÷ 2 = 69½, say 69.

2 Allow 3cm/1¼″ (or the desired measurement) for the button and buttonhole bands, and calculate from the tension the number of stitches in this measurement: 3 × 3 (cm) = 9sts; 7½ × 1¼ (″) = 9⅜, say 9sts.

3 Subtract half this number from the number of stitches obtained in step 1: 69 − 4 (or 5) = 65 (or 64). This is the number of stitches to be cast on for the right and left fronts.

4 When the sections are completed, pick up stitches (see page 212) on each centre front, and work a button/buttonhole band to a depth of 3 cm/1¼″. Alternatively, cast on a number of stitches to equal 3cm/1¼″ (if the bands are worked in rib, the number will probably be greater than the main tension), and work each band vertically to the required length. Sew each band to the centre front edges.

To convert a cardigan to a pullover, work the front as for the back up to the neck shaping. The shape of the front neck will be similar to that of the cardigan left and right fronts, but you must add stitches at the centre to equal the width of one button band. Calculate this using the main garment tension. It is advisable to work out this shaping on graph paper (see page 219).

CARDIGAN TO WAISTCOAT

This is best attempted on a cardigan with a fairly close-fitting set-in sleeve, so that the armhole will not be too deep. You simply eliminate the sleeves, then before sewing up the side seam, you pick up stitches around the armhole and work armhole bands in rib or another suitable pattern.

Converting a waistcoat to a cardigan is more difficult, as it involves designing a sleeve to be set into the armhole. (See 'Tapered Shaping', page 218.)

Pullover to cardigan

Cardigan to waiscoat

Tapered to straight sleeve

Remember that buttons and buttonholes on men's and women's garments are on opposite sides. Women's garments have the buttons on the left side; men's garments have them on the right.

If you are working a button/buttonhole band vertically, to be sewn on, it can be tricky gauging how long to make it. To be sure of a smooth fit, work the band until it is about 4cm/1½" shorter than the garment edge; do not break the yarn, but slip the stitches onto a safety pin. Sew the band to the edge of the garment as far as possible, stretching it slightly, then continue knitting until it fits exactly – which is easy to judge over the short remaining distance.

TAPERED SLEEVE TO STRAIGHT SLEEVE

If you prefer the fullness in the sleeve to be added just above the ribbing, instead of gradually at the side edges, this can easily be accomplished. Simply subtract the number of cast-on stitches from the number on the needle in the last row just before the sleeve head shaping. On the last rib row, increase by this number of stitches, spacing the increases evenly across the row (see page 217). Work straight up to the sleeve head shaping.

Converting a full sleeve to a tapered one is somewhat more complex; see page 219.

ESTIMATING PICKED-UP STITCHES

When picking up stitches along the side edge of a piece of knitting, the general rule is to work into 3 out of every 4 row ends. In some cases, depending on the tension and the yarn used, the proportion may be 4 out of 5. Count the row ends and calculate the number to pick up before beginning the work. If it looks like too many or too few, adjust the calculation slightly, unravel the stitches and begin again. With experience you will become more skilled at estimating the number accurately.

TAKING MEASUREMENTS

A bust/chest – measure around fullest part
B waistline – measure loosely
C hips – measure around fullest part
D neck – measure around base of neck
E armhole – measure all the way around
F upper arm – measure around fullest part
G wrist
H crown of head
I back neck to waist
J shoulder width – measure to armhole at top of shoulder
K shoulder depth – measure from top of spine to line J
L garment front neck depth
M skirt length (extend for trousers)
N garment length – measure from neck to chosen lower edge
O neck to sleeve edge – measure from top of spine to sleeve edge with arm down

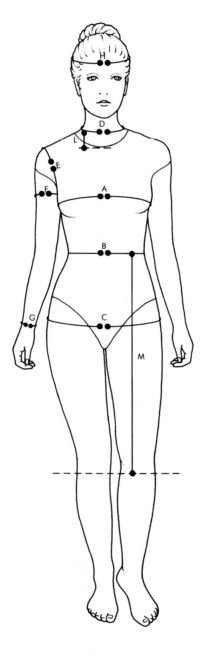

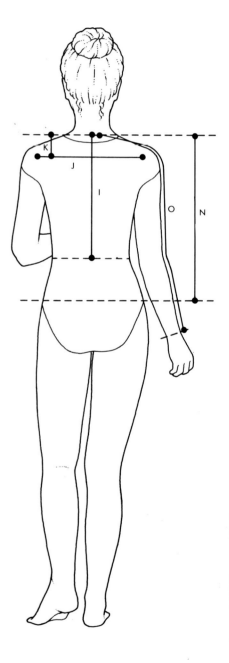

TAKING MEASUREMENTS

Whether you are planning to design original garments or simply need to make occasional alterations to existing patterns, you will need to have a set of accurate body measurements.

The diagram given opposite shows two sets of measurements on one figure. Those in black are body measurements; those in blue relate to garments and will thus be determined when you are beginning a project. Use this as a guide when taking your own measurements and when planning original designs.

To find your own measurements, enlist the help of a friend or relative. Wear comfortable undergarments and use a good-quality tape measure. Stand straight, but not rigidly at attention. Ask your helper to identify the measurements by the letters provided with the diagram.

Similarly, record the measurements of any adult for whom you knit regularly. In the case of children, measurements should be taken just before the project is begun. It is also a good idea to check adult measurements if there has been any gain or loss in weight. Keep the measurements in a folder in a place where you can find them easily.

SIZE ALTERATIONS

Many people do not precisely fit the 'average' proportions for which knitting patterns are designed. They may be short-waisted, for example, or have longer-than-average arms, or upper arms that are plump in relation to their other body measurements. If you normally have trouble finding ready-made garments that fit, you will probably need to make one or more adjustments to a knitting pattern. In any case, it is wise to check the measurements given in the pattern and compare them with your own, just to make sure no alterations will be needed.

The first rule in getting a good fit is to buy a pattern that will fit the bust/chest measurement.

Alterations to length are much simpler than those to the width (unless, of course, the garment is knitted sideways).

Remember to allow for ease. Most garments are designed to be somewhat larger than the chest/bust measurement in order to fit comfortably. The amount of ease provided varies considerably, according to the type of garment: a pullover will normally have less than a cardigan or jacket, which must fit over more layers of clothing. A sun top worked in a rib pattern will have 'negative' ease, being smaller than the body measurement in order to fit snugly.

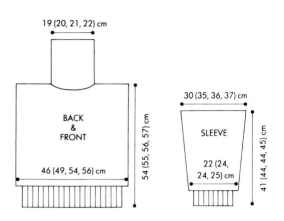

MEASUREMENT DIAGRAMS

Before you can decide what adjustments are required, you will need to find out the measurements within the pattern. Some patterns include a measurement diagram, which shows the main pieces with the principal measurements. Compare these measurements with your own (see above), and make a note of any that you would like to change. If the pattern does not include such a diagram, you can easily make one.

Certain key measurements, such as the garment chest/bust measurement and the sleeve length from the shoulder, will be given at the head of the pattern. Others may be contained within the pattern. In some cases you may need to calculate a measurement by referring to the tension. For example, if the row tension is 26 per 10cm/4", or 2.6 per cm/6½ per inch, then 'work 10 rows' indicates approximately 4cm/1½".

ALTERATIONS TO LENGTH

Where possible, length adjustments should be made in a part of the garment that is worked straight. On the front and back of a pullover or cardigan having no shaping between the top of the ribbing and the beginning of the armhole shaping, a length adjustment can usually be made simply by working to a different measurement. For example, instead of working straight until the back measures 30cm/12", as instructed by the pattern, you might choose to work only until it measures 28cm/11".

The same method could be used to lengthen or shorten a straight sleeve. On a sleeve that includes gradual shaping between the wrist and underarm, there will usually be a short straight area just below the underarm where this adjustment can be made. In other cases, the length adjustment must be spread over the whole length as described below.

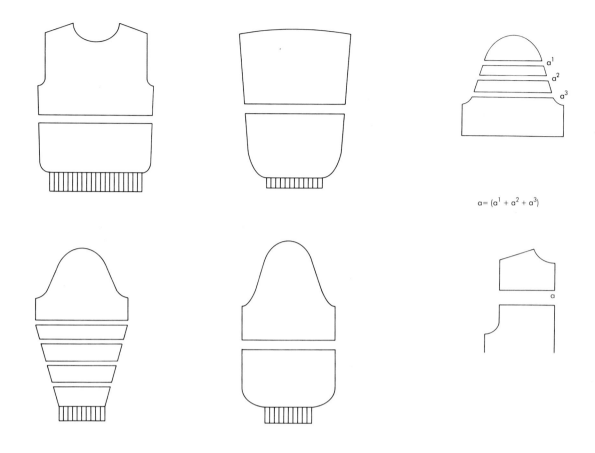

$a = (a^1 + a^2 + a^3)$

ADJUSTING VERTICAL REPEATS

If the stitch pattern has a noticeable vertical repeat (for example, a repeated Fair Isle border pattern), it is important to make sure that the pattern will match at the armhole seam. If you are lengthening the back and front but not the sleeves, for example, you may need to begin the stitch pattern or colour pattern in the middle of the repeat, so that the first complete repeat after the beginning of the armhole shaping is aligned with the first complete repeat in the sleeve head shaping.

Suppose that you wish to add 2cm/¾″ to the length of a sweater which has a vertical repeat pattern of 20 rows. The row tension is 40 rows to 10cm/4″, or 4 rows per cm/10 rows per inch.

1 Calculate the number of rows to be added: 2 (cm) × 4 (rows) = 8; ¾ (″) × 10 (rows) = 7½, say 8. Therefore you need to add 8 rows immediately above the ribbing.

2 Determine the pattern row on which to begin: subtract 8 (rows) from 20 (number of rows in pattern): 12 rows. Begin working on the next, 13th, row. After this partial repeat, which adds the length, you then begin working whole repeats. If you were *subtracting* 8 rows, you would simply begin on the 9th row of the first pattern repeat.

CORRESPONDING SIZE ADJUSTMENTS

If the armhole depth must be altered, a corresponding adjustment must be made in the sleeve head, so that it will fit. But whereas the armhole will usually include a straight section, in which the adjustment can be made simply by working to the new measurement, the sleeve adjustment may be more complex. A set-in sleeve will require a shaped adjustment of the type described below.

In some cases a length adjustment may dictate a corresponding adjustment in width on the adjacent piece. An example of this would be a straight sleeve set in with French shaping (see illustration above). If the armhole is made smaller or larger, the width of the sleeve's cast-off edge must be similarly adjusted in order to fit.

ALTERATIONS IN SHAPED SECTIONS

If a piece requiring alteration consists mainly or entirely of diagonal or curved edges, the length alteration must be spread out between the increases or decreases, in order to retain the gradual shaping.

Suppose that you must add 18 rows to a sleeve, and the pattern instructions require you to increase 1 stitch at each end of every 10th row 9 times.

1 Divide the additional 18 rows by the number of sections between increases: $18 \div 9 = 2$. This is the number of additional rows between increases.

2 Add 2 rows to each section, and change the instructions so that you increase on every 12th row.

ALTERATIONS TO WIDTH

If only a slight adjustment is needed, it may be possible to achieve this simply by changing the tension – provided that this can be done without spoiling the texture of the fabric.

Suppose, for example, that you would like the front and back each to measure 50cm/19¾″ across, rather than 48cm/19″, and that the stitch tension is 32 stitches to 10cm/4″, or 3.2 per cm/8 per inch. Suppose also that the number of stitches across the front/back is 154. Divide the number of stitches by the desired measurement: $154 \div 50 = 3.08$ sts per cm; $154 \div 19\frac{3}{4} = 7\frac{63}{79}$ sts per inch, say 7¾. Therefore, the new tension would be 31 stitches to 10cm/4″, a difference of only 1 stitch from the specified tension.

The orthodox way of adjusting a width measurement is to keep to the stated tension but adjust the number of stitches on the needle. You will first need to annotate your measurement diagram to show the stitches at certain key points in the pattern.

Using the tension, calculate the number of stitches you will need to add or subtract in order to get the required measurement.

Suppose that you wish to increase the total chest measurement of a pullover by 8cm/3″. The stitch tension is 22 stitches over 10cm/4″, or 2.2 sts per cm 5½ per inch. The total garment width measurement is 104cm/41″; the front and back each 52cm/20½″.

1 Divide the increase by 2, and add the result to the front and the back measurements: $8\text{cm} \div 2 = 4\text{cm}$; $3\frac{1}{2}″ \div 2 = 1\frac{3}{4}″$. Therefore the front and back sections should each measure 56cm/22¾″. Write this new measurement on the diagram.

2 Calculate the number of stitches you must add to each section: $4 \text{ (cm)} \times 2.2 \text{ (sts)} = 8.8 \text{ (sts)}$, say 9; $1\frac{3}{4}(″) \times 5\frac{1}{2} \text{ (sts)} = 9\frac{5}{8}$, say 9 (or 10).

3 Amend the instructions and the diagram to include the additional stitches. You may simply add them to the number of cast-on stitches, or you may add some to the cast-on and some at the top of the ribbing. If the hip measurement is slim, you may prefer to add all the stitches just above the ribbing, where there is usually a mass increase (see page 217).

The altered number of stitches will also affect the armhole, shoulder and neck shaping. As a general

rule, the number of stitches left for the neckline will be the same as in the pattern. (If this measurement, too, requires adjusting, it may be better to design the garment from scratch.) Decrease for the armhole as instructed. When you divide for the neck opening, half of the increased stitches should be included in each side. If the shoulder is shaped, you may need to add the extra stitches in several groups to the cast-off instructions to preserve the shaping.

CENTRING THE STITCH PATTERN

If the stitch or colour pattern has a noticeable repeat, you must amend the instructions – or chart – so that the effect is still symmetrical. If possible, simplify the task by adding or subtracting a complete repeat. If this is not possible, you must add or subtract stitches evenly at each side edge.

DESIGNING A SIMPLE SWEATER

As in all creative activities, it is best, when designing your first original garment, to try something simple. Avoid complicated shaping or an elaborate colour pattern; stick to something composed mainly of rectangles. Some of the most attractive knitted garments are designed in this way. If your garment fits properly and is well knitted in good-quality yarn (though it is unwise to be wildly extravagant at this stage), it will almost certainly be becoming.

INITIAL IDEAS

Begin by putting down on paper as much information as you can about the garment you have in mind. A sketch – no matter hows simple – will help you clarify your ideas. If you find this too daunting, you can use a photocopy of a similar garment and draw any modifications on top of it. Jot down any criteria that apply to the garment (for example, 'horizontal inside pockets', 'Irish moss stitch', 'double rib', 'Aran-weight yarn'). You may find that some of your ideas change as you proceed with the designing; this is a natural part of any creative process.

Next, buy a ball of your chosen yarn (or alternative yarns), and make some samples. Cast on enough stitches for a generous-sized tension swatch (see page 25), and work a sample in your chosen stitch pattern, using appropriate needles (see chart, page 221). Change the stitch pattern and the needle size if necessary until you are satisfied with the result. Also make a sample for any other stitch to be used, such as ribbing (normally worked on needles two sizes smaller than those used for the main fabric). Make a note of the needle sizes, and measure the main fabric tension. Write this information down and keep it close at hand; the tension you have obtained will be the key to designing the sections of the garment.

To illustrate the process of designing, we have used a T-shape pullover made of four rectangles: an identical front and back, plus sleeves. The straight sleeves are attached to the combined back and front as indicated by the diagram, forming a dropped shoulder. A few rows of garter stitch have been included at the upper edges to prevent the slash neckline from rolling. A flat rib pattern, worked to a slightly greater depth, would achieve the same purpose. This should be the same rib pattern as is used for the cuffs and welt. If the main fabric were stocking stitch, the welts, etc., might be worked in a fancy rib for textural variety.

MEASUREMENT DIAGRAM

On a sheet of paper draw the basic shapes required for the garment; these need not be precisely to scale, but you may wish to use graph paper to make them neat and symmetrical. Mark an arrow on each section to show the direction of the knitting (normally from the lower edge upwards).

Consult the body measurement chart (see page 212) for the relevant measurements, adding ease where required. Take any additional measurements specific to this garment (e.g. length of main sections and sleeve, neck opening), and add these to the list of body measurements.

In some cases, you may not be sure what dimensions you wish the garment to have. Measuring the relevant part of a similar existing garment may help you to decide. Lay the garment flat to measure it. Remember to double measurements where necessary (when measuring the width of a sleeve, for example). Above all, do not attempt to mix metric and imperial figures; choose one system or the other (metric, if you wish to avoid fractions), and then stick to it throughout the project.

Write all the measurements on the garment measurement diagram.

WRITING THE PATTERN

Your measurements and your tension will determine the number of stitches on the needle at any given point and the number to cast off or decrease or increase when shaping. To find the number of stitches for any dimension, multiply the measurement by the number of stitches or rows per centimetre/inch.

Thus, for example, if the front/back section is to measure 52cm/20½″ and the tension is 36sts to 10cm/4″, or 3.6 per cm/9 per inch, you would multiply 52 (cm) by 3.6, which gives 187; or 20½ (″) by 9, which gives 185 (occasional slight differences result from rounding off some measurements).

If you wish, you can use this number for casting on and continue on the same number for the main section. A ribbed welt worked on needles two sizes smaller than those used for the main fabric will naturally fit more snugly than the main fabric; and many sweaters have no increase above the ribbing.

However, if you wish the garment to blouse slightly, you should cast on fewer stitches for the ribbing, then work a mass increase on the last (wrong-side) row of the ribbing (see below). To determine how many stitches to cast on in this case, take half the body width measurement (that is, subtract the ease) and multiply this by the tension.

A sleeve nearly always involves a mass increase above the ribbing, in order for the wrist to fit snugly and the main part of the sleeve to be reasonably comfortable. For a simple straight sleeve put all the increases in the mass increase row; for a tapered sleeve shaping see page 219.

When you have calculated all the stitches for each part of the garment, write your pattern, using a published pattern as a guide to style. For example, your opening instructions, based on this example, might read as follows: 'Using smaller needles, cast on 171 sts. Work in K1,P1 rib for 7cm.'

CALCULATING YARN REQUIREMENTS

Estimating the amount of yarn you will need for an original design is somewhat tricky. The only rule is to estimate generously; for you must get all the yarn at the outset, from the same dye lot. Begin by checking the yarn requirements in patterns for similar garments worked in similar yarns, then round up generously. If possible, buy from a shop where they will either reserve a quantity of yarn for you or allow you to return unused yarn within a reasonable period. You can then estimate the yarn more precisely using the following method.

1 Take 1 ball of the yarn and start knitting the back with it. When you come to the end of the ball,

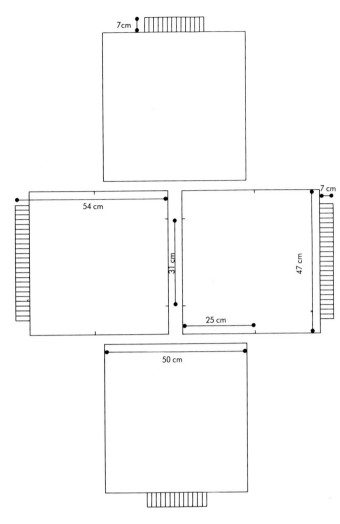

measure the area of the knitting. Let us suppose that it measures 52 × 15cm/20 × 6″.
2 To find the area, multiply the two measurements; this gives 780sq cm/123 sq ″.
3 Now calculate the area of each piece of knitting, using your measurement diagram. Add the resulting figures together to get the total area.
4 Divide this by the first figure you obtained (780/123) to get the number of balls you will require. Double-check your calculations, and add an extra ball to be on the safe side.

WORKING OUT A MASS INCREASE

A mass increase is a number of increases worked across a row, usually at the top of the ribbing. The increases should be spaced evenly (although slight irregularities will not be noticeable). If you are figuring out the increases for your own design, the calculations are slightly easier for a 'Make 1' type of increase than for an ordinary bar increase.

As an example, suppose that you have 99 stitches on the needle and wish to increase by 20 stitches to make 119 stitches. The steps are as follows:

1 Divide the number of stitches on the needle by the number of groups between increases, including the groups at either end. This figure will always be 1 more than the number of stitches to be increased – in this case 21: 99 ÷ 21 = 4.71.

2 If the result is a whole number, you could proceed to step 4. However, in this case (as often) it is not. Round the result up to the nearest whole number – in this case 5. Multiply this figure by the number of groups between increases *excluding* the end groups – here, it is 19: 5 × 19 = 95.

3 Subtract this figure from the number of stitches on the needle: 99 – 95 = 4; this is the number of stitches left for the end groups. Divide it by 2 to get the number of stitches at each end: 2. (In some cases there may be a difference of 1 stitch between the two ends.)

4 You now have the number of stitches in all the groups between the increases. As a check on your calculations, represent the row on a sheet of paper in this form (M represents an increased stitch):

2M5M5M5M5M5M5M5M5M5M3M5M5M5M5M5M5M5M5M2

5 Finally, write the instructions for the row: 'Rib 2, ☆M1 by picking up strand lying before next st and knitting into back of it, rib 5, rep from ☆ to last 2 sts, M1, rib 2.'

TAPERED SHAPING

If you are designing a garment that involves diagonal or curved lines, you will need to plan the increases and/or decreases carefully in order to produce the desired shape. This is best done on a sheet of graph paper, allowing each square to represent 1 stitch. If you wish, you can use a tension grid for this (see page 208), but this is not really necessary; just remember that on ordinary graph paper the proportions will be somewhat elongated, compared to the actual knitting.

It is not necessary to chart the entire garment in this way – only the shaped sections. For example, if you were planning a pullover similar to the one shown on page 216, but wished to give it a round neck and a tapered sleeve, you would chart the front neck and the sleeve up to the armhole; if you wanted a set-in sleeve, you would chart the whole

Leftover yarn can be used for all sorts of things: a patchwork blanket or afghan, a toddler's sweater or slipover, stuffed animals, scarves, gloves, cushion covers....

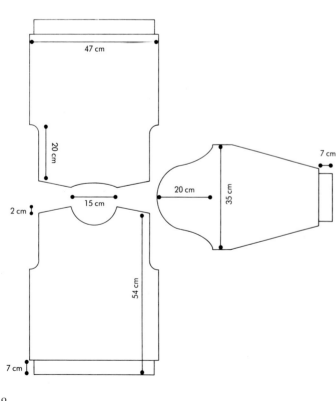

sleeve and the front and back from the armhole shaping upwards.

More measurements are required for this type of garment than for one composed of rectangles. For example, for a round neck you would need the neck measurement (d); for a shaped shoulder, the depth of shoulder (k); for a set-in sleeve, the upper arm (f) and shoulder width (j), in addition to the basic measurements required for the T-shaped pullover on page 216.

THE BASICS OF SHAPING

The basic procedure in shaping consists of 4 steps:
1 Establish the number of stitches on the needle just before the shaping (stitch tension multiplied by the number of centimetres/inches).
2 Similarly establish the number of stitches after the shaping is completed.
3 Establish the number of rows to be worked between the first and second measurements; in many cases this may include a straight section; an armhole, for instance, will be charted up to and including the shoulder edge, and may include a section worked straight.
4 Plot the shaping in steps on the graph paper. To illustrate this process, let us take the example of a tapered sleeve.

CHARTING A TAPERED SLEEVE

Let us assume that the sleeve is to fit a dropped shoulder and therefore has a straight upper edge. The lower edge consists of 43 stitches; the top edge, of 129. The total length of the sleeve is 50cm/19½″, including a ribbed cuff 8cm/3″ deep. The tension is 23sts and 32 rows to 10cm/4″, or 2.3 and 3.2/5¾ and 8 respectively.
1 Subtract the cuff depth from the total length to get the length in which the increases must be worked: 50 (cm) − 8 (cm) = 42cm; 19½ (″) − 3 (″) = 16½″.

In most cases you will also need to complete the shaping a short distance below the armhole seam (although this is more important in a tighter, set-in sleeve than in a full sleeve such as this one). For the moment we shall allow 2cm/1″; so the increases must be completed within 40cm/15½″. This allowance may need to be changed later.
2 Subtract the number of stitches at the lower edge from the number at the top: 129 − 43 = 86. This is the number to be increased.
3 From this number subtract those to be increased (if any) at the end of the ribbing in a mass increase. For this example 16 stitches will be increased at this point, leaving 59 stitches (43 + 16) on the needle. Therefore 70 stitches (86 − 16) must be increased

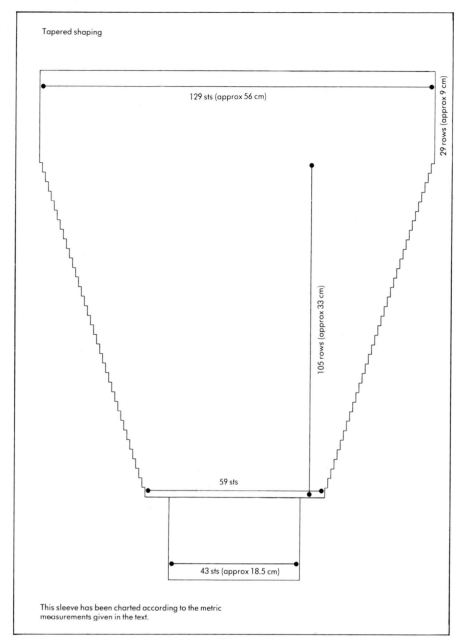

Tapered shaping

129 sts (approx 56 cm)

29 rows (approx 9 cm)

105 rows (approx 33 cm)

59 sts

43 sts (approx 18.5 cm)

This sleeve has been charted according to the metric measurements given in the text.

over 40cm/15½″.
4 Divide the number of increases by 2 (because they will be worked in pairs, at both sides of the sleeve): 70 ÷ 2 = 35. There will therefore be 35 increase rows over a length of 40cm/15½″.
5 Calculate the number of rows in this length: 40cm × 3.2 rows = 128 rows; 15½″ × 8 rows = 124 rows. (Use the figure for your chosen measurement system!)
6 Subtract the number of increase rows to get the total number of straight rows: 128 − 35 = 93 rows (metric); 124 − 35 = 89 rows (imperial).
7 Divide this number by the number of increase

rows to get the number of rows between increases: $93 \div 35 = 2.66$ (metric); $89 \div 35 = 2.54$ (imperial).

Since we must choose a whole number, let us try 2 rows between increases – that is, increasing on every third row. This will mean, however, that the increasing will be completed somewhat before 40cm/15½″. If we multiply 3 rows by the number of times we increase – 35 – we get 105 rows, which measure 33cm/13″ (number of rows divided by tension). This leaves a straight section of 9cm/3½″ (42cm/16½″ – 33cm/13″) – somewhat more than the original 2cm/1″. This may be acceptable, in which case you can chart the sleeve shape accordingly and write down the pattern instructions.

If, however, you preferred a more gradual shaping, and rounded the 2.66/2.54 up to 3, with the increases worked on every 4th row, the main sleeve section would end up too long: 140 rows, or 44cm/17½″. In this case you could solve the problem in one or more of the following ways: put more stitches into the mass increase, thus reducing the number of increase rows in the main sleeve section; shorten the ribbing to allow for a longer main section; narrow the sleeve by a few stitches to eliminate some of the increases.

As you can see, there is a degree of trial and error in designing shapes that involve tapering – and even more where a curved edge is required. Your experience in following published knitting patterns will give you some familiarity with the classic shapes of knitted garments and how they are achieved. It may help to make charts of garment shapings from some of your favourite patterns. Of course you will not be able to use these as exact patterns for your own designs, unless the tension and measurements are the same; however, they will give you an idea of the shape to aim for when designing, say, a set-in sleeve or a V-neck.

RECOMMENDED NEEDLE SIZES

A commercial knitting pattern will specify the size(s) of needles recommended for achieving the stated tension. However, if you are making some experimental tension swatches, perhaps with a view to designing an original garment, you may find the following guidelines helpful. Bear in mind that the recommended size for a given weight of yarn is just a starting point; you may wish to move up or down one or two sizes in order to achieve the best effect with the yarn and stitch pattern you are using.

YARN	NEEDLE SIZE
2-ply	2mm
3-ply	2¾mm
4-ply	3mm
double knitting	4mm
Aran	5mm
chunky	6mm
extra-chunky	9mm

EQUIVALENT NEEDLE SIZES

Knitting needles sold in Britain today are sized according to the metric system, and these sizes are specified in patterns. However, if you have inherited some needles sized by the old English system, or are using an old pattern, you will need to consult a chart such as the one shown here to find the metric equivalents.

	METRIC
14	2mm
13	2¼mm
12	2¾mm
11	3mm
10	3¼mm
9	3¾mm
8	4mm
7	4½mm
6	5mm
5	5½mm
4	6mm
3	6½mm
2	7mm
1	7½mm
0	8mm
00	9mm
000	10mm

CHOOSING A CIRCULAR NEEDLE

When using a circular needle for tubular knitting, it is important to select one that will comfortably accommodate all the stitches. The table shown gives the minimum number of stitches required for various lengths of needle. This number varies according to the tension: the fewer stitches per 10cm/4", the shorter the needle required.

To use the chart, first find your stitch tension in the left-hand column. Then find the first number to the right that is *less* than the number of stitches in your knitting. The measurement at the top of that column is the longest needle you can use. For example, if your tension is 16 stitches to 10cm/4" and there are 130 stitches in the work, the longest needle that you could use would be one 80cm long. However, you could also use a 40cm or 60cm needle, as a circular needle will hold many more than the recommended minimum of stitches.

A word of warning: some stitch patterns entail temporarily decreasing the stitches at a certain point. Read through the instructions to see if your pattern does this, and choose your needle for the minimum number of stitches, rather than the maximum.

TENSION LENGTH OF NEEDLE
(in centimetres)

sts to 10cm/4"	40	60	80	90	100
	number of stitches				
16	64	96	128	144	160
18	72	108	144	162	180
20	80	120	160	180	200
22	88	132	176	198	220
24	96	144	192	216	240
26	104	156	208	234	260
28	112	168	224	252	280
30	120	180	240	270	300
32	128	192	256	288	320
34	136	204	272	306	340
36	144	216	288	324	360

CARE OF KNITS

After putting many hours of work into a knitted garment, you will want to ensure that it retains its shape, colour and texture for as long as possible.

Always save the ball band from a knitted garment. Tie a short length of the yarn to it for quick identification. The band will normally include symbols indicating the recommended care of the yarn; the symbols most often used are shown here.

Many yarns are now machine washable (on wool yarns look for the word 'superwash'); however, hand-washing is usually preferred, especially if the fabric is delicate. Use a mild detergent specially intended for knits, and cool to warm water. Squeeze the suds gently through the knitting; do *not* wring. Rinse the garment thoroughly, then squeeze out as much water as possible. Lay the garment on a turkish towel and roll it up for about half an hour to allow the towel to absorb excess water; then lay the garment on another towel and pull it gently into shape. Leave it to dry flat, away from direct heat. Depending on the yarn and stitch pattern, a light pressing may be appropriate (see page 34).

Special care may be needed for multicoloured garments. It is a good idea to knit a small swatch using all the colours and then wash it to make sure none of the colours run into the others. If they do, you will need to have the garment dry-cleaned.

Always store knitted garments flat to preserve their shape.

WASHING SYMBOLS

Machine/hand wash warm (40°C)
Medium machine wash, normal rinse and spin

Machine/hand wash warm (40°C)
Minimum machine wash, cold rinse, short spin

Machine/hand wash warm (40°C)
Minimum machine wash, spin

Hand wash only warm (40°C)

Do not bleach

Cool iron

Warm iron

Hot iron

Do not iron

Dry-clean only

Dry-cleanable in all solvents

Dry-cleanable in certain solvents; consult cleaner

Do not dry-clean

MAIL-ORDER SUPPLIERS

You may be fortunate enough to live near a shop that sells a good range of knitting yarns. If not, you can avail yourself of the mail-order service offered by many shops. Among these are:

Best (Woolshop)
26/28 Frenchgate
Doncaster, S. Yorkshire DN1 1QQ
tel. (0302) 367410
stockists of Hayfield, Patons, Sirdar
no credit card orders

R. & D. Bishop and Sons Ltd.
2nd & 3rd Avenues
Pioneer Market, Winston Way
Ilford, Essex IG1 2RD
tel. (081) 478 0515
stockists of Hayfield, Jaeger, Patons, Phildar, Robin, Sirdar, Solo, Wendy
credit cards: Access, Visa

S. N. Cooke
11 Meer Street
Stratford-upon-Avon, Warwickshire CV37 6XB
tel. (0789) 292155
stockists of Argyll, Slalom Aran, Patons, Jaeger
credit cards: Access, Visa

Creativity
45 New Oxford Street
London WC1 1AA
tel. (071) 240 2945
mail orders: 15 Downing Street
Farnham, Surrey GU9 7PB
tel. (0252) 714856
stockists of Avocet, Colinette, Forsell, Jaeger, Kilcarra, Lopi, Patons, Rowan, Scotnord
credit cards: Access, Visa

Liberty
Regent Street
London W1R 6AH
tel. (071) 734 1234
stockists of Jaeger, Kilcarra, Patricia Roberts, Rowan
credit cards: Access, American Express, Visa

Ries Wools of Holborn
242 High Holborn
London WC1V 7DZ
tel. (071) 242 7721
stockists of Jaeger, Patons, Pingouin, Rowan
credit cards: Access, American Express, Visa

INDEX

ACKNOWLEDGMENTS

Senior editor: Linda Burroughs
Art editor: Sandra Horth
Designer: Pauline Bayne
Production controller: Alyssum Ross
Illustrators: Terry Evans, Coral Mula, Gillie Newman
Special photography: John Slater

Photo credits: The Octopus Publishing Group Ltd/Fiona Alyson 173/Carol Sharp 103,
105, 107, 119, 125, 135, 137/John Slater 7, 9, 11, 13, 14, 16, 17, 18, 19, 20, 21, 22-23, 24,
25, 27, 32, 34, 36-37, 38-39, 40-41, 42, 48, 49, 50-51, 52-53, 54-55, 56, 63, 64-65, 66, 69,
72-73, 74-75, 76-77, 81, 84-85, 86, 89, 98-99, 208, 209; Woman's Weekly, IPC Magazines:
139, 143, 147, 179, 181, 191, 193, 197, 199

This edition published 1992 exclusively for Colour Library Books,
Godalming Business Centre, Woolsack Way, Godalming, Surrey GU7 1XW.
Tel : (0483) 426266, by Octopus Illustrated Publishing, Michelin House,
81 Fulham Road, London SW3 6RB, part of Reed International Books

ISBN 0 86283 929 7

Produced by Mandarin Offset
Printed and bound in Hong Kong

The Complete Step-By-Step Knitting Book

ELEANOR VAN ZANDT

Colour
Library
Books

The Complete Step-By-Step Knitting Book

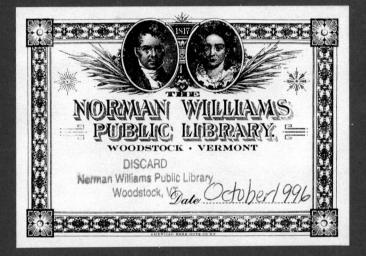